Medieval Regions and their Cities

Josiah Cox Russell

Texas A & I University

Indiana University Press

Library of Congress catalog card number 70-172025

ISBN 0-253-33735-6

Printed in Great Britain

🁢🁢🁢🁢🁢🁢🁢🁢🁢🁢🁢🁢🁢🁢🁢🁢🁢🁢🁢🁢🁢🁢🁢🁢🁢🁢🁢🁢🁢🁢🁢

Contents

🁢🁢🁢🁢🁢🁢🁢🁢🁢🁢🁢🁢🁢🁢🁢🁢🁢🁢🁢🁢🁢🁢🁢🁢🁢🁢🁢🁢🁢🁢🁢

Tables

Figures

Abbreviations

b	burgesses or burgages
f	heads of families
fr	freemen
h	hearths
hyp est	hypothetical estimate of city size based normally on the size of the largest city
km	kilometre
m	men (males)
o	oathtakers
p	persons (usually estimated total population)
pop est	population estimate
km²	square kilometres
s	soldiers
t	taxpayers
un	unze, unit of payment supposedly based on hearths

Preface

THE IDENTIFICATION OF functional regions is an increasingly important approach to the study of society. My interest in it developed accidentally while studying the size of cities for my *Late Ancient and Medieval Population*. Within areas certain cities stood out for their great size, while others exhibited a rank-size pattern in the area. This, I found after looking over the work of W. Christaller and E. Ullman, is characteristic of many modern areas. Since any consistent pattern of population is normally the result of certain conditions, the medieval pattern and its implications deserve study. The investigation of a problem naturally has three stages: collection of data, classification of data, and interpretation of their function and relationship.

The collection of data about the population of medieval cities and larger areas is already well advanced. Large collections have been made by Beloch for Italy, Lot for France, Keyser for Germany and by myself for Britain. The largest collection has been assembled by Mols in his *Introduction à la démographie historique des villes d'Europe du xiv*e *au xviii*e *siècle* (1954–6): somewhat less is found in my volume on *British Medieval Population* (1948). But since the publication of these works many more studies have appeared, noted in the text of several chapters.

Classification of data for study of regionalism is primarily on the basis of the populations of cities and countrysides and of their geographical conditions. Many of the problems involved in determining urban populations have been discussed carefully by Mols: the interpretation of the value of sources is his chief interest. However, he finally declined to make estimates of population sufficiently definite for rank-size study —a quantitative effort which must be made if further advances are to be achieved in the subject.

Notwithstanding obvious problems inherent in the evidence, estimates of city sizes can be made as accurate as most statements which medievalists make without apology. Geographical classification, limited as it will be in this study to the largest dozen or so cities in each region, is a matter of simple maps which illustrate locational relationships.

Interpretation of the functions and relationships of cities within regions was considered in part in my *Late Ancient and Medieval Population*, in a rather uncomplicated way. The understanding of factors such as migration into cities from the countryside and from one city to another, is a more complicated problem. The rank-size pattern requires an explanation: why should cities in a region offer something like a descending order of size (such as 100, 57, 39, 30, etc)? Linking this with a pattern of migration indicates a circulation of people within a region and with it a circulation of ideas and institutions which give currency to regional habits, dialects, customs, and even physical characteristics. Regionalism thus becomes an important factor or condition of society, explaining many of its most distinguishing characteristics of diversity by geographical areas.

This study deals, with two exceptions, with the century before the outbreak of the plague in 1348, a period of relatively active population growth in most areas. By about 1300, population had actually reached the limit of effective use of available lands in large parts of Europe and began in some places to approach overpopulation. Rapid urbanisation brought with it, as urbanisation usually does, rapid development of civilisation: the period AD 1000–1348 saw the appearance, as is well known, of the Gothic cathedral, the university, the climax of the medieval Church, great legal development and an interesting group of inventions, such as the eyeglass, gunpowder, improved navigation techniques and equipment, the compass and the wheel-barrow. With this advance one would have expected an increasingly sophisticated society of ever greater complexity. Regional integration of economic activities was a part of it all.

The area covered in this study may seem an arbitrary collection of countries from Ireland to India. In fact, it includes regions along the great trade routes from Ireland to India in the century, that is, from about AD 1250–1348, before the fourteenth-century attack of the plague. Asia Minor, the Balkans, Slavia and Scandinavia are omitted, largely because of lack of time to study them.

The chapter on India is earlier in time (AD 629–645), but indicates the impossibility of that country possessing the enormous population that it is accorded for the middle ages by some authorities.

This, then, is a tentative study of late medieval regionalism, an examination of the spatial distribution of cities, a discussion of other regional characteristics, and an explanation of the possible reasons for the development of regions at that time. Some of the detailed arguments may be altered by later research and interpretation and, indeed, some of my own ideas on the subject have changed radically in the course of the study. For instance: was Dijon rather than Lyons the metropolitan city of an upper Rhône-Burgundian region or was there a region at all in that area then?

However, this study should make clear the importance of quantification as a tool in the understanding of medieval history. Without a careful study of city size, awareness of the fact of rank-size arrangement with all of its implications, would be impossible. It is strange that quantification, one of the essentials in all of scientific advancement, has not become a part of much historical writing; perhaps the humanists have prided themselves too much on the quality of the material which they study rather than upon its quantity. In any case, failure to consider quantification has resulted in our missing many of the essential qualities of historical development.

The help given over the years by the American Philosophical Society lies behind much of the work in this study. It financed nine months of study on my *British Medieval Population,* published my *Late Ancient and Medieval Population,* gave me the summer of 1961 in Europe and published an article on the region of Barcelona in 1962. Both of its referees, Sidney Painter and J. R. Strayer, made valuable suggestions on the manuscripts. This gave me much help and encouragement during a time, particularly in the earlier period, when population was not receiving the attention which it receives today and when it was not very popular with historians and especially medievalists.

For a historian to participate in a geographical series is both a personal pleasure and a welcome gesture towards interdisciplinary co-operation. I owe especial thanks to Dr Alan R. H. Baker and Dr. J. B. Harley for the invitation to participate and for many helpful suggestions and improvements of the text. I appreciate the editing of the David & Charles staff, The editors of *Demography*, Beverley Duncan and of *TAIUS* (Texas A & I University Studies), George F. Cook, have kindly given permission to reprint material from articles in their publications. Finally, my wife, Ruth, has helped greatly all along the way from discussing ideas to reading page proofs.

1

The Structure of the
Medieval Region

A REGION, THE dictionary says, is a large tract of land. This would have satisfied a nominalist in the great medieval debate, but the realist would have added people to the land and have insisted that the region had a distinctive landscape and a common life of its own. With the realist, the geographer and the regional planner would today agree. They have produced a voluminous literature, illustrating or planning regional activities. Today these activities are heavily industrial, educational, recreational or residential. Regionalism in the Middle Ages was different since 85–90% of the people lived in agricultural villages. Cities existed, kept up by what are termed 'basic factors', like markets, castles, monasteries, simple manufacturing, which brought in money from outside of the city.[1] These cities tended, furthermore, to be arranged in a definite order by size within the region, called a 'rank-size series'.[2] These are essentially demographic factors, which along with migration[3] and spatial arrangement, will constitute the main emphasis in this study of medieval regionalism.

THE REGION AND ITS STUDY

In many respects the medieval region was like its modern counterpart, described by R. E. Dickinson
    a geographical unit of economic and social activity and

---

[1] Notes and references for this and succeeding chapters appear on page 249

organisation. We have defined it as an area of interrelated activities and kindred interest and organisation. It is an entity of human space relationships, which are effected through the medium of the route pattern and the urban centres. Such a region, therefore, embraces the complex and closely woven fabric of intercourse by which are effected the transfer of goods, and the distribution of services, news, and ideas, the very bases of society. This conception does not involve the idea of a water-tight compartment, nor does such integration mean that the linear boundaries can be defined in reality. It does maintain that such a region has a core and that it is normally centred upon the principal cities. Such a region is a unit in the sense that its people are bound together economically and socially far more than with adjacent areas. This unity is due to three sets of conditions: first, the predominance of a group of activities—agriculture, industry, commerce and service—that are the same or complementary and interdependent through the interchange of goods and services; the second, the dominance of both movements and activities by one or more great cities, that are at once the chief centres of affairs and the chief centres of radial routes and traffic; third, the common bonds of historical associations and tradition—both in the economic and cultural senses, in spite of the fact that these associations often cut across old-established political boundaries.[4]

Modern regions are often delimited by such criteria as the circulation of metropolitan newspapers, the relationship between central and outlying banks or the market and supply areas of wholesale and industrial concerns. Not all of these phenomena delimit the same territory exactly: thus the limits of regions are often indefinite. Furthermore, regions seldom, at least in the United States and in some continental European areas, coincide with political boundaries, and so do not necessarily have an integrated political life. Thus, the regions are not as well defined as the state or nation. Nevertheless the subject has developed a large literature and is the basis for extensive planning projects to adjust society to its ecological background, a very complex problem.

Compared to society today, medieval society was much simpler in its relationship to land and water, but it was already complicated by human competition for economic opportunities. The solution stemmed eventually from the sense of territoriality so prominent in nature. The male bird sings to indicate, in part, the area which he will defend because he needs it to support him and his family. The most elemental example of this in human history is the idea—tenacious in peasant history—of ownership of enough land to raise a crop and support animals. A village protected itself from too much use of its lands, pastures and forest by limiting the number of holdings in it and not allowing a man to marry until he had one. The city guilds admitted only those who could be supported by the trade of the city. The Church advanced to the holy order of priesthood only those who had cure of souls. Thus the human race until modern times took great care to prevent overpopulation. Unless evidence of it can be found in southern Italian cities, medieval society did not produce the mass urban proletariat, poverty-stricken but prolific, which plagues modern underprivileged society and poses a very serious question for the entire world. Based on the fundamental concept of population control, medieval society had a healthy structure with its elements functioning effectively from top to bottom as far as control of its numbers was concerned.

What prescribed boundaries to regions? For islands, it was obviously the limits of the land, as in the cases of England and probably Ireland. Sicily, however, was united with southern Italy, more connected by the sea and coast than with its interior so broken up with ranges of mountains and rugged hills. The northern French plain was obviously the base for the region of Paris. River basins were important factors in areas such as those of Cairo, Milan, Dijon, and Cologne. The high meseta of northern Spain, the region of Toledo, stands in contrast to the Mediterranean coastal regions of Barcelona and Montpellier. Thus the geographical factor was very important both for the characteristic physical features which affect the culture of regions and through the mere fact of location. Factors of historical development— many of which must be attributed to chance must also be

B

considered. The fact that areas over the centuries showed widely differing conditions of life and of attitudes and cultures indicates that physical resources and location are not the sole factors. Even in the short period of 1250–1348 startling changes occurred within the regions: Paris rose to prominence, Magdeburg declined, as the south-eastern German cities grew. Augsberg was being overtaken by Nürnberg, Valencia began to rise in competition with Barcelona, and Seville in respect of Cordoba. Montpellier was supported by quite accidental conditions and the English lesser cities failed to grow.

The problem of understanding the structure of the region from a demographic standpoint requires a study of the *size* of cities, of the *spacing* of cities in respect of each other and within the population of the region, and of the *functioning* of demographic factors such as migration and differing economic groups within the cities and region. This study will examine these three aspects of regional demography during the medieval period.[5]

For the Middle Ages, French human geographers, notably Vidal de la Blache, developed the idea of regions from somewhat different bases.[6] They noticed that certain geographic areas—which they called the *pays*—had common characteristics, such as dialects, social customs, building patterns and eating habits. These also provided reasons for setting up divisions of society along regional lines rather than utilising political boundaries. These common characteristics led naturally to common feelings of unity and affection for their home areas. The French especially enjoyed an affection for the *patrie*: indeed, the tenacious affection for their local areas made them one of the least effective imperialist nations, since so few citizens desired to emigrate. The emphasis here was upon the countryside rather than upon the city, as the basis for the region, as was natural in a state where agriculture remained so important for so long. On the other hand the great cities tended to stand for larger units such as the nation in the case of Paris or for extensive areas in the case of Marseilles, Lyon and Toulouse. In any case it is easier for medievalists to locate areas of dialects, social customs, building patterns and eating habits than to discover those arrangements—such as circulation of newspapers, banking connections, business affiliations and forms of transportation and travel, which are used by modern regionalists to define modern regions.

Another approach to regional development in Europe is made by those who emphasise 'core-areas', as forerunners of the modern state. However profoundly they may have been modified and their expansion influenced by the forces of modern nationalism, most European nations in fact grew by a process of accretion from germinal areas which have come after Derwent Whittelsey, to be called 'core-areas'. Since expansion is a human rather than a territorial occurrence, this means that the ruling groups occupying favourable lands for defence and manpower have spread out over the surrounding areas eventually to found in many instances the modern nations. However, as N. J. G. Pounds and S. S. Ball have pointed out, the factor of landownership operating through marriage and inheritance, is strong and explains many of the anomalies in lack of coincidence of modern nations with areas obviously appropriate for the development of nationalism. Nevertheless, the expansion of ruling classes in core-areas tended to be along lines of least resistance which means easier advances into areas of marked similarities and ancient traditions of unity of language. French expansion, for instance, extended over areas not only where the French language was spoken but also where French kings held vague rights long before they had actual control.[7]

Of these two approaches, neither the *pays* nor the core-area concept makes use of quantitative data or of patterns of the data to understand the medieval scene. One should not have to defend the idea that quantitative data and analysis of their components should be used. Much of modern science is based upon these methods. It assumes that regular association of data in a definable pattern is not only to be expected but should have proper scientific explanations. It is quite possible that at times society may have been without definite organisation of villages and cities in areas, but this also should be capable of statistical proof.

There are great advantages in setting up patterns which represent a number of situations, assuming that they are sufficiently similar to satisfy statistical requirements. One, of course, is that it enables one to classify a new case if it conforms reasonably to a pattern already defined. A second advantage is that deviations from the pattern offer valuable indications about the difference between the case and the pattern, often providing clues to peculiar qualities of the case itself. For instance, a pattern of mortality from a cemetery alleged to come from a plague period, would be seriously questioned if it did not conform to the patterns of plague periods. The rule proves the exception.

It must also be remembered that the use of patterns which are based upon an increasing number of instances offsets the mistakes of the individual figure. If several people throw darts at a target, the target centre is evident from the places where the dart holes are made, even though no one may hit the exact centre. Thus the discovery of errors either of the evidence itself or of the person in copying the evidence need not have much effect upon the result. This is in contrast to much of historical evidence, particularly of the pre-modern period, where important conclusions are drawn from a small amount of evidence and its interpretation. Here either an error in the original evidence or a mistake in interpretation often results in widely held errors. The variety of interpretations of the crowning of Charlemagne as Roman Emperor in AD 800 is a good illustration of this.

Another great advantage of the identification of patterns is that one may often interpolate missing elements in a case which seems to fit the pattern. One of the best illustrations of this is the reconstruction by archaeologists of the appearance of ancient buildings from often relatively few remains. The reconstruction over a period of years of the great Romanesque Church of Cluny shows how this can be done. The idea is not new; it was stressed by Langlois and Seignobos in their famous book on historical criticism of two generations ago.

DATA AND THEIR LIMITATIONS

To define the position of cities in a rank-size series, one needs relatively accurate medieval estimates of city populations. Scholars are notably hesitant to accept estimates on the ground that they are not accurate. Many who refuse to believe in figures of city population feel free to fill their studies with statements which are quite as questionable as population estimates and feel no qualms about them. In fact all value judgements with a quantitative base about the Middle Ages are about as uncertain as population estimates. Yet it must be remembered that most medieval estimates are quite rough—15,000, for instance, is apt to mean anything from 14,000 to 19,000. Statistically, however, the average estimate is apt to be relatively close to accuracy. The nature of the evidence about urban populations of the period explains why there is a question about accuracy. The most extensive study of evidence for civic demography is that of Mols.

Some medieval cities preserved lists of new citizens which give evidence of city size. If these can be assumed to be about the average number of men for a year of age between 20 and 25, an estimate can be made of total population from life tables. We assume also that the previously published life table of English landholding classes (born about 1276–1300) is reasonably accurate for all cities of that period.[8] In that table (adding for an equal number of women) there was a total of 62,590, with 609 a year between ages 20 and 25, or about one per cent. However, since the percentage of the burgess class in the cities was normally about 70%, the one per cent should be reduced to .7%. This assumes that both sons of citizens and newcomers to the cities were included: if many were not included it would show in the percentage of the group. The small size of the sample for one year would make it an uncertain index for total population, but if there were a long run of years the results would be more impressive statistically. Data from twenty years, for instance, should give 14% of the population. The data are especially significant when comparing evidence for neighbouring cities where conditions were probably much the same, as in the cities of the region of Lübeck.

The most accurate estimate for civic population was, of course, an entire list of the inhabitants. Although none remain for cities before the fifteenth century, they were taken for several cities—Nürnburg, Strasbourg, Nordlingen, Pozzuoli and parts of Ypres—in that century. These figures give a very definite indication of the size of cities in that century: their smallness provided quite a surprise when the lists were first edited. Certain poll taxes, such as the poll tax of 1377 in England, covered about two-thirds of the population: there are also comparable documents available for the Low Countries.

A common tax of the pre-plague, as well as of the post-plague period, was the tax on hearths, heads of houses, families, taxpayers, or soldiers. These pose a wide variety of problems, and usually need to be considered on a local basis. The number to the household depended primarily upon the social customs of housing: the smallest units occur where such relatives as grandparents and single unmarried persons lived by themselves. If names are given in lists the presence of large numbers of feminine names (15–25%) usually indicated the lowest number, often about 3.5. If others than the man-wife-children group lived with the household, the index rises and may at the end of the period number five or six. There are other problems, such as the fictitious character of many of the 'hearths' or questions about how many escaped taxation by virtue of poverty or superior social class.[9]

Another type of evidence comes from estimating the areal size of medieval cities. Modern maps were studied by Püschel many years ago for fifteen cities of Germany. He found that the pattern of streets did persist through the centuries in most cities and thus the street patterns could be used to estimate size.[10] This modern pattern is peculiarly useful because of the historical development of the cities. Few cities retained their street pattern after the decline of Rome, although there were exceptions, like Saragossa. From small beginnings before AD 1000 cities grew, gradually adding walls to contain the newly-settled areas. Most cities reached their widest limits in the thirteenth and fourteenth centuries. The decline in population induced by the plague froze the street pattern for centuries. When, normally in the early modern period, cities extended beyond their medieval streets, they showed a different street pattern with straighter streets. The walls were often razed, leaving traces only where boulevards ran through the city. It is desirable to have proper historical studies of the evolution of city plans, but in lieu of them topographic plans may be used. The most readily available ones are in the *Enciclopedia Ilustrada Universala*, the great Spanish encyclopaedia, whose editors were more interested in city maps than were those of other publications. Most estimates of city size which are based on maps come from this source unless otherwise stated. The International Commission for the history of towns has launched its project for a series of historical atlases of urban centres in the various European countries with a volume of English cities under the editorship of M. D. Lobel, and this, too should yield new data.

For cities which have only data from after 1348, estimates can be made for the earlier period by allowing for plague losses. In general population dropped about 20% in the first epidemic of the years 1348 to 1350. Later epidemics occurred at intervals of about 3.8 years (a rodent cycle) and their multiples and gradually reduced the population until the low point was reached after 1400 at 50–60% of the pre-plague level. From about 1460–70 the population began to rise, reaching the pre-plague figure in the first half of the sixteenth century. Again local conditions have to be kept in mind since the results were not everywhere the same. Drier areas normally had less mortality than the damper areas, for instance. There are, of course, no ways to test the statistical limitations of most of these sources of information about medieval civic population. In general, modern study of civic areas and of other methods of quantitative surveys have shown a remarkable consistency in the results of such use. The correlations of space-size series are generally quite reliable and satisfactory.

SPACING: RANK-SIZE PATTERN

It has long been obvious that cities and villages were distributed over the countryside in something like a pattern: villages every few miles, small cities a day's journey or so, and larger cities at less frequent intervals. They obviously satisfied the needs of people on a number of levels: smaller for more frequent and smaller demands and larger for less frequent and usually more expensive needs. These relationships invite mathematical study. What was not so obvious until such study was broached was that within great areas cities bore definite relationships to each other. Many modern countries show a relationship defined as:

$$n_r = \frac{c}{r}$$

where n r is the population of city n in a series of cities in an area with rank r

    r   is the rank of the city among cities of the country

    C a constant, normally the size of the first city in the series.

Thus if the size of the first city was one million, the size of the second city would be half of a million, that of the third a third of a million, and so on. While this seems to hold for certain modern areas, it does not seem to hold for the cities of the late medieval period. As will be seen in the tables for each region, the second and succeeding cities are larger than this formula suggests, probably because the pre-industrial society did not provide as much means for keeping up the larger city's size. For the medieval period it is therefore necessary to reduce the numerator. Since the city is a two dimensional area, some form of square root reduction of the numerator seems in order and is given below. The form is that suited to the more sophisticated regions, such as Florence and Venice. It seems best to set up an hypothetical model rather than to reduce all of the data to a formula based upon all types of regions:

$$n = C \times \left(\frac{1 + \frac{\sqrt{r-1}}{10}}{r} \right)$$

where n = population of city with rank r

        r = rank of city

        C = population of the largest city

The data in respect of the cities of each region can be seen in the tables set up by regions in this study. The size of cities diverge from the hypothetical size in many instances, as can be expected of any statistical concept in practice. Local circumstances vary considerably, shifting the actual population from the ideal. Indeed the variations are often important and interesting in pointing to the economic and other circumstances of the cities.

The rank-size series seems to have as a fundamental basis this reasoning. In any area which enjoyed a circulation of trade, some goods were very specialised, so that only a small number of persons could pay for them or were interested in them. The persons who wanted them would go to the city to buy them, or an agent would circulate in an area to sell them. Obviously if there were room for only one agent in a region he would either sell in one place or circulate with one place as his residence. Now if he sold more in a larger place, as would be natural, he would tend to fix his residence in that place. If there were room for two men in the field, the chances are that he would find shorter distances to his market-places or more customers in a second place; and so on as the market widened. However, the largest place would tend to attract more of the agents who sold very specialised wares and thus it would tend to grow more rapidly than other cities, assuming that other factors of basic economics were equal. The second largest city would tend to develop in the second most populous or wealthy area. This tended to scatter the location of cities. Against this pull toward scattering is the chance that a basic factor (manufacturing, mining, etc) existed or appeared, which attracted a larger number to a particular place, and produced a city outside of the established rank-size series.

The development of a regular rank-size distribution thus depended upon the building up of specialised goods and demands on the part of a people. This, of course, rested upon a considerable wealth on their part and a rather human desire to use the wealth to display their affluence and social status. Thus the appearance of a rank-size pattern was an indication both of wealth in the group and of the desire to exhibit. The example given below of the use of leather in Tuscany is an excellent illustration of this: a generalised use at the beginning of the thirteenth century for a wide variety of goods, including saddles, windows, bags and clothes, was succeeded by the more specialised employment of materials such as glass, cotton and silk, during the course of the century.[11]

The original concept of rank-size assumed that the metro-politan city was also a 'central' city in the area. However, some great cities which are obviously the metropolitan cities of areas are not near the geometric centre of their regions. This is very clear in the case of Dublin, for instance, unless one assumes that it is the centre for the coast of Wales and other British areas across the Irish Channel. Today the same would be true for instance, of New York in the United States. These we shall call *portal cities,* the gates to regions.

In dealing with rank-size pattern of city-sizes, one must remember that cities had two sources of strength: their position as local centres of agricultural populations and their influence as components of the regions. If regional commerce and in-dustry were not great, not many of the cities were above the average size (a few thousands) of local centres. In most regions the lesser cities were essentially at a distance of a day's journey from each other, that is, from about 35 to 60 kilometres distant from each other. Thus the size of cities was an indica-tion of the industrial-commercial status of regions. The tiny size of the Carolingian cities illustrated the primitive character of society at that time.

Sometimes, if one city does not fill the place in a rank-size series, a combination with a nearby city seems to offer the proper population. An objection raised to this is that it is a mere manipulation which can easily be made. But, in the modern period no one would question the unity of metropolitan complexes such as the New York-Jersey City-Hoboken-Newark complex, or to give a European example, Budapest. The com-bination must be of cities that seem too close for cities of their size and which share in the same market or serve the same function, so that they fill jointly the need for a large city in the area. These are in fact not very common. On the other hand, the great cities of the Low Countries, the textile cities, preserved their identities so sharply that one could hardly regard a combination of them as fitting into a rank-size order unless one set up a sort of super-region in north-western Europe.

In general the cities would have been distributed more evenly in the Middle Ages than at present, since there were fewer concentrations of basic industries to disturb a fairly regular pattern. Centres for the processing of salt from springs, ocean water and occasional mines tended to be outside of a normal pattern. Similarly, castles or monasteries in remote places

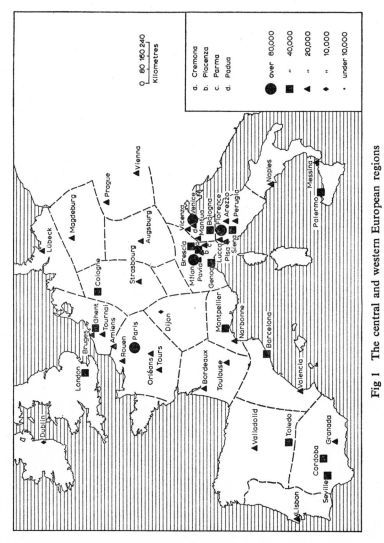

Fig 1   The central and western European regions

produced local centres, but they were not usually of large size. Thus the determining factor in respect of location of settlements from the smallest to the largest was distance. The hamlet or village was within walking distance of the fields and, even within the area, the frequency of visiting the areas affected location: pastures were farther than gardens. Market towns appeared within easy walking range, perhaps every ten kilometres or so. The length of the day's journey, thirty-five to fifty-five-odd kilometres, fixed the location of cities.

The rank-size pattern enables one to identify regions by including the territories obviously dependent upon the cities in the pattern (Fig 1). The problem is often that of the boundaries of two regions in an area with a certain territorial unity, such as the regions of Venice and Milan in the Po Valley. Or take the case of Dijon in France: did it belong to the region of Paris or to a region of its own? It did not fit easily into the pattern for the region of Paris but was sufficiently large to be head of a modest-sized region in Burgundy and to the south. Among the Indian cities the upper Ganges Valley had two very large ones and enough smaller ones to fit the pattern for two regions rather than for the one originally set up for that area. The use of rank-size series is the more valuable because for the Middle Ages the data for determining regions today (newspaper circulation, bank arrangements, wholesale and retail relations, among others) were either non-existent or provided few data. They supplement evidence showing that regions were usually definite territories with physical and often historical unities.

Dickinson has published a map of the modern regions of Germany, which naturally differs considerably from the estimate of medieval regions in this study.[12] The number of regions, for instance, is much greater than the five which are suggested for the Middle Ages. The regions of Munich, Nürnburg, and Stuttgart are essentially the same as the southern region, based on Augsburg. The illustration indicates part of the difference: the three modern cities, of which only one, Munich, was important in the medieval period, and that late, are now great centres of industry. The concentration of great industrial concerns in the Essen-Cologne area show also how the development of basic industries has overshadowed the medieval pattern of more widely distributed cities, based primarily on services, commerce and the basic factors of politics and religion. The medieval pattern ought then to conform more easily to a theoretical base for the distribution of cities within a region. Dickinson mentions this but does not carry the concept very far.

One question arises. Should all of Europe be included within regions or ought some parts be considered as non-regional? Presumably, if the area had few characteristics of a region, it could be considered non-regional. There are areas so rural in Scandinavia, for instance, that one might question whether regions existed there, in our sense of the word. In any case, no effort has been made to set up regions in that peninsula. Similarly, after an initial effort, the attempt to consider Scotland as a region was abandoned. It might seem that southern Scotland was really a part of England, so close were some of the relationships. The Highlands were apparently so hostile to the Lowlands that they could hardly be a part of the same regional complex. Edinburgh stood out as a sizeable city, but without those relationships which seem to make a region. In a sense Glasgow had the same kind of relationship, even more complicated because of its relations with the region of Ireland.

It has been asked whether Dublin might in fact be part of a maritime region that includes London and cities in the Low Countries. This could also be asked of the maritime possessions of Venice and Genoa about the Mediterranean, of course. The Hanseatic League, especially in the Baltic, is another case, while the Barcelona region might be envisaged as extending to such ports as Cagliari and Palermo besides Palma de Mallorca and Ibiza. Carriage by water was less expensive than by land so that communications, even over considerable distance, were cheaper. It raises the question of how relatively important the non-commercial aspects of regionalism were, for water did in fact prevent the continuous mixing of the populations of adjacent areas, a process which operated to fix distinct regional characteristics.

A type of non-regional city would seem to be illustrated by Metz and perhaps by its historical associates along the Franco-German frontier, Verdun and Toul. Metz was quite a large city by the end of the thirteenth century, with perhaps a population of 20,000; by 1500, and probably much earlier, it had a wall enclosing some two hundred hectares.[13] It was about 200 kilometres from Cologne and Dijon, 300 kilometres from Ghent and Paris and more than 350 from Augsburg. It was a little less than 225 kilometres from Strasbourg but across a range of mountains from that place, although on a main highway between that city and Paris. Indeed, it was the focus of an intricate network of Roman roads which made it a natural centre of commerce. It was capital of Lorraine for a time and the seat of a powerful bishopric. Had it been in a less mountainous area and not along the language and historical division between German and Romance, it might well have been a regional centre of considerable importance. As it was, it seems to have been the victim of both physiography and history.

In between the definitely regional areas and what might be called non-regional areas are the less densely settled areas apparently associated with regions, but with few sizeable cities. Holland as a part of the region of Ghent, the Central Massif of the regions of Paris, Dijon and Toulouse, the mountainous areas of Italy, the northern areas of the regions of London and Dublin—these were often associated with the more densely populated areas of the regions more on the political side than the social or economic. One wonders if these areas provided more manpower in the thirteenth-century fighting forces. Or was their importance more in supplying wool, hides, and meat for the cities of the region? The fact of their existence does stand out, however, rather more prominently at the end of the period covered by this study than it did at the beginning.

FUNCTIONS: PATTERN OF MIGRATION

The evolving of a rank-size pattern is obviously connected with patterns of migration.[14] One possibility is that a specialist craftsman or tradesman in the largest city in a region sent a member of his family or group to start the same craft in a smaller city. There is, of course, much evidence of the migration from one city to another as well as of the more important migration (in terms of numbers) of persons from the immediate countryside. A second possibility is that an agent selling a speciality from one market day to another in a series of places would settle in the largest place where he might spend more time. The rise in population of a city thus might be speeded as more and more of the circulating agents settled in the city. This movement would have been a serious factor in reducing the size of lesser cities within easy distance of the larger and growing city.

There are thus two types of migration to consider: local from the countryside into the nearby city, and intercity, mostly of persons who carry certain economic ideas or skills, usually within a family, from city to city. In the case of the migration from countryside into the city, a notable barrier existed to going beyond the nearest large city, the cost of staying overnight in an inn, since one's relatives were apt to be in the nearest city. The first barrier was probably in the city itself. Cities did not replace themselves normally and thus attracted persons from the countryside, both men and women. Despite a total numerical superiority of males (perhaps 120 to 100), nationally or regionally, women outnumbered men in most cities.[15] Once a relationship was established, it would have been easier for other relatives to come both to live free with relatives and to profit from their positions within the city. But the barrier to the next city was much greater, not least because of distance. It might be only 10 to 20 kilometres to the nearest city but the second city must have been normally more than half the distance from city to city (35 to 70 kilometres) or much farther if one went beyond the nearer cities. In addition, intermarriage and frequent associations tended to build up local customs and ideas and the factors of language and habits developed so that men felt strange in farther cities.

The migration into sizeable cities (and the reverse countermigration from cities into the countryside) was largely proportional to distance. It would tend to set up cultural areas of perhaps thirty-five to sixty kilometres in diameter. The migration from the lesser cities to larger in the rank-size group created a circulation within the region, and thus gave the region its essential characteristics. The influence of this migration was reinforced by the medieval affection for family-visits between the original city where the family lived and their migrant relatives. Migrants frequently used their influence to provide places for promising relatives in their new homes.

If the migrant went beyond the nearer cities, however, he

found himself at home only in small colonies of his fellow citizens in those farther cities, not in the intermediate villages or even quite small market towns. In the larger places, nuclei developed of persons of common origins or interests. Although almost any obstacle could hinder movement, it was those who surmounted local barriers within an area who gave it its regional characteristics. Along the French-German border it was those who spoke or tried to speak both languages who circulated through the entire area and propagated the dialect which gives the region its characteristic *patois*. Middle English became standard English; it could be best understood by those to the south and the north; Tuscan became Italian, in part for the same reason, although its sheer beauty was a factor to the beauty-loving Italians.

A third type of migration, colonisation, was a large-scale movement to fill areas either thinly inhabited or vacated by pushing or driving inhabitants from an area. Some were very conspicuous, like the German *Drang nach Osten* in the marches to the east of that country, or the large scale Slavic movement into the north-east of Europe before the Teutonic Knights took over that area. A large migration of Castilians, mostly north of Toledo, helped fill the southern Iberian cities from which Moors were expelled. There was some movement of the French into the Holy Land, and in Egypt movements along the western edge of the Delta and up the Nile river. In Spain there was the 'population' by land grants into territory vacated by the retreating Moors. Closer study of these movements is necessary in order to understand their extent.

Regions were, then, areas in which certain types of migration took place easily. Distance itself was a factor; in the smaller places most of the migration came from the immediate country-side and even in the larger cities a considerable migration of that type occurred.[16] But beyond the local migration, distance was only one factor, although a quite important one. The principle of the least effort operates here as in most of life. Migrations moved more easily along trade routes than across them, and along rivers than on roads. People were more readily attracted to areas which spoke the same language than to areas of a foreign language. Of course, once relatives were established in a place it was easier to migrate there and get a start with them or with their assistance and advice. Actually, several factors were complementary: distance, relatives, language and even types of employment. A man equipped with particular skills went to a city where relatives existed, who spoke his language and were employed in the same type of work. The net result was to build up groups over a geographical area having common customs, languages, and employment.

This was being done rapidly in the period between AD 1000 and the Black Death of 1348 because the population increased its total at least two and perhaps three times in the period. Much of the urban increase was the result of migration from the countryside since medieval cities, like most cities, had trouble in just replacing their population. Cities usually had more women than men, a lower marriage rate and consequently fewer marriages and less children than the countryside. The rapid increase of urban population accordingly indicates a very considerable increase of migration. Girls came in to acquire a dowry as maids in the wealthier households. Boys migrated from the countryside to fill the ranks of the workers. Families moved to take advantage of better opportunities in the larger cities. As Mols has pointed out in his excellent study of migration, the larger the city, the more distant the area from which the migrants came and, of course, they brought with them ideas and customs from larger areas, as the chief bases for the development of the region.[17] The particular importance of the population movement of this period was its great size, compared to that of the preceding feudal period and the consequent strong development of regions.

For the medieval period we are not attempting a quantitative study of migration since the figures are not extensive and the problems of calculation quite difficult. The lists of new citizens, already mentioned, provide some of the best information. They do not tell much about the girls and women, so numerically important, nor even much about boys who came as apprentices, although they may appear in the lists when admitted as masters. If the total population of a city can be estimated, a certain death-rate can be assumed although the instances are mostly of the plague period, highly exaggerated for the pre-plague era. Nor does one know much about emigration from the city—the number for instance, retiring to their home villages or seeking new locations. Many families carried names of their home towns as surnames, indicating that they or their ancestors came from the towns. But the medieval personal name might indicate, as well as place of origin, things such as colour (Black, White, Brown), trade (Smith, Weaver), father (Jones, Davidson) or residence (Attewood) so that the evidence of migration from this source is limited. It is sufficient then merely to indicate that the migration was extensive and probably provided at least a quarter to half of the population of any growing city in this period.

FUNCTION: BASIC-NONBASIC FACTORS

Within cities themselves quantitative measures may be considered for two types of factors: positions produced by outside income and those supported by needs of the first group. These are called basic and nonbasic. Today it is understood that if a factory moves into a city, and sells its products outside the city, that it will increase the city's population by about six or seven times the number of its employees; thus a factory employing a thousand workers will increase the civic population by about six or seven thousand. Each worker represents a family of approximately three or 3.5 plus a nonbasic worker with the same sized family to support him. The largest cities today exhibit a somewhat different proportion, but they are very much greater in size than the medieval cities. It must be noted that this definition of basic and nonbasic is not the exact equivalent of production and service personnel: the latter term is not suited to the medieval period. An illustration of a basic factor would be a monastery set up in a village which would increase the size of the village by about the same number of families as there were monks in the house. The same would be true for a castle with its courtiers and its garrison: about an equal number of families in the near-by village as there were courtiers and garrison. One need not say that the village growing up near a castle did so because of the 'protection' available; the village just supplied an economic need.

The schedule of basic persons needs some explanation. The basic persons, as noted above, were those whose support came from outside the city. The income of the king, for instance, largely from payments from all over the country although, of course, some came from the city itself. Income for the bishops, for most of the monasteries, cathedral chapters, and nobility came from lands which they possessed outside the city itself. Merchants and guildsmen who produced primarily for outside purchase, such as the textile workers of Ghent, were also basic. Small farmers who lived in a city barely supported themselves and their families and so were merely counted as

TABLE 1: VERY TENTATIVE SCHEDULE FOR BASIC FACTORS IN A CITY

Factor	Basic Persons	Dependents	Nonbasic Persons	Total.
King	200	500	700	1,400
	500	1,250	1,750	3,500
Bishop	40	100	140	280
	200	500	700	1,400
Monastery	20		70	90
	100		350	450
Cathedral	20	50	70	140
	50	125	175	350
Duke	30	75	105	210
	50	125	175	350
Count-Earl	10	25	35	70
	30	75	105	210
County officials	5	12	18	35
	15	22	38	75
Basic merchant	5	12	18	35
	50	125	175	350
Guildsmen, basic	1	2.5	3.5	7
	10	25	35	70
Small farmers in city	1	2.5		3.5

parts of the population in addition to an estimate based on the basic support. Nonbasic guilds (providing for the city people alone) and such groups as priests of city churches (which had no outside city support), dock workers and intra-city porters either were not counted as in an estimate based on basic factors or, if all were counted, as part of the total.

In the scale of basic factors the permanent presence of a royal court ranks high. Capitals have seldom been studied as sources of population but their importance cannot be doubted.[18] Not only was a court with its members, often numbering several hundred, responsible for adding perhaps seven times its number to the city, but many other people were drawn there for political, social, and financial reasons. This usually set the capital above other cities, as in the cases of Cairo, London, Paris, and Palermo. Conversely, the failure to establish a more or less permanent centre, as in Germany or Iberia, often operated against the rise of outstanding centres in this period. The presence of parliamentary assemblies was also a factor of some importance.[19] On going to Avignon, the Papal Curia apparently had about 450 *curiales* which should have added about 3,000 to the population of that city.[20] The establishment of a capital often brought feudal nobles to it; with no capital they were often a factor in less important cities.

One of the causes of the rapid rise of north Italian cities in the thirteenth century must have been the voluntary or enforced move of great feudal families into the cities. They brought not only sizeable groups of members and retainers but also a large buying power. They built those impressive palaces which are now the tourist attractions of the cities. A palace holding fifty to a hundred people supported by income from agricultural holdings outside of the city would be basic for at least another fifty to a hundred nonbasic people within the city; given the family wealth, the nonbasic element depending upon it might even be more. And once in the cities the families soon turned to the interests of their neighbours, commerce and industry. They often provided a more aggressive leadership for the cities, a development not quite so happy for its future. However, the attitude of nobles and gentry differed very widely over Europe,[21] so that each city had its own experience with its feudal neighbours, but the relationship had quite important demographic significance.

Another facet of the population picture is the importance of the textile industry in the period. Some of the greatest of the cities, notably in the Low Countries, had the industry not only as the chief basic factor, but as on overwhelming part of the factor. It was likewise very important in the regions of Florence, Venice, and Milan in Italy as well as in the regions of Montpellier and Barcelona. The development of a hierarchy of cities rests heavily upon diversification of industry and multiplication of products. This was very true of the thirteenth-century textile industry with multiple bases of clothing, not merely the ancient wool trade, but the newer linen, silk, and cotton. People seemed to relish producing both the tremendous variety of types of weaving of the cloth and the variety of colours, especially with the brilliant new red just then on the market.

Another developing industry of the late thirteenth and early fourteenth century was the paper industry. Fortunately it made use of watermarks almost from the beginning, apparently from Jativa. C. M. Briquet's great collection (*Les filigranes*)[22] enables one to follow the spread of paper-making over Italy, France, Germany and Britain, showing again, the influence of space and thus of regionalism in its development. Unfortunately, Briquet omitted Spain and thus did not understand the very great importance of that country in paper history. *Catalan* paper was widely used even in southern France in the late thirteenth century and much of the fourteenth century.[23] For many documents vellum was still used; the prevalence of cattle and sheep made it relatively cheap at that time. The addition of paper to vellum represents again a multiplication of types within the industry.

The extensive textile trade, and perhaps even more the great wine and paper trades, indicate the growing wealth and accompanying sophistication of the thirteenth century—part of the new secularisation of society. More and more people were not content with the homespun cloth or locally worked leather clothes of their ancestors. Furthermore, very many had money to buy the more expensive and very popular cloth imported first from the Low Countries and then from Italy or the Pyrenees region. Similarly local wine, beer, or other alcoholic drinks were not good enough for those with more money. As life became somewhat more secure over wide areas with the cessation of local fighting, as in France or England, money formerly spent on fortifications became available for the purchase of luxuries. One reason for the obviously slow development of German trade must have been that Germans spent more on defences in the pre-plague period as anarchy and local government persisted in the area. Despite these variants from more secure conditions, a widespread long-distance commerce developed for the first time since the disappearance of the Roman Empire in the west.

The relation of basic factors to the region was often quite significant. A region with only one political ruler (as London), which had a well-developed bureaucracy (for the Middle Ages), would tend to have a large capital city. Regions divided among several political leaders (such as the German regions) might not have such dominant metropolitan cities in them. Great concentrations of basic factors as in the Italian regions or the Low Countries might increase the town's share of the total population of the region. This approach to the region has been strictly demographic. It does have the advantage through the rank-size series of defining the area of a region, although in most cases it must be left to elements of the trade and commerce beyond the limits of the region.

The determination of the relative size of cities also enables one to compare the urban population with the population of the whole region. In this study we use the size of the largest ten cities as an index of urbanisation in comparison with the regional population, calling it the 'urban index'. If the normal size of the largest city was about 1.5% of the total population of a region, the urban index was usually 4.9%. A greater urban index than this would raise questions about the reasons for the larger number. This was true for the northern Italian regions and for the Netherlands, since both had extensive physical geography to suggest the limits of the region.

This chapter has set up the outlines of the structure of the region as it appeared in the Middle Ages. With the increase of population there was an increase in the size of cities which tended to form a rank-size pattern. This will be illustrated in the succeeding chapters for many of the regions of the medieval world. The effort here has been to explain why such a pattern appeared and how it was ordered. It will be demonstrated that in many of the regions such an order apparently did not appear until in the thirteenth century. The advantage of using such a pattern as a base is obvious. Conformity to it indicates a considerable urbanisation. Deviations from it are most interesting and indicate peculiar conditions in the particular region.

2

Central and Southern Italy:
Florence and Palermo

ITALY IN MOST respects was the most advanced country in
Europe, probably even in the world during the period AD
1250–1348. It occupied a central position in the European-
Mediterranean area at a time when the northern European
states were advancing rapidly and learning much from the
Mediterranean culture. Such a shift in development was bound
to affect the status of various regions, often changing the
relative importance of cities within them. The great increase
in population occurred primarily in Italy, France, Germany
and the lesser countries in this period. It also occurred as
rapidly in Egypt as in the West, but probably much less rapidly
in Asia Minor, the Balkans, Syria, and North Africa west of
Egypt. The way in which the reshaping of cities within a region
occurred is perhaps best illustrated by the region of Florence
in the thirteenth century, while the partial disintegration of a
region is shown in the decline of Palermo in the south of
Italy.

Information about Italian population is, in comparison with
most European countries, quite considerable. The great
historian, K. J. Beloch, made population his main interest in
his later years, preparing a great *Bevölkerungsgeschichte
Italiens* which was published by friends after his death in three
substantial volumes. He carried his study into modern times,
but the medieval sections are quite impressive, bequeathing
a great mass of information for the medievalist. After his

death an Italian committee made an extensive survey of demographical materials (*Fonti archivistiche*) which reveals material which even Beloch did not discover. World War II disturbed some archives, such as those at Bologna, but, for the most part, the wealth of data is still there. It is doubtful if enough new material exists to change the outline of population development as now defined; probably more change will result from further study and different interpretations of the existing evidence.

Medieval Florence and Tuscany have been much favoured by scholarship of the last half-century for a variety of well-known reasons, especially the period from AD 1250 to the end of the Renaissance.[1] At the beginning of the thirteenth century the larger cities were in the range of five to twenty thousands with none notably larger than the others. By the end of the century Florence had outstripped the rest. What is more interesting is that the pattern of sizes of cities approaches a standard arrangement by rank-size and was thus like many other medieval regions.

In general the history of Tuscany has a certain unity except in the period before the thirteenth-century integration. It was the core of the Etruscan lands with its special traditions of settlement and life and seems to have maintained its traditional unity throughout Roman days. It has an obvious territorial unity, bounded on the west by the Mediterranean, and on the north and east by the Apennines. Only on the South was the limit uncertain as it merged with papal territories.

The physical geography of a region influences the spacing of the cities (Fig 2). Tuscany has two peculiarities. The first is that the mountains with their low population density have a limiting influence as a barrier to the north and east, creating a question as to Tuscan relationships with the cities just across the Apennines. As it is, a line of the Tuscan cities lies quite close to the mountains which apparently cut off land normally a part of the region. The pattern of Tuscan cities thus has a skewed distribution. Probably the economic activities of Bologna (or other Po Valley cities) actually filled the normal position of one or two places in the Tuscan pattern. Thus the seventh position (in Table 3) is assigned to Bologna in part. Even assuming that some of the activities of the city of Bologna belonged to the region, by any standard the Tuscan area was small for a region.

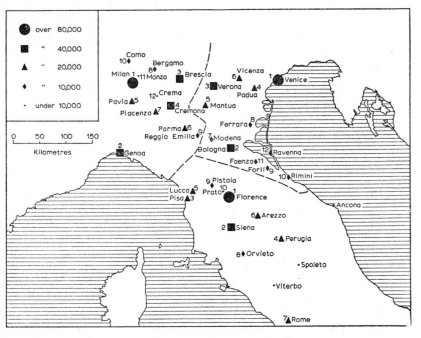

Fig 2   The regions of Florence, Venice, and Milan

The second peculiarity is that the Tiber river valley parallels Tuscany to the east and south so that it is uncertain whether such cities as Perugia and Orvieto belong to it or to the region of Rome (assuming such a region, which is doubtful). They are included here in the Tuscan region, adding about 7,000 km² to the area. This also assumes that the political connections of the two cities with Rome were so independent and loose that their economic interests, tied in with the Tuscan cities, were of more importance. Rome was primarily a city of religious and pilgrim interests with a minimal economic life.

The population of these cities has already been studied by

authorities whose opinions about size have been generally accepted. The problem of the number of persons to a house, to a holding or in the family of an oathtaker remains, but the range of interpretations is being reduced, in spite of marked variations in historical documentation. Perhaps more uncertain is the relation of population to the areas within city walls. Hilltop cities, such as Siena, Perugia, and San Gimignano seem more densely settled, perhaps because space had always been at a premium.

Florence was much the largest city in Tuscany at the end of the thirteenth century. But to maintain a perspective we begin a study of population about AD 1200 with Pisa, which, at least up to AD 1200, maintained its undeniable status as the largest and commercially most advanced city in Tuscany—a status enhanced further by its rapid overseas expansion. Yet Herlihy suggests a population of only about 11,000 in AD 1164 and 15,000 plus in AD 1226.[2] The estimate for AD 1164 might be upgraded. The army of 3,000 horsemen and 400 footsoldiers might well be multiplied by as many as four, which would suggest at least 13,000, while the number of persons to the hectare in a prosperous, rapidly growing city could be at least 125, which would give Pisa's 114 hectares about 13,250 persons. Indeed, it is rather difficult to conceive a port of Pisa's great importance having less than 15,000. The treaty of AD 1228 was sworn to by about 4,271 Pisans, which, it has been assumed, indicates from 15,000 to 40,000 inhabitants. The poorest 30% may well have not been included, as being too poor. This would suggest somewhat over 20,000 circa AD 1228 and about that number around AD 1200.

In comparison with these, the second circle of Florentine walls begun in 1172 and carried rapidly to completion, enclosed about 80 hectares.[3] At about 125 to the hectare (it could hardly have been more) Florence would then have had a population of only about ten thousand. The city was, however, growing rapidly and must have had at least 15,000 by the end of the century. Although Siena was the largest city in southern Tuscany, its population is hard to estimate. Even circa 1300 the enclosed area seems to have been only about fifty hectares, but the peculiar morphology of the city, sited among relatively steep hills, makes definition difficult. Fifty hectares, even at a high density of 400 to the hectare, would only give 20,000 persons. The area seems to have been built over by 1200; so that half of that number, or 10,000, is suggested. Pistoia's wall, built about 1240, enclosed 114 hectares, and earlier, in 1219, 3,206 male citizens swore to maintain a peace treaty with Bologna. Both the area enclosed by the wall and the number of citizens suggest a population of about 11,000. This would give about 100 to the hectare, which was slightly low for a growing and prosperous medieval city. From a map of Lucca the first line of walls, presumably before 1200, might have enclosed about 54 hectares to hold about 10,000 at most; a later line of walls included about 75 hectares. The walls of Perugia, Arezzo, and Orvieto and Prato, together with their later population, suggest roughly the figures assigned to them. The fifteenth-century size of several other cities suggests populations of about the size of San Gimignano. The obvious lack of pattern among the sizes makes the accurate definition of size of less importance than if there had been evidence of a pattern (Table 2).

TABLE 2: REGION OF TUSCANY ABOUT AD 1200-1230

Rank,	City	Pop Est 1,000s	Hyp Est 1,000s	Area hectares		Beloch vol. 2
1	Pisa	15–20	20	114	1228–4240 C	161
2	Florence	15–20	11	105		128
3	Siena	10–15	7.6	50		150
4	Pistoia	11	5.9	114	1219–3206 m	169
5	Perugia	10?	4.8	72		62
6	Lucca	10?	4.1	54		165
7	Arezzo	8?	3.5	45		
8	Orvieto	7	3.2			
9	Prato	6?	2.9	66		170
10	San Gimignano	5	2.6	20	1457 m	

Pisa: Herlihy, *Pisa* 36. Florence: Herlihy, *Pisa* 35, 41. Siena: map in *EUI*. Pistoia: Herlihy, *Pistoia* 74, 76. Perugia: map in *EUI*. Lucca: Herlihy 42–3: map in *EUI*. Arezzo: map from Library of Congress map F 531.9–4 3281 1935. Orvieto: Carpentier, *Orvieto*, map on p 24. Prato: Herlihy, *Pistoia* 74: map in Library of Congress map F 532 9–4 01,766. San Gimignano: Fiumi, *San Gimignano* 155: Herlihy, *Pistoia* 73 ; map in Library of Congress, map GSGS 4280 1943.

The twelfth and even more so the thirteenth century saw the cities spreading their influence over the surrounding *contados*. Unlike the feudal leaders of northern countrysides, the Italian feudal group tended to move into the chief city of the *contado*, building there the *palazzos* which are so typical of the cities. The results of this movement were very important. From a demographic point of view, it meant adding to the rapid growth of the city; each great family moving into the city probably added from fifty to several hundreds to the city population, of basic and nonbasic elements. Many families, with living conditions too dangerous in the countryside were forced within the city walls. These families provided much of the more aggressive leadership of the cities, again a notable difference between their activities in Italy and in the north.

TABLE 3: REGION OF FLORENCE NEAR END OF THE THIRTEENTH CENTURY

Rank,	City	Pop Est 1,000s	Hyp Est 1,000s	Area hectares		Beloch vol 2
1	Florence	96	96	630		128–30
2	Siena	52	52.8	50+	1328–11,710	150
3	Pisa	38	36.4	185		161
4	Perugia	28	28.2	72	1285–5,529 h	
5	Lucca	23	23	75–95	1333–4,736 m	165–6
6	Arezzo	20?	19.6	99		170–2
7	Rome, or part of Bologna		17.2			1–3
8	Orvieto	14	15.2	106	1292–2,816 h	45–6
9	Pistoia	11	13.7	114		169
10	Prato	9	12.5	66	End xiv[c]–1,070 t	170
	Viterbo	9			1449–ca.6,000	57
	Spoleto	6?				62

Florence: Herlihy, *Pisa* 35, 41, 43. Siena: *Bowsky* 8, 11. Pisa: Herlihy, *Pisa* 36. Perugia: *Waley* 85.n.3 ; Carpentier, *Orvieto* 3. Lucca: Herlihy, *Pisa* 42–3. 23,800 proportionate to Siena's heads. Arezzo: map in Library of Congress F 331. 9–4 3281. Orvieto: Carpentier, *Orvieto* 30, map on p 24. Pistoia: Herlihy, *Pistoia* 74 ; map in Library of Congress F 331. 9–4 01766.

The cities grew rapidly in the thirteenth century (Table 3). Florence outstripped the others and had about 96,000 at the end of the century. On the basis of a reinterpretation of the Siena data, the AD 1328 list of 11,710 heads of families for that city yields an estimate of about 52,000, which does not include 'the very poor, transients and the religious population'.[4] For Pisa there was a total population in 1293 of about 38,000[5]. For Lucca the range is between an estimate of about 15,000, based upon the 4,746 men who swore fealty to King John of Bohemia and his son, Charles, in March 1333, and about 40,000 based on Lucca's consumption of 168,000 barrels of wine in 1334, assuming five or six barrels a person. The city walls add some evidence. The 630 hectares of the Florentine walls gave about 150 a hectare. The walls of Siena apparently never included more than fifty hectares, but the city seems to have had extensive suburbs—its hilly location made their enclosure difficult. The walls of Pisa eventually included about 185 hectares, which would give about 205 persons to the hectare. Lucca's walls also enclosed a relatively small area, some 75 hectares, but it must have had some suburbs: about twenty more hectares were included in the sixteenth-century walls, where the heavy fortifications would have destroyed evidence of earlier edifices. Seventy-five hectares and 15,000 persons would give 200 to the hectare; 30,000 and about 100 hectares would give about 300 to the hectare, probably too dense.

The first three cities conform closely to the hypothetical pattern of the rank-size order. While Lucca has been estimated at between 15,000 and 40,000 and thus included, the 23,000 suggested for the fifth ranking city is near the 23,800 estimate of Lucca's 'men' if they were proportionate to Siena's 'heads'. Perugia would seem to fit into the fourth place since it had about the right number of hearths—5,529—for the suggested number of persons. The calculation for the population of Arezzo is more devious. It had only 1,776 *allirati* (taxpayers) in 1390 after several epidemics of the plague, but there was a sizeable exclusion on the basis of lack of property. Assuming five to the taxpayer and a 30% exclusion, the number in 1390 should have been about 12,700, and a 40% decline during the plagues should indicate a pre-plague population of about

20,000; the walls enclosed about 106 hectares. It is possible that Bologna—the nearest and a very large city across the Apennines—occupied with a part of its activity in commerce, education and political power the place of the seventh city in the region of Florence. Actually Bologna occupied an anomalous position. It hardly had a region of its own but lay on the edge of the regions of Florence, Milan, and Venice (it has in fact been tentatively included in the last region). The ninth and tenth positions seem to have been those of Pistoia and Prato. There is a definite failure in the region to have cities in the range of five to ten thousand, probably because the region was too small and the intense economic life concentrated near the mountains. The total number assigned to the top ten cities of the region thus increased in the course of the century from about 102,000 to about 310,000, a threefold increase. Even if Bologna (in part) is eliminated and San Gimignano substituted, the number is still near 300,000. The number is very conjectural, it is true, but the chances are that the estimate is within twenty to thirty thousand of the actual number. The increase in any case was very large in comparison to the civic population of the region. Now the problem arises as to the total population of the region: the 21,000km² of Tuscany and an additional 7,000 of the *contados* of Perugia and Orvieto. This is probably a minimum area for the region since it may have incorporated some territory to the east, albeit in part rather thinly settled mountainous country.

Of the total population of Tuscany alone, wide variations in estimates appear. Beloch thought that the population of the countryside was not notably different in the sixteenth century from what it had been in the thirteenth and thus would have been about 912,700. Another suggestion, of 1.2 millions, is based upon the average density of population in all of Pistoia's territory. At a greater extreme is the suggestion of two millions, based on the estimate for the lands of San Gimignano. The trouble with these is that the civic population of both cities occupies a much larger proportion of the total population of their areas than is true for all Tuscany. The population of the countryside seems to have remained fairly stable or even to have declined in the thirteenth century.

When the population of the larger cities has been subtracted from the total population of the areas held by those cities, the average density is not great. The relatively thickly settled countryside of Pistoia averaged about 38 to the km², while that of San Gimignano was about the same. Even Florence's 120,000 for the country people, divided into its 4,250km² gives only about 28 to the km². The 266 Sienese *contado* communities, whose number of farms *(mazzarizio)* are known, had 10,453 farms; the total (295 communities) should have had about 11,600. At 6 to the farm the population would have been 69,900, an average of about 16 to each km² of Siena's 4,500km². The thirteenth-century population of three small areas in Pisa's *contado* seems to have been about two-thirds of their sixteenth century population. If this percentage were the same for all of the Pisan lands outside of the city, the *contado* would have had only about 26,000 in the thirteenth century in its 1,430km², an average of about 18 persons per km². This was a low density but compatible with the wooded and swampy character of that countryside. Under the circumstances it is doubtful if the land outside of the cities in the region of Florence averaged more than 30 to the km², even including the smaller cities. For 28,000km², including the territories of Perugia and Orvieto, the population would then have been about 840,000. Adding the larger cities would give the total area about 942,000 persons early in the century and about 1,140,000 at the end. This would give a density including the cities, of about 41 per km².

If one assumes that the top city in a normal medieval region should have had 1.5% of the total population, the first ten cities, as discussed earlier, should have had about 4.7%, one kind of urban index. In the region which we have considered, leaving out the possibility of Bolognese territory as part, the first ten cities in the early part of the thirteenth century had about 10.8% of the total population, more than double the normal degree of urbanisation. For the latter part of the century this index rose to 26.3%, a really stupendous one. The only other regions which were likely to match such an index were the regions of the Po Valley and the Low Countries. The region of Barcelona shows an index somewhat above normal (see Chapter 8). Even within the Florentine region it can be seen that the Arno Valley could not have supported five such cities as Pisa, Lucca, Pistoia, Prato, and Florence and that their support must have rested in part upon their international finance and commerce.

The difference between the pattern of population of the greater cities in the region in the first half of the thirteenth century and the second half requires explanation. One of these differences was the apparent simplicity of life in the first period, commented upon extensively at the end of the century. Cities of ten to twenty thousand, which were of considerable size for the Middle Ages, could satisfy the needs of the people in the first half of the century. For instance, the heavy dependence upon leather, so propitious for Pisa, declined when paper was substituted for parchment, glass windows for oil-soaked leather ones; pottery, glass, or metal for leather-lined bottles; silk and linen for leather purses; iron for leather armour and shields; wool for leather clothing, particularly for trousers; only the saddlers continued to work extensively in leather.[6] But until the new styles came in, the need for specialisation by glass, paper, ceramic, silk, linen, metal and wool workers did not exist. And, of course, as the commerce of the cities reached far across the sea, the need for more sophisticated methods of trade and finance developed.

Political conditions before the thirteenth century had favoured civic individualism. There was a county of Tuscany in the tenth and eleventh centuries, but it had never been an effective political unit. The gift of the county by its last countess, Mathilda, to the pope, precipitated a struggle between the pope and emperor, which enabled the rising communes of area to secure their independence with a minimum of struggle, at least compared with that of the Lombard communes. The region had too many archbishops, at Florence, Pisa, and Siena, to make for ecclesiastical unity. Thus the twelfth century saw about as intense a particularism after AD 1114 in that region as existed in Europe at that time. The move to develop the Papal States as a political unit in the thirteenth century came too late to affect the region of Florence very much.

Political particularism was probably increased by the divergent interests of the several cities. Pisa was a great seaport with extensive trade with Sardinia, North Africa, and the

Levant. Pistoian interests lay with the great passes over the Alps and the iron industry. Lucca early developed the manufacture of silk, while Florence specialised in textiles and banking. Arezzo and Siena were centres of agricultural areas with interests in wool, as were Perugia and Orvieto. Antagonism between Guelf and Ghibelline inclinations and occasional wars helped widen the breaches among them. As long as they were fairly small, they could live within their *contados* and devote their time to local interests. The roads ran along the foot of the mountains and avoided, until the road building of the thirteenth century, the mud of the open country.

Increasing European prosperity made for more travel along the main roads to and from Rome and some of these went through the larger cities of the region of Florence. It was hard to get to Rome by land from the north without going through Florence or Arezzo and it was better to go by Pistoia or even Lucca. The era of better roads required less energy than in the period when one had to climb over the foothills. These better roads also tended to draw the cities together. The importance of wider trade is evident in the effort to maintain a relatively stable coinage by the chief cities.

Commerce involved even the smaller cities. 'The figure of the merchant of San Gimignano,' Fiumi noted, 'does not differ from that of the merchants of Pisa, Lucca, Siena, Florence and Pistoia'.[7] They did not limit their activities to local and mutual commerce, but maintained *(correvano)* their commerce over the highways of the world. International commerce, if we may call it that, was a unifying influence. Throughout history the merchant has united, while the political leader has divided, a kind of dissonance in history. The participation of the small city of San Gimignano in overseas commerce was probably rather exceptional, but it does indicate something of the common commercial interests of the area which would operate to create a regional economy. For, after all, the merchants of San Gimignano, with the merchants of other inland cities, would have had to use the shipping and probably other facilities of Pisa as the one seafaring city of the area. And the extensive credit facilities of Florence must likewise have been needed by other cities as well. Tuscan colonies abroad in the

Pisan and other *fattorie* would have been a source of mutual profit and understanding.

From 1250 to 1300 the political development of overriding significance was the rise of the *popolo*. Following the death of Frederick II in 1250, 'a torrent of popular uprising breaks out'.[8] A few years later the restoration of Hohenstauffen power re-established aristocratic governments, and this in turn was followed by a popular reaction in 1266. Thus in these and ensuing upheavals there was a chain of reaction, although individual cities, like Pisa at times, remained outside the general movements. Common action produced a Guelf League. Even politically the cities acted integrally on occasion, and struggles were as often among intramural groups as among cities.

Florence, Siena, Pisa and Perugia extended also gradually their control over more and more smaller cities, regulating trade and apparently even encouraging it, in such subordinated cities as Pistoia. The reduction of the area to a few great spheres of influence did much to unify the region, continuing the regional unification which had proceeded in other fields of interest. Along with these, often encouraged by political interests, went the great cultural development. The architects, sculptors and even the poets of the area tended to learn from each other, and the cities competed to embellish their churches and other buildings. Their young men went first to Bologna and Padua and then to Arezzo for their legal and other education. All of these are phases of the spread of ideas.

The high index of urbanisation, as mentioned earlier, shows the dependence of the cities of the region of Florence upon a far wider area than its own region. The danger, of course, was that other cities would develop textile and financial facilities in areas served by the Tuscan cities and, profiting by shorter hauls and nearer markets, would reduce the base of Tuscan economic strength. As long as Tuscan names carried prestige for sophisticated goods, they could probably maintain their position for luxury goods. The achievement of the pattern of hierarchial character, the rank-size order of cities, shows that the area had attained economic integration as a region.

The account of the development of Tuscan into the Italian language is of interest. Uusually it is assumed that this occurred because Dante chose to write in it.[9] and because it was the most beautifully spoken dialect. The high degree of urbanisation of the area could have been an important factor. It gave large numbers of men and perhaps women the wealth and consequent leisure to devote time to such cultural pursuits as writing poetry, and, eventually, as painting and sculpture. Furthermore, the very wealth produced many patrons for such literature and art. Normally, to have one Dante an area should have a thousand others who were trying to write poetry and who could appreciate poetry: this is a statistical concept which underlies nearly all important human effort. But statistics makes provision for the accidental in the curve of chance. There is naturally the question of motivation: why did the Florentines in the course of the thirteenth century, apparently a typically obdurate group of Italian merchants before 1250, suddenly turn their attention to art and literature, especially poetry, along with ever rougher politics, rather than continue with the making of money as virtually their only interest?

The inclusion of Perugia and Orvieto, which technically were in the Papal States, suggests the possibility that the entire area within papal jurisdiction south of Romagna might be considered in the region of Florence. This would be mainly the March of Ancona, the Duchy of Spoleto and the land immediately about Rome, possibly doubling the territory of the region. It would be an attractive addition since it would add to the region's list of cities a series containing about 5,000 to 12,500 persons in population where the present regional list is weak: Ancona, Pesaro, and Spoleto. It would also suggest that any reference to Bologna might be deleted and the city of Rome substituted in its place. The most serious problem is the size of Rome itself. Obviously Rome was connected closely with the cities to the north through which the continuous stream of pilgrims and merchants came to the city.

Rome's first recorded census was of the year 1526 and showed 55,035 persons.[10] The only other data, for the early fourteenth century, give about 3,000 clerks (including about 1,200 monks and nuns) with another 1,966 *hospitalerii*. The 1526 population was the result of consolidation of the administration of the Papal States over the preceding century and Rome's growing attraction as a seat of religion. Yet simply being a great pilgrim centre did not necessarily produce a large population: the second great focal point for pilgrimages, Santiago de Compostela, had apparently only about 7,000 in the thirteenth century. As basic factors, the religious can usually be multiplied by only three or four—suggesting about 5,000 for Rome. The Papal Curia could hardly have been the haven for more than another 5,000, even as the administrative hub of the Papal States. It is thus quite possible that thirteenth-century Rome did not have more than the 17–20,000 needed for the position in the list now suggested for Bologna. Another possibility is that the populations of Perugia and Lucca should be estimated by 4.5 persons to the unit (as in Siena) which would reduce them to 24,000 and 21,000 respectively. Thus Rome's population could be estimated as high as 30,000 and fill the fourth place in the list.[11]

Rome, as well as the rest of the Papal States cities, suffered from the residence of the nobles in the country rather than in the cities. Each noble of considerable wealth, coming from extensive lands, should have had a retinue of 30 to 40 at least which, multiplied by seven, would have added about 210 to 280 to the city for each noble household. If they were in the city, they had a tendency to go into business and thus help even more to build up the city. When the popes were building up a centralised government for the whole area through rectors or other officials for political divisions like the March of Ancona and the Duchy of Spoleto, these officials did not settle or stay long at Ancona or Spoleto but lived in the smaller cities. Under these circumstances, all cities in the Papal States were handicapped in their growth and influence. Thus the Tuscan part of central Italy dominated the papal part throughout the thirteenth century and, of course, the presence of the Curia at Avignon from 1305 to 1377 was an inhibiting factor in Roman development.[12]

THE REGION OF PALERMO

The region of Palermo seems to have included, in the thirteenth century, Italy south of the Papal States and Sicily (Fig 3).[13] The Norman kings had dominated most of the territory since about AD 1090 and their administration had created elements of common life for the whole area, despite the peculiar physical features of the kingdom. The great range of mountains split southern Italy with Apulia as a plain to the south-east and Campania in the north-west. In the island of Sicily there were plains in the Syracuse-Catania area and occasionally elsewhere. The cities might be expected to be in those areas, at least the larger cities. Communication was largely by water, although lines of old Roman roads connected Campania with Apulia and other places beyond the mountains. The period considered for this region is essentially from about AD 1250 to the time of the Black Death, although a case might be made for the gradual separation into regions after the Sicilian Vespers of 1282.

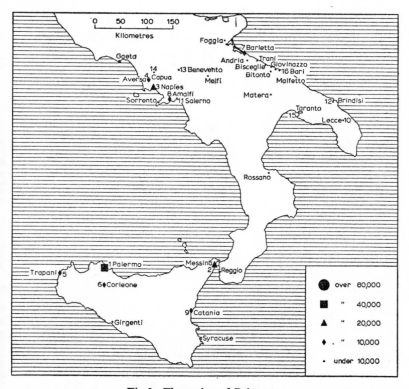

Fig 3 The region of Palermo

The sources of information include records from several

taxes levied over the whole area in the period, primarily upon hearths but unfortunately at an even rate only for districts. So one of the chief problems is the interpretation of the taxes for use in the study of population. Since in some cases the taxes were upon the whole district rather than upon the city alone, a continuation of the ancient city-state idea, a problem remains here also. In some cases the information about the size of the city is important.

TABLE 4: REGION OF PALERMO

Rank,	City	Pop Est 1,000s	Hyp Est 1,000s	Area hectares	Base	Beloch vol 1
1	Palermo	50	50	200	1276–2,201.4 un	151, 159
2	Messina	30	28.5	200	1277–1,330 un	152, 159
3	Naples	25	19.5	200	1277–500 un ; 1320–500 un	169–70, 178
4	Aversa	15	15	56	1320–300 un	235–7, 274
5	Trapani	13.6	12	90	1277–680.6 un	150
6	Corleone	13.2	10.2	56	1277–660 un	119
7	Barletta	13	9.8	96		272–3
8	Amalfi	13?	7.9			243, 273
9	Catania	10	7.2	96		145
10	Lecce	7		96		
11	Salerno			60		
12	Brindisi			56		
13	Benevento			45		
14	Capua			41		276
15	Taranto			30		273
16	Bari			30		

Palermo: Traselli. Naples: Dopp, abh.3. Aversa: Egli 36. Amalfi: much of the city disappeared into the sea in 1344. Citarella 531. Catania: Ruocco. Bari: Egli 89.

Beloch[14] has presented information about Palermo in the late medieval period and this is supplemented by interesting information from Professor Traselli (Table 4).[15] Beloch estimated the population at about 50,000 or about 8,800 hearths in 1276 based upon the tax return of 2,201.4 *unze*. The tax apparently was about a quarter *unza* to the hearth in Sicily. However, 50,000 seems rather high for 8,800 hearths. Since the walled area under Charles of Anjou (1266–85) was about 200 hectares, even 40,000 persons would mean an average of 200 to the hectare. Yet Palermo was an Islamic city in its prime and for such a city, 200 to the hectare was not high. Professor Traselli shows that Palermo in the middle of the thirteenth century was a depressed city with delapidated houses and even open spaces in the city. The division of Sicily from mainland Italy by the Sicilian Vespers of 1282 would certainly not help Palermo's prosperity. Still, the city could have had 40,000 inhabitants and have shown vacancies from an earlier population of 50,000. Like most Islamic court cities, it had a large number of noble families living within it, but the parliament moved from city to city, being most often in Palermo and Messina.[16]

For the fourteenth century Professor Traselli believes the population of the city was down to about 10–15,000.[17] In 1335, in anticipation of a siege, the city procured grain which he estimates would support 11,000 persons for fifty days, but he admits that certain elements of the city would have provided for themselves. Since neither the anticipated length of siege was known nor the percentage of the people to be supported, the data does not seem much help. If only a third needed to be supported for fifty days, the population would be about 33,000. Similarly, the troops requested by King Peter about the same time show really very little about the city's population. Since Palermo had in 1347 some 4,082 houses paying the subsidy, its population could hardly have been less than 18–20,000,[18] which should indicate a pre-plague population of about 30,000 assuming a loss of about a third. And in 1478 the city had a counted population of about 26,000. So unless there was a catastrophic decline in the thirteenth century and a recovery when most other cities were barely holding level (in the period 1370–1470), Palermo should have been a large city in the late thirteenth century. But Professor Traselli shows readily why it had declined from fifty to thirty thousands in the century. A rapid increase of population occurred between 1476 and 1548 for which there seems no very good reason. Perhaps here is an example of the loss of population control which has since produced one of the greatest problems of modern society, overpopulation.

Messina was the second largest city of Sicily and apparently of the kingdom in 1277. It was rated at 1,330 *unze*, according to Beloch,[19] thus representing about 5,320 hearths or about 30,000 people. Two Sicilian cities are rated as above 10,000 in population in 1277. Trapani and Corleone paid 680.6 and 660 *unze* respectively which, by the same calculations as for Palermo and Messina, should give about 13,600 and 13,200 persons respectively.[20] In subsequent centuries, both cities failed to become outstanding cities because of the proximity of Palermo. Corleone was a rather typical inland Islamic city, such as Kairwan or Fez, while Trapani, occasionally the residence of Aragonese kings later, was always an important port because of its convenience. A surprising feature of Sicilian city size in the thirteenth century was the smallness of the south-eastern cities, such as Syracuse and Catania, but probably Messina dominated the shipping, and malaria may have reduced the population of the plain.

Compared to the Sicilian cities, especially of the west, which seem to have grown under Islamic influence, the cities of the mainland were small. In 1277 Naples paid only about 500 *unze* which, if it were at the same rate as Palermo, meant only 4,000 hearths and a population of 20–25,000. The rest of the small tax district paid another 186 *unze*, about one-third of the sum given by Naples. The area of Naples raised to be his capital by Charles of Anjou was about 200 hectares, appropriate for a city of 25,000 since he would normally include an area of low density, looking forward to future growth. Apparently it did not grow much before the Black Death, even though the Angevins had made it into a kind of capital where many parliaments were held.[21] The seas in the period were largely dominated by Genoa and Aragon so that Naples could hardly grow by its commerce. Unfortunately, only a further widening of the city walls, finished in 1498–99, indicated that the city had made up the losses of the plague. Indeed the enumeration of the city in 1547 gave a population of 212,325 persons, which shows why it had experienced a famine at the time. What is needed is a study of the city's growth, since this is the first clear evidence of overpopulation creating the slum city, so characteristic of southern Italy since that day.

One of the chief problems is the apparently large size of the series of Apulian cities from Barletta to Bari.[22] The number of *unze* for these cities and the area of the district were as follows:

		km^2
Barletta	622	147
Andria	243	
Trani	509	102
Bisceglio	250	
Giovinazzo	224	
Bitonto	503	185
Molfetta	258	
Bari	455	74
	3,064	

Assuming the cities paid three-quarters of the district totals, this gives 2,298 *unze* for this group. If each *unza* represented eight hearths and each hearth five persons, the total population was 91,920. In a line barely forty miles long there would then be eight cities averaging more than 11,000 persons each. In size this line would include the second, third, fourth, fifth, seventh and eighth cities in southern Italy! This is simply unbelievable. A simple solution would be to assume that the unit of taxation was double in Apulia and hence to reduce the size by a half: the population would still be large with cities so close to one another. And one has the problem of explaining just what kept them alive—what was their basic support? They were on the sea, the one common factor: perhaps fish, salt-making, some mineral resources?

An examination of the history of these cities shows a very considerable interest in the area in this period of the Middle Ages. Nearly all of these cities, as well as Brindisi and Otranto farther south, built large cathedrals in this period, indicating much prosperity. Frederick II built castles at Trani and Andria in the period and had Andria as a favourite residence where two of his wives were buried. Other castles appeared in Barletta, Bisceglio, Molfetta, Otranto and Brindisi. Barletta was an outstanding financial centre, showing nine members of the Peruzzi and Acciaraoli companies in 1336-41. Only Naples with thirteen members had more representatives in south Italy.[23] Avignon had about the same number. Perhaps the chief reason for the urban development in the area was transhumance, the great movement of sheep to and from the mountains to the plains. It is the one place in Italy where extensive high mountains are reasonably near open plains. If, as alleged, there were a million sheep participating in this movement, with five herders for each thousand, the five thousand herders and their families as a basic element would provide a basis for a population of forty thousand. But this was merely the base, since the sheep imply a very large wool trade. The concentration between Barletta and Bari probably derives from their nearness to the mountains and to the highway through the mountains to Naples and other eastern ports. This would appear to be a development which like that of the later *meseta* in Spain. These cities also offer the longest haul by water between Durazzo and Naples and conversely the least by land. During this period, also, the kings had their eyes on the Byzantine possessions just across the Adriatic.

An earlier document shows that Giovinazzo had in AD 1278–80 about 734 men, which should indicate a total population of about three times as many, or 2,200. In 1320 Giovinazzo paid a sum of 224 *unze*.[24] To simplify matters then we assume that the total population of the Apulian cities was about nine times the number of *unze*, a trifle higher than the earlier assumption of eight to the *unze*. This would have given then, following the earlier calculation, about 40,000 persons for the series of eight cities along the Apulian coast in a line of forty miles. Even this creates an odd situation. In the list we are crediting rather uncertainly, two cities: Barletta in seventh place and Brindisi in twelfth.

Of the other cities in south Italy, Aversa seems to have been the largest, although it is hard to estimate its size since the tax includes both the city and a surrounding area of about 201km.[2] Aversa paid 448 *unze* in 1320 when Naples paid 692, but the other towns of the district of Aversa, even though near Naples, probably had a larger percentage of the district's population than did those in the district of Naples. If we assume that Aversa had about 300 unze as a tax, its population (comparable to that of Naples) should have been about 15,000.

Amalfi, with some suburbs, was apparently between ten and fifteen thousands in population; its history at an earlier date had been important.

The total population of Sicily was estimated by Beloch at half a million as a minimum at the end of the Hohenstauffen period, AD 1266,[25] while he was willing to assign about two millions to the mainland.[26] These are admittedly very round figures for the kingdom. Now, if the total for the largest ten cities is, as seems from the table, to be about 190,000 persons, the urban index is about 7.6. This is considerably above the 4.7 which is about normal for a purely agricultural area. It is possible that the population of the cities is overrated. From the estimate for Palermo 10,000 could be taken without much disturbance of the evidence; possibly 5,000 from that of Messina. On the other hand, life along the Mediterranean was heavily dependent upon the sea for food and much of the rest could easily have come from the mountains with their extensive pastures. The larger cities, although not centres of great mercantile families, did however participate largely in the great transit opportunities provided by the ships of Genoa, Barcelona, other northern ports to the east and ports towards Tunis.

Since the kingdom of the mainland was divided into northern and southern divisions the areas of the two halves as well as that of Sicily are as follows:

		km^2
North:	Terra de Lavoro	6,540
	Principato Citra	5,731
	Principato Ultra	3,644
	Abruzzo Citra	4,223
	Abruzzo Ultra	8,010
	Molise	3,004
	Capitanata	8,364
South:	Terra di Bari	5,312
	Terra d'Otranto	7,240
	Basilicata	9,384
	Calabria Citra	7,453
	Calabria Ultra	7,513
Naples and district		322
		———
		76,740

Sicily	Val Mazzara	10,237
	Val Demone	6,728
	Val Noto	8,499
		——
		25,464
		102,204

At 2.5 millions for an area of 102,204km² the average density would have been about 24.5 persons to the km²: without the top ten cities the density was about 22.6 to the km². The classification by the two geographical areas provides a surprise. Sicily, in spite of its disproportionate number of larger cities, had a density of only twenty to the km², while the mainland had an average of about twenty-six to the km². Since the population density of Tuscany, which is thought to have been one of the most densely inhabited areas of the time, had only about thirty to the km², the southern half of the peninsula had a fairly large population, and the population explosion at Naples was to be expected. However, before this is assumed, the tax returns and their interpretation for demographic purposes should be carefully scrutinised.

The kingdom under Charles of Anjou, who preferred Naples to Palermo, saw a decline in the latter city to the advantage of Naples. Then the Sicilian Vespers of 1282 wrenched Sicily from the Angevins. The long and violent struggle between them and the house of Aragon made co-operation between Sicily and the mainland difficult. Sicily then became a part of the Aragonese Empire and must have profited to some extent from it. Yet Palermo can hardly have been as important as capital of the sub-kingdom of Sicily as it had been as capital of both Sicily and southern Italy before 1282. A case could be made for the region of Palermo after 1282 actually being two regions, with the mainland part as a separate region with Naples as its metropolitan centre. Certainly they were two regions politically, each with its own assembly. The parliament of Sicily was to have a remarkable history.[27] The size of the south Italian cities before 1348 would suggest, however, a rather backward area.

Messina, like Palermo, must have declined as Reggio, across

the strait, grew and her trade with the mainland lessened. If Palermo declined to 35,000, perhaps Messina went down to about 20,000. The Sicilian cities then would run approximately this way: Palermo, Messina, Trapani, Catania, Corleone, and Syracuse—a short list.

Conversely, Naples grew rapidly. Perhaps the other southern Italian cities remained much the same; evidence about their size appears in the latter part of the period, so only their apparent size is given here:

	hectares
Naples	200
Barletta	96
Amalfi	part disappeared in the sea
Lecce	63
Salerno	60
Brindisi	56
Aversa	56
Benevento	45
Capua	41
Taranto	36
Bari	30

The size of some of these, Bari and Taranto for instance, may cause some raised eyebrows. There is obviously room for a careful series of historical geographies of the southern Italian cities, like that of Dopp for Naples.

3

Regions of Northern Italy:
Venice and Milan

TUSCANY, A PART of north Italy, has been treated earlier; its beautifully integrated life, developed in the thirteenth century, was an excellent illustration of the rank-size pattern of regions, while its very high urban index showed that its economic life was rooted in commerce and banking, activities extending far beyond its own boundaries. The many cities of the Po Valley and its environs also offer interesting problems in their relationships.[1] The cities were often unusual. Venice set its limits politically at the edge of the Adriatic: was Padua to be considered really a part of a Venetia urban complex? Could Genoa be considered a part of the north Italian pattern of cities at all? Was the commerce over the steep passes to Milan sufficient to cause Genoa to be regarded as part of a Po Valley complex? And what about the passes to the north over the Alps and their effect upon patterns of the Italian cities? Fortunately, the work of Beloch, and others to a lesser extent, enable good estimates to be made of the sizes of the cities of north Italy.

The cities of the Po Valley have less demographic information from the thirteenth century than those of Tuscany. Direct information is available about several of them, however, even for that century. The next best information comes, as usual, from maps of the cities showing their medieval morphology. For comparison with populations of later periods, it is assumed (with some exceptions) that the population just after the brunt of the plague (1380–1420) was about two-thirds of the pre-plague number, that the populations reached pre-plague figures about 1500, and that the numerous surveys of about 1550 show about 125% of the pre-plague estimates. Here, as in so many places in these studies, further research will fix the estimates more accurately, but what exists is probably sufficient to provide the base for an effective study of demographic relationships of the century just before the plague.

THE REGION OF VENICE

The chief problem in outlining the limits of the regions of Venice and Milan in the thirteenth century (Fig 2) lies in defining the boundary between the two regions, particularly with such borderline cities as Brescia, Parma, and Reggio Emilia. The two regions were hemmed in by the Alps, the Appennines, and the sea. Essentially the regions were of the Po Valley and the smaller eastern valleys contingent on the Adriatic. The great Roman roads determined largely the particular location of cities, but the routes through the Alpine passes were also very important in the two regions. In the fifteenth century, when Venice became a continental power, it included territory as far west as Bergamo and Crema but did not include Bologna and cities lying to the west along the old Aemilian Highway. However, in the thirteenth and in the early fourteenth century, Venice was strictly a maritime power and its influence was commercial rather than political. Bologna and its western neighbour, Modena, are thus included within the Venetian region as well as Verona and Mantua. The biggest problem is Reggio Emilia, which is assigned to the region of Milan on the theory that, because Parma was larger then, it had more influence on Reggio than smaller Modena had to the east. Both Venice and Genoa had extensive maritime possessions which are not considered as parts of the Italian regions.

Venice was presumably the largest city in northern Italy at the time, although Florence was not much smaller by the end of the thirteenth century (Table 5). It had been a large city for a long time and probably had not increased much in size over that century. In 1338 it was alleged to have had 30,000

TABLE 5: REGION OF VENICE

Rank, City	Pop Est 1,000s	Hyp Est 1,000s	Area hectares	Base	Beloch
1 Venice	100	110	324	1338–30,000 s	vol 3, 3, 6
2 Bologna	60–70	66–77	419	1249–20,000 h	2, 91–2
3 Verona	40	44	150–436	1502–38,500 p	3, 102, EUI
4 Padua	33	33	350	1302–11,000 s	3, 67, 74
5 Mantua	30	26.4	215	1463–26,400 1559–36,200 p	2, 287–8, EUI
6 Vicenza	22	22.4	62–84	1548–21,000 p	3, 87, EUI
7 Modena	18	19.5	72,150	1306–5,356 or 5,600 s	2, 260, EUI
8 Ferrara	17	17.4	104,150	1520–41,000/3 p	2, 108, EUI
9 Forli	13.8	15.7	99	1371–2,300 h	2, 85, EUI
10 Rimini	13.4	14.3	35,48	1371–2,240 h	2, 85, EUI
11 Faenza	11.6	13.2	80	1371–1,926 h	2, 85, EUI
12 Ravenna	11.5	12.2	110	1371–1,743 h	2, 85, EUI

Verona: Allen 385 ; area, early 12thc about 206 hectares, in time of Can Grande 436 hectares. Ferrara: area from Baedeker, *Italy* (1879) 104. Rimini: area from Baedeker, *Italy* (1879) 302.

armed citizens between the ages of 20 to 60, which must have indicated a population of about 100,000. A fragment of a manuscript in London gives names of Venetians of about 1363–68, thus following a period in which Venice had suffered two severe attacks of the plague.[2] It suggests a population of about 65–70,000, which also would indicate a pre-plague number of about 100,000. With the acquisition of the continental holdings after the plague, Venice was to grow to be a larger city, but it still had only about 85,000 persons in 1424, 105,000 in 1509, and 130,000 in 1540.

Venice's refusal to acquire land on the mainland of Italy probably accounts for its total population being lower than the hypothetical 110,000 suggested by the size of most of the other cities in the first ten. For with the very extensive maritime empire of the city, it should at least have had its place in the hypothetical pattern. Indeed, one might have expected that it would have been substantially larger, given the great size of the Po Valley cities. On the other hand, Padua is probably somewhat larger than a city so close to Venice (40 kilometres) should normally have been. The superiority in size of Venice over Genoa was probably the result of a greater market in its own region and in the region of Milan, as well as its access to transalpine regions, through the easy passes to the east. It also had no rivals on the eastern side of Italy except the cities in Calabria, the commerce of which might cross the mountains to Naples. Genoa, on the other side from Venice, competed with Pisa, Marseilles, Aigues-Mortes, Montpellier, Narbonne, Palma de Mallorca and Barcelona, to mention the main contenders for western European trade on the north-west coast.

The population of the second city of the region, Bologna, is not so easily estimated. It was growing rapidly early in the thirteenth century: its walls enclosed about 208 hectares in 1200, while the next addition built in the fourteenth century included about 409 hectares. A fragment of a register of circa AD 1249 seems to indicate about 20,000 hearths in the city. Since the names of many widows and other women appear in it, the number to the hearth may be low, possibly about 3.5.[3] Still this gives a total population of 70,000. The 409 hectares within the wall would suggest a smaller population. The *des-*

criptio of 1371 gives 8,000 hearths, which at the rate of 4.4 to the hearth, as in Florence of that period, would suggest 35,000, and perhaps 54,000 for the pre-plague period. It had apparently about 50,000 persons in 1495.

The population of Verona was first checked in terms of persons in 1502, when it had about 38,500. In 1471 the number of hearths had been 4,849, indicating, as one would expect, a somewhat smaller population. Verona had enjoyed a very prosperous period before the plague, so that 40,000 seems a reasonable estimate, with which the area of the city then, about 436 hectares, is compatible.

Padua was near Venice but separated from it by Venice's firm decision in the early period to undertake no political responsibilities on the mainland. In 1320 a census showed some 11,000 men in the city; the list of approximately 7,635 families including them makes it clear that the men were soldiers and that the index number for them would have been about three, bringing the total population to about 33,000. Venice's decision to move on to the mainland naturally had an adverse effect on Padua, which seems to have had only about 18,000 persons in 1411 and 27,000 by 1500. Like Padua, Mantua's earliest remaining censuses came at the end of the fifteenth century and show that the city had a population somewhat less than 30,000 officially registered then, which suggests a similar figure for the pre-plague period. The walls in 1242 enclosed only 150 hectares, but did not include several of the suburbs developing in the thirteenth century. Like the two previous cities, Vicenza must also be judged from its later census: in 1548 and 1556 estimates of about 21,000 and 28,000 were made; four-fifths of the second would give about 22,000 for the pre-plague period. The area its walls enclosed was about 62 hectares, but there were suburbs.

Unlike the cities just mentioned, Modena had some valuable contemporary evidence for the pre-plague period: a list of armed men, aged 16 to 70, of AD 1306, totalling either 5,357 or 5,600. This should represent about 16,000 persons, to which might be added others not required to serve. Beloch suggested 20,000, but it might well have been less, perhaps 18,000. Modena's wall, enclosing 150 hectares, was of the sixteenth century, when the population of 1539 was about 15,675. The city of Ferrara has a curious history: it had grown by three times its fourteenth-century size in 1492 and a generation later it had a population of about 41,000. A third of that would be about 17,000 persons; its ancient wall (south west of the Corso della Giovecca) contained about 150 hectares.

After these there are a group of cities in Romagna which were the subject of an enrolment of their hearths in 1371. It is assumed that each hearth represents four at that time and six in the pre-plague period.

The region of Venice thus conformed to the ranksize pattern in a most interesting way. This is not surprising since the pattern had been a long time in developing. Venice had been the largest city in a great eastern trade which connected with the Brenner Pass to the north and to the Po Valley by way of Verona and Bologna. The cities were, for the most part, independent and prosperous in the pre-plague period. Possibly Bologna had grown faster than some of the others, with its great law centre and university, and it was in the best position to profit by the rapid rise of Tuscany in medieval commerce and finance. Perhaps the most surprising element in the history of that region was Venice's persistent refusal to use her tremendous strength to overpower or dominate the cities of the mainland.

THE REGION OF MILAN

The region of Milan occupied the upper Po Valley. Milan has usually been seen as the most populous site in northern Italy, but its advantages seem to have been less in the thirteenth century than either earlier or later. In that century, the region of Milan and the adjacent region of Venice were full of relatively large cities. Furthermore, those cities disliked Milan's connections with the emperor, and developing a kind of balance of power, held Milan in restraint. Communication was less favourable, too. Cities to the east such as Bergamo and Verona were nearer to the eastern lower Alpine passes and to the Venetian market. The goods which came in from Genoa had to go over the mountains; even for this trade Pavia competed for a time. In the new textile industry, it faced the formidable competition of Florence and the local cities. It never

TABLE 6: REGION OF MILAN

Rank, City		Pop Est 1,000s	Hyp Est 1,000s	Area hectares	Base	Beloch
1	Milan	75	110	500	1288–12,500 doors	vol 3, 175–6, EUI
2	Genoa	60	62.7	293	1500–11,500 h	3, 267, EUI
3	Brescia	48	42.9	252	1493–48,560 p	3, 122
4	Cremona	40	33	165	1502–40,000 p	3, 302
5	Pavia	30	26.4	158+	1250–4,735 (in part)	3, 212–3
6	Parma	22	22.4	201	1395–4,500 h	2, 238 ff
7	Piacenza	20	19.4	120	1546–25,000 p	2, 249
8	Bergamo	14	17.4	119	1548–17,707 p	3, 142
9	Reggio Emilia	13.5	15.7	100	1473–9,201	3, 209
10	Como	12.3	14.3	96	1375–2,048 h	3, 235
11	Monza	9.6	13.2	56	1576–12,000 p	3, 202
12	Crema	8.8	12.2		1548–11,000 p	3, 158

Pavia: Professor C. Cipolla kindly loaned the author his map of the city, showing a considerable inhabited area outside of the walls. Piacenza: for area, Baedeker, *Italy* (1879) 266. Reggio Emilia: area, Baedeker, *Italy* (1879) 268. Crema: Bertossi.

developed—until the Visconti took over much of northern Italy—many of the facilities and sources of basic support often achieved by metropolitan cities of regions. With these handicaps in the pre-plague period, it would have been surprising if it had achieved the normal size of such a city in an expected pattern.

Milan is reported to have had 12,500 entrances with doors (*hostia cum ianuis*) in 1288, which should mean hearths. Multiplying by four gives 60,000 doors (Table 6). However, four is a post-plague figure from Florence; the chances are that before the plague the number would have been about five, giving a total population of somewhere near 66,000. Between the 1203 walls, enclosing 234 hectares, and the sixteenth-century walls of 794 hectares, the map shows a curious encirclement, enclosing about 500 hectares, which looks like an arrangement for a temporary boundary which should have included the pre-plague area of settlement, and for this 75,000 would be about right. Of course, when Milan at the end of the Middle Ages became the second political power in the Po Valley, the city became much larger. A problem of Milan's position is that a series of sizeable cities lay so close to it: Pavia, 32 kilometres away, Como, 42 kilometres, Monza, 13 kilometres and Lodi, 34 kilometres. On the map Milan is included in the 80,000 group.

Pavia's walls, enclosing 140 hectares, would indicate that the 30,000 suggested by Beloch is a little large and the city's post-plague population reinforces this: 25,000 is therefore suggested. However, this was the period of its greatest medieval prosperity, so that 30,000 might not be too high an estimate. Como in 1375 had 2,048 hearths which, multiplying by six, gives about 12,300 as its pre-plague number; its walls included about 96 hectares. Lodi had already been subdued by Milan by the thirteenth century. The only estimate is 80% of the 7,000 number of 1542, or about 5,600. If Monza had 12,000 in 1574, its pre-plague population might be estimated as below 9,600. However, it is possible that all of the last three might be raised somewhat, assuming that the great growth of Milan in the fifteenth to sixteenth centuries impinged on the revival of its neighbours.

Genoa apparently had about 11,500 hearths in 1500, which

should have given it a total population of about 57,500 at five to the hearth. In the late thirteenth century, the city was at the height of its prosperity and could presumably have been somewhat larger, say 60,000. It was tightly limited within an area of 293 hectares and had, on the average, more than two apartments to a house. Professor Heers[4] believes that the city had over 85,000 persons even though the city in the sixteenth century had only 60,000.[5] Genoa, like other Italian cities, housed the castles of its leaders, the nobles, within the walls. The great turbulent families, such as Doria, Fieschi, Grimaldi, and Spinola, and many other families, added to the Genoese population but maintained some of their castles in the country-side. Their adventurous leadership contributed many brilliant if somewhat erratic chapters to the history of Genoa,[6] yet somehow the city seemed to have operated within the region of Milan.

Very late medieval data remain for the three next cities. Brescia had about 48,500 in 1493 which we assume must have been about the pre-plague figure; its wall, containing 252 hectares, would have been about right for that number. In 1502 Cremona was said to have had 40,000, again to be expected for a pre-plague figure. Its wall was torn down for later military construction and seems to have enclosed only about 165 hectares but there may have been suburbs also in the built-over area. Pavia's *catasto* of 1250-54 shows 3,790 hearths with 4,735 taxpayers, many widows and many poor. The *castasto* only includes 44 of the 105 divisions of the city.[7] Assuming that the 44 are representative, the city should have had about 9,000 hearths. Since the percentage of widows and poor is high, 3.5 persons may be assumed for the hearth, giving a total population for the city of about 32,000.

Parma is said to have had 3,000 hearths in 1395 with a third of the people too poor to pay and thus not enrolled. Doubtless many of the poor were widows, or heads of other small families, and thus the 4,500 estimated families should be multiplied by about 3.5 to get a total population of about 15,750. By 1404 it was about 15,000. This suggests a pre-plague population of about 22,500 even though its pre-plague walls enclosed 240 hectares, which might suggest a larger number. Piacenza had walls enclosing about the same area.

In 1447 it had an alleged 6,000 citizen soldiers, which Beloch says suggests at least 25,000 for total population. However, it had only about that number in 1546, which might indicate a pre-plague figure of about 20,000, small for the extent of its walls. For Bergamo, again, the earliest figures are of 1548, about 17,707. If we assume 80% of this is a pre-plague estimate we should have about 14,000. Reggio Emilia, with a population of about 9,200 in 1473, should have had a pre-plague population of about 13,500; the study of a document of 1315 from that city (mentioned in 1748) would seem to corrobor-

TABLE 7: AREA AND POPULATION OF THE REGIONS OF VENICE AND MILAN

Region of Venice	Area	Population Pre-plague	Other	Density	Sources Beloch
Romagna	10,180	550,000	1656–561,840	vol 2, 125, 122, 98	
Modena	2,597	36,800	1620–55,283		2, 284, 276
Mantua	2,301	105,000	1511–105,000		2, 296, 300
Treviso etc	3,501	125,700	1548–157,166		3, 58
Feltre, etc	3,138	45,400	1548–56,800		3, 64, 59–63
Padua	2,552	121,700	1548–152,168		3, 79, 80
Rovigo	1,775	20,360	1548–25,451		3, 83, 85
Vicenza	2,564	100,000	1548–124,760		3, 100, 97
Verona	3,022	112,200	1473–102,000		3, 118, 118
Friuli	7,025	155,600	1548–194,510		3, 40
Venice	100	100,000			
	38,755	1,472,760			
Region of Milan					
Milan, etc (Cremona, Pavia, etc)	16,981	504,900	1542–126,229 hearths		3, 242, 200
Genoa	4,191	267,625			3, 303
Piacenza	3,030	100,000	1546–124,400		2, 252, 249, 257
Parma	2,509	44,600	1509–45,000		2, 244, 243
Reggio Emilia	2,291	33,200	1620–49,797		2, 284, 276
Bergamo	2,376	106,000	1548–132,511		3, 153, 158, 141
Brescia	4,827	288,831	1493		3, 140, 135
Piedmont	14,778	400,000	14thc		3, 273, 252
	50,983	1,745,156			

ate this. Finally, Crema with about 11,000 in 1548, should
have had about 8,800 before the plague.

In contrast to the region of Venice where a well-integrated
rank-size pattern existed in the thirteenth century and might
well have gone back two centuries beyond that, the region of
Milan presents problems (Table 7). There is no doubt that
Milan had been the largest city, except in brief intervals of
destruction, through the twelfth and thirteenth centuries   it
had been the largest city even in the Roman Empire, in the
Po Valley. However, it had lost its dominating position apparently in the twelfth century largely as the result of some balance of power politics from which its near neighbours, Pavia
and Como, had especially profited. Lodi had gone down in
defeat in the period. Now, it can be seen that unless one com-
bines with Milan its neighbours, such as Pavia, Como and
Monza, it does not reach 110,000, which fits the pattern of
the other cities quite well. This was reasonable for Como
which is really the base from which trans-Alpine commerce
started through several passes. Similarly Pavia to the south,
an ancient Lombard centre, was an important way-station to
Genoa.

Nor can the problem be solved by eliminating Genoa and
assuming that the upper Po Valley is a region without Genoa.
That arrangement in comparison with the rank-order would
be:

	Pop Est in 1,000s	Hyp Est in 1,000s
Milan	75	75
Brescia	48	42
Cremona	40	28
Pavia	30	23
Parma	22	18
Piacenza	20	15
Bergamo	15	13

It can be seen that Milan would have had to have 88,000
population to be right with Brescia's second place and higher
to meet the requirements of the others, while the population
of Milan was actually estimated generously. Thus Milan does

not even occupy the position of a metropolitan city with respect to the upper Po Valley cities. It would be only with the development of political power by the rulers of that city that it increased vastly in size after the medieval period.

The thirteenth century saw the effort of Frederick II to reduce the cities of northern Italy to obedience. Suppose that he had succeeded and had selected Bologna, probably the most appropriate of the northern cities, since it had a great law centre, as a capital. Could he have concentrated basic factors, such as government, industry, and commerce to have produced something like that in northern Italy?

	Pop Est *in 1,000s*	*Hyp Est* *in 1,000s*
Capital	228	228
Bologna, Parma, Reggio, Cremona, Piacenza, Modena, Mantua		
Venice-Padua	130	130
Milan	75	74
Brescia	48	51
Verona	40	39
Pavia	30	31
Vicenza	22	25

It is hardly possible that such an extensive capital would be created even as capital of the Roman Empire then. However, it does suggest that something like an amorphous region was developing in northern Italy which was potentially the most impressive economic unit in Europe at that time.

The two regions were remarkably similar in their density of population. The density of the region of Venice was about 38.0 persons in the whole population and 29.4 for the area without the largest ten cities. For the same densities the region of Milan had 34.5 and 27.8. There are, of course, the problems of defining the limits of the two regions. Both impinged upon extensive mountain areas, so that it is a question of whether these areas should be added. However, the two regions were reasonably similar so that the comparison is rewarding. In Europe the only area with an apparently higher density was that of the region of Paris and possibly the region of Florence which was a somewhat smaller area, again facing mountains which perhaps ought to be considered even more a part of the Florentine region than portions of the Alps in the northern Italian regions. In part the strength of the Italian regions must be considered as deeply rooted in the large agricultural populations of the peninsula.

The urban index (percentage of total population of regions of the largest ten cities) is naturally high with the large size of the cities. If one takes the larger area (that is, including Friuli in the Venetian region and Piedmont in the Milanese) the urban index is 23.4 for the Venice region and 19.1 for the Milan region. These are not as high as the 23.3 for Tuscany. In any case it is clear that Tuscany and the Po Valley regions formed the most highly urbanised area in the thirteenth century, not merely in Italy but even in the European-Mediterranean world of that day.

The three regions, in fact, had in their great cities a kind of industrial quadrilateral: north, Como to Venice; east, Venice to Siena; south, Siena to Genoa; and west, Genoa to Como. The northern side faced the many passes through the Alps to Germany and Switzerland; the east had the passes to France by way of Aosta and the seaway by the Mediterranean; on the south the ways to Rome and the Mediterranean routes to Africa and the east, while the east faced the Adriatic way to the Byzantine and Islamic world. The great size of the cities indicated the importance of the commerce moving along those ways. But the chief addition of the thirteenth century was the rapid development of the new industrial and commercial (even banking) cities of the regions of Milan, and especially of Florence and its satellites. During that century they dominated the economic life of Europe. In the fourteenth and fifteenth centuries they largely controlled trade and banking from Constantinople and Alexandria to Bruges and London in the west.[8]

The three northern regions of Italy also constituted the largest market of the period, at least in terms of the size of the urban part of the population. The top ten cities of these regions had over a million people in thirty cities, a very considerable fraction of their 4.5 million population. Distances were not great, and much of their commerce came by sea through the great ports: Venice, Genoa, and Pisa. It was a wealthy agricultural area which, in itself, produced a sizeable surplus for the people there. Cheap grain came from over the sea, and there was a large supply of fish from the Mediterranean itself. As yet its energy was not dissipated by overpopulation, although the density increased markedly in the course of the thirteenth century. The only real competitor in the western Mediterranean was the combined Montpellier-Barcelona-Toulouse area but there cities were smaller, the agricultural base not quite so fertile, and the distances greater. In the north the Netherland area, with Ghent as the centre, manufactured for a much greater total population, perhaps fifteen millions at the end of the thirteenth century, but the city population was less than a million, perhaps two hundred thousand less, and the surplus over subsistence much less than in Italy. It is not surprising then that the late medieval period was a great age for northern Italy and that it led the other European states in so many phases of economic and intelligent life.

The language situation accorded relatively well with the regional arrangement as outlined above. The Venetian group of dialects were all in the region of Venice. In the region of Venice were the districts whose dialects are considered Emilian except for those of Piacenza and Parma. In the region of Milan were the Lombard dialects as well as the closely related Ligurian. The region of Milan also included the two Emilian districts mentioned above. As usual, of course, there is a question of how different the groups of dialects actually were. Were the Emilian and Venetian so different that the speakers of one had difficulty understanding the other? Was it possible that Bologna was in fact the metropolitan city of a quite small region in Emilia and Romagna? Bologna, however, was a crossroads city par excellence, possibly the centre of Roman law jurisdiction as well as law study; its university was certainly an international educational centre much as Florence was an international financial centre.

For both of the northern Italian regions there was a quite extensive hinterland. Venice not only shared in the southern slopes of the Alps into the Trentino which has remained Italian-speaking to this day but also in the area of the old

Patriarchate of Aquileia. This would have included the March
of Verona, Friuli and perhaps much of Carniola. Similarly
the region of Milan shared the even more severe slopes of the
western Alps and that territory, so hazily defined on the maps
between Lombardy and the territory of the counts of Savoy,
whose centre was Turin, later known as Piedmont. The leaders
of this area eventually were responsible for the unification
of Italy, a very dynamic group. The share of the medieval
mountain men still needs definition.

4

Border Regions:
Augsburg, Dijon, and Cologne

GERMANY, AS THE country in which ideas of rank-size pattern
early developed, has been the subject of many regional studies
but mostly of the regions of the modern period. The larger
cities, at least, of Germany have changed much from the
medieval period. Great modern cities, such as Berlin, Munich,
Hamburg, and the Ruhr and Saar cities, were only small places
in the Middle Ages; their early counterparts were Cologne,
Magdeburg, Augsburg, and Prague. Medieval Germany had
little of the industrial life which characterises the country now.
Even the countryside was of modest quality as farmland, while
a large part of the country was still in forest and a considerable
part in very hilly or mountainous terrain. In this and the next
chapter the border regions of the first Roman Empire (Augsburg, Dijon and Cologne) are considered and the more eastern
frontier region (Prague, Magdeburg and Lübeck). As usual,
to understand the situation, one must replace one's concept of
the modern French-German divisions by the more hetero-
geneous medieval Empire.[1]

In the tables of city sizes much has come from the *Deutsche
Städtebuch*, edited by Professor E. Keyser. So much of the
data have been used that the citations are given in the tables
themselves. Even so, a few of the cities have not been studied
by the collaborators in the project and, although the writers
were given standard instructions, the results are not even.
Sometimes the areas are not stated, sometimes they are given

very exactly in terms of places in the city itself, but with no estimate of the number of hectares enclosed at those times. In most cases numbers of households or armed men are given together with the total population based on this estimate. In other cases rather general guesses have been made, some apparently far too large—as in the case of the 30,000 attributed to Magdeburg in 1400. The area, as well as other estimates, is supposed to be for the pre-plague period; it is often for the time of the building of the walls. The problems remaining suggest that there is plenty of room for sound studies in the historical geography of these settlements.

There are two ways of estimating total population of the central European areas: one by determining density of particular areas and using them as samples for all, and the second by assuming that the cities have a certain proportion of the population. Leaving the first for a moment, let us turn to the second. The hypothetical approach assumes an average density of population based on city size; this Germany might seem to have. In the Rhineland the density has always been high, but this was certainly not true of the southern area nor, indeed, of the extreme northern area. During the Middle Ages the sheer failure to produce a city larger than Cologne—with perhaps forty thousand persons—indicates a lack of urbanisation. The results of the estimate are something like the following. The five largest cities had a total of about 140,000 which, at 1.5% of the total, should indicate that Germany had about 9.3 millions. If the top ten cities of the regions are considered, the total was about 527,000, which would indicate a total for Germany of about 12.2 millions if the urban index were 4.7. The larger figure came in part from overestimates of the population of some of the lesser cities while the smaller suffered because the regions were not well enough integrated to have a metropolitan centre of full size.

Germany had, from the tenth century, a good chance both to integrate as a well-organised state and to expand permanently to the east. Nor can its failure be attributed to the kind of family chaos which distinguished the Merovingian and later Carolingian lines with the division of the state among numerous heirs. The theory of election prevented that, but the cost of the election was a continuously heavy burden, even

though the German kings from Henry I to VI had a remarkably long average tenure of office. First, the cost of
the *Romfahrt* and then the heavy involvement in Italy after
the Hohenstauffens became kings of Sicily distracted the
sovereigns from their unification of Germany. Despite this,
the German kings might have advanced against their feudal
rivals if they had been willing to join the cities in a common
cause. The cities generally went their own way; failing unity
with the kings, they failed also to join with the lesser lords.
A surprising number were free. Few German cities built up
extensive possessions, such as those of Milan and Venice in
later medieval Italy; most did manage to escape control by
German feudal lords. The political base then for the cities
was usually small.

The Rhineland (except for its lowest reaches) was a part of
the north-western Roman frontier, facing the Germans. The
limes cut across from the Rhine to the Danube, including
much of the later region of Augsburg. That city lay on the
great highway behind the *limes* which ran between Mainz and
Carnuntum near what is now Vienna. The other great road
through Augsburg came up from the Brenner Pass and Switzerland and on northwards through the frontier, the route by
which many Roman traders carried their goods into the
German areas. In addition the road from Italy through Basel
and the Alps entered just west at Ulm. To the late medieval
person the 'Empire' usually meant the axis: Regensburg-
Nürnberg-Frankfurt-Mainz-Cologne-Aachen. But this was later
than 1350, since Nürnberg and Frankfurt had replaced
Augsburg and Strasbourg.[2] Later Munich took over as the
largest city and the capital of Bavaria, and even earlier Nürnberg in the north became the great city of the area. It profited
by being the crossroads city of the Mainz–Prague highway
east and west and the north–south highway to the north coast
cities and Magdeburg. It probably resulted in part from heavy
migration, filling the better lands to the north of Ulm and
Augsburg. In any case, Augsburg was the centre of the older
urbanised section of central Europe.

The border provinces occupied the upper reaches of three
great European river systems: the Rhine, the Rhône and
the Danube. The position of the Rhine was far and away the

most important as the strong and large cities along it proved. The small size of the cities of the region of Dijon, especially Lyons, and the somewhat larger cities of the upper reaches of the Rhine and Danube suggest that the Rhine-Alpine pass commerce was rather small. It was perhaps more important for themselves and for the inter-city commerce originating in the region than for the Mediterranean commercial cities, perhaps even more important than for the Low Countries-French trade.

The German regions seem to have coincided fairly accurately with language divisions: Low German with the region of Lübeck, Upper High German with that of Magdeburg, East Middle German with that of Magdeburg and that of West Middle German with the region of Augsburg. The language lines for the later Middle Ages were not entirely clear and did not coincide exactly with urban regions, especially since these regions themselves were indefinite. Many of the German tribes had moved about considerably before they settled into their relatively permanent sites and disintegrated into feudal fiefs of almost uncounted number. Beginning then with fairly marked differences in dialect from other tribes, their associations in regions would tend to make regional linguistic limits more clear.

The German area included the Roman frontier *(limes)* along the Rhine and Danube rivers. The cities on these rivers naturally grew up on the Roman side of the river and were joined by roads along the bank as well as by the river itself. The pattern was thus firmly fixed by the end of the Empire and it was the roads rather than the rivers which fixed the cities on the western bank of the Rhine and the southern bank of the Danube. The persistence of the road was not as unalterable as the persistence of the street within the city but it was nevertheless enduring. Along the frontier road occurred centres at which Roman roads either crossed the frontier or came in from other parts of the Empire, as at Cologne, Strasbourg, Augsburg and Vienna. Four of these have retained their positions as great centres and only developments at Munich and Nürnberg reduced the position of Augsburg over the centuries since the late medieval period.

If one turns to the traditional type of house and homestead

to indicate regions, one finds much the same situation. The Saxon type appears from the lower Rhine and stretches north-east even along the Baltic coast and thus suggests that this was essentially a region. The Rhineland almost as far as Basel has the Frankish type which, indeed, crosses the central part of the country and goes on into Bohemia. The southern region is distinguished by three types, respectively Alemannic (or Swabian), Swiss, and Bavarian, all representing sufficient similarity to be called the South German type. The houses of the Magdeburg region are of the Middle German type (several buildings on two or more sides of a rectangular yard), much like those of the Rhineland. The division of regions based upon house or homestead types illustrates units of thought of the persons concerned, presumably the result of tribal history in some cases.[3]

The problem of the Westphalian cities is a puzzling one. It would seem that they were on the border between the northern-Baltic group and the Rhineland region. Perhaps Osnabruck and Münster can be assigned with least difficulty to the Baltic region: similarly Dortmund might best go with the Rhineland district. Soest was the most difficult. It was quite independent at first and an influence even upon Lübeck, which would seem to associate it prominently with the Baltic area. However, it went, along with Angria, to the archbishop of Cologne after the fall of Henry the Lion at the end of the twelfth century. So with some hesitation it is assigned to the region of Cologne. It was a true border city in that much of its commerce was with the central German area. Dortmund and Soest were on the great east–west highway known as the Hellweg which ran from Bruges and Cologne to Paderborn and Magdeburg, but there were no good highways passing through them from north to south.[4]

Metz constitutes an interesting problem. At first sight its position in the Moselle Valley and nearness to Treves might suggest that it was part of the region of Cologne, essentially that of the Rhine Valley. Yet it was almost equidistant from Cologne, Augsburg, Lyons, and Paris. It was a key city in the Roman system of defence and in the defence of modern France, a part of the well-known triangle: Metz, Toul, and Verdun. It seems better then to regard Metz as outside of

F

any of the regions. An alternative would be to consider it the metropolitan city of a region: its walls originally enclosed seventy hectares in the Roman period and 221 in the thirteenth century. It must have had an approximate population of twenty thousand then, as later.[5] But what other cities would have belonged to its region? Probably it may be regarded as a border city among the regions which owed its strength to the peculiar position which it possessed then and now. Its unusual characteristics deserve more study.

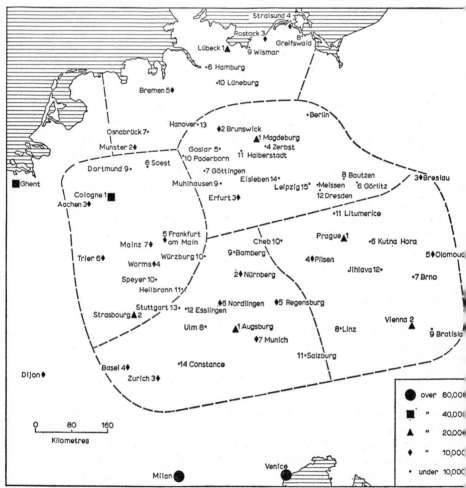

Fig 4   The regions of Augsburg, Cologne, Lübeck, Magdeburg, and Prague

THE REGION OF AUGSBURG

The southern region of Germany is not so well covered in the *Deutsche Städtebuch* as are the western and northern divisions, in part because some of the cities are now a part of Switzerland rather than Germany. The region of Augsburg (Fig 4) had an ancient unity as a part of the Roman frontier and in the early Middle Ages was largely the territory of the Swabians and the Bavarians. A similar change to that marking the northern region appears also in the southern. Augsburg, Zurich, and Basel formed a natural patterned group for the top three of the area. The surprising development is the rise of Nürnburg during the thirteenth century, perhaps the result of the increasing importance of the regions to the east in Bohemia and the Marches (Table 8).

Augsburg occupied a key position in the Roman Empire at the junction of roads along the frontier and from Italy. Roads later extended to Ulm, Strasbourg, and Paris and the northern highway went to Nürnberg, dividing there to the north German cities. The only real handicap was that it lay in a rather thinly settled area by lowland standards and was some distance from the greater cities. Thus it was in a somewhat similar position to Lyons to the west. In 1364 Augsburg had 2,249 houses with 5,176 taxpayers.[6] There were only 99 vacant houses, so the loss of families in the first attack of the plague cannot have been too great. Schreiber estimates the population as about 26,000, multiplying the taxpayers by five. This would mean at least ten to the house, much too high. Probably the population then should have been about 15,000 with the population before the plague about 25,000. The area seems to have been at least 178 hectares and probably was somewhat larger. This would be approximately right for a population of 25,000.

The study of the whole population of Nürnberg in 1449 was the first accurate count of a city population of the Middle Ages. It gave a count of very nearly 20,000. Another document, of 1431, which can be compared to some extent with that of 1449 indicates that the city was growing rapidly. The history of the city would not indicate that before the plague it

TABLE 8: REGION OF AUGSBURG

Rank, City	Pop Est 1,000s	Hyp Est 1,000s	Area hectares	Base	Sources
1 Augsburg	25	25	178–200	1364–5,176 t	Herzog 187; Püschel 211 Schmidt 18; Schreiber 139
2 Nürnberg	14	14.2	138–60	1431–4,142 h	*IXH*; Schmidt 89; Weczerka 71
3 Zurich	13	9.7	54–70+	1357–2,806 t	Mols 3, 106; Egli 149
4 Basel	11	7.5	49–100	1429–2,500 h	*LAMP* 51; *WEC* 65
5 Regensburg	11	6	95		Püschel 210
6 Nordlingen	10	5.1	93	1456–1,059 h	Keyser 313–4
7 Munich	10	4.4	90		Püschel 211; Hamm 56
8 Ulm	8	4	66–84		*DS* IV, 2, 262; Püschel 211;
9 Bamberg	8	3.6	70–80		Herzog 174; Schmimmelpfennig
10 Würzburg	7	3.2	72	1407–860 h	Herzog 153; Keyser 313–4
11 Salzburg	7	3	58		
12 Esslingen			55		*DS* IV, 2, 69
13 Stuttgart			50		*DS* IV, 2, 215
14 Constance			50		

had more than 15,000 for its 138 hectares.[7] Like Nürnberg, Zurich has preserved excellent information, but from much nearer the plague. In 1357 it had a total of 2,806 taxpayers. If we set 3.5 persons to the taxpayer, assuming that as at Augsburg there were more than one taxpayer to the household, the total after one attack of the plague would have been about 9,800. This figure allowing for a 25% loss, would give a pre-plague population of about Fourquin's estimate of 12,375.[8] Zurich was one of those cities somewhat between regions which causes some doubt as to whether it should be included in an adjacent region, such as that of Dijon or even Cologne and the Rhineland. It is actually large for the third city in the region.

Regensburg (Ratisbon) and Basel are two cities whose populations are not easy to define in pre-plague period. Basel built a wall in 1280 which enlarged the city area to 49 hectares, and constructed an addition in 1400 to bring the total to about 100 hectares. This would assume a rapid increase from 1280 to 1348, since it is doubtful if the city actually increased in population from 1348 to 1400.[9] The population of Basel then should have been about 11,000 before the plague. Regensburg had its splendid days in the tenth century when it increased the area within the walls to ninety-five hectares.[10] It probably suffered from competition of the other cities in the regions of Augsburg and Prague and so remained around 11,000 in size in the pre-plague period. These were Roman frontier cities which had profited by their earlier Roman associations, especially the Roman roads, but lost their advantages with the development of the territory beyond the old Roman *limes*.

The seventh city in size in the period was probably Munich. It was large enough to have a mint in 1158 and was evidently the centre of a salt trade. The duke of Bavaria made it his capital in 1255 and surrounded it with a wall. This wall seems to have enclosed about ninety hectares which should have meant, for a rapidly growing city and ducal seat, about ten thousand persons. Its growth, encouraged by the duke, was probably also stimulated by the development of the economic life of Germany to the north and Bohemia to the east in this period. Thus it began to compete effectively against the older cities of the region to the south: Augsburg, Ulm, Regensburg, and Salzburg. However, it had greater success against the nearer cities, Regensburg and Salzburg, in part perhaps because of the rise of Vienna as a centre to the east. The great thirteenth-century increase in the Italian economic centres must have funnelled more commerce through Augsburg as the great centre to the south so that, if it did not increase as fast as Munich and Nürnberg, still kept it ahead throughout the pre-plague period.

Three cities, apparently having a population of 7–10,000, provide something of a mystery. Ulm got an early start and has, of course, become a considerable city, but it is alleged to have had only 4,000 persons in 1300 and 7,000 in 1345. It had between 66.5 and 84 hectares in area, however, so it is assumed that it had about 8,000. Salzburg was in early times the site of an archiepiscopal see and an important place, yet it only enclosed 58 hectares which suggests perhaps 7,000 persons. On the other hand Nordlingen, which is still a very small place and had no claim to importance in the Middle Ages, had a wall enclosing 93 hectares and presumably had about 5,295 persons for its 1,059 hearths in the year 1456. Both of these suggest a population of about 10,000 in the pre-plague period. These are rather rough guesses presented with some qualms about their accuracy.

The area of the region for which Augsburg was the centre may be limited as follows:

	km^2
Bavaria	75,870
Parts of Switzerland not in the region of Dijon	28,324
Wurtemberg	19,512
Salzburg	7,163
	130,869

Again there is little information which can indicate the density of population, unless the size of the cities gives clues. The size of Augsburg, if 25,000, suggests a regional total of about 1.67 millions. This would give a density of about 12.7 to the km^2, which would be reasonable for the area with its extensive woodlands. Without the ten largest cities (117,000), the density of population would be about 11.9 to the km^2. The urban index would be about 6.5. This is obviously high because other cities were advancing faster than the metropolitan city and may indicate that the population may have been somewhat higher, perhaps near two millions.

As with other German regions there was some linguistic unity in the region—the group known as the Upper High German series, containing the Alamannic, the Bavarian-Austrian, and the Upper Franconian dialects. The frontier character of the area had doubtless contributed to this unity, since life along a frontier is apt to be of a composite type. There the lines of communication moved both along the frontier of the Roman Empire and across the frontier from Italy into the Germanic country. Even though the Germans eventually dominated the whole area, the breakdown of the frontier probably still left enough of the older population who would have handled commerce and perhaps even local administration for a time to have maintained a unity of commercial action and communication.

THE REGION OF DIJON

The city of Lyon is one of the great French cities today, the metropolis of eastern France, as it had been during the Roman occupation of eastern Gaul. In the later Middle Ages, it was a border city between France and the Empire. In spite of its magnificent site on the Rhône and Saône rivers, it remained a small city. The metropolitan city then was Dijon, capital of the Duchy of Burgundy. Burgundy was divided among the Duchy of Burgundy, the county of Burgundy (Franche-Comté) and the French counties of Dauphiné, Forez, Auvergne, and Valentinois. Evidently Burgundy dominated the region and Dijon was thus a natural metropolis, even though it was at the northern end of the region. Although the political division seems to have had a deleterious effect on the region, it still possessed a certain geographical unity with the upper Rhône, upper Saône, the Doubs and western Swiss territory as the core of an area extending well into the neighbouring mountains. Ecclesiastically, the region included much of the vast province of Lyon as well as most of the provinces of Besançon, Vienne and even a part of Bourges.

The problem then is largely why the region of Dijon failed in the thirteenth century to profit more from the Italian-Low Country-French trade. Through it went three lines of commerce from the south to France and other northern areas: the Avignon-Lyon, Genoa-Mont Cenis and Milan-Simplon routes.[11] The larger trading city was Venice, rather than Genoa, and its trade to the north tended to cross the lower, eastern Alpine passes, like the Brenner, directly to the German cities and even to the Fairs of Champagne, largely bypassing the Dijon region. The Roman road along the east bank of the Rhône had its influence in that the major cities south of Lyon remain on that side of the river. The trade of Montpellier, a considerable city, presumably went by Lyon-Dijon to the north. The cities of Béziers and Narbonne had two possible land routes north: by way of Millau-Clermont and by way of Toulouse. Neither Dijon nor Lyon was much of an industrial centre in the middle ages although the local wine, especially of Beaune, was among the best in Europe and much went south to Avignon and other towns. The cities of the area never formed, either separately or under the leadership of Burgundy, city leagues such as protected the Hanse commerce. Thus a combination of unfavourable circumstances prevented the economic development of the region of Dijon, although it was protected by the Duke of Burgundy.[12]

TABLE 9: REGION OF DIJON

Rank,	City	Pop Est 1,000s	Hyp Est 1,000s	Area hectares		
1	Dijon	17	17	104	1376–2,353 h	*LAMP* 120, *WEC* 340
2	Lyon	10.5	9.7	72	1300–3,000 p	Mols 3, 99, *EUI*
3	Besançon	8	6.6	99		Baedeker
4	Autun	7	5.1	80		Baedeker
5	Le Puy	6	4.1	50(27)	1300–1,200 h 1367–912	Mols 1, 255 *IXH*
6	Valence	5	3.5	40		Lot 1, 114
7	Clermont-Ferrand	5	3.0	38		Eychart 162
8	Vienne	5	2.7	36	1391–959 h	Lot 1, 122: *IXH* 76
9	Mâcon	4	2.4	36		Duby 683
10	Geneva	3	2.2	45	1356–491 h	Lot 1, 38-9, Binz 107
11	Chalon-sur-Saône	3		24		*WEC* 344
12	Grenoble	3		20	1383–532 h	*IXH* 76

Lyon: mid 13th c. Steyert, II, 393 ; about 1388, Dénian at end.

Well up in the valley of the Saône, Dijon had a strong economic position and gradually became a sort of capital of Burgundy (Table 9). In 1376 the city was taxed for 2,353 hearths which at five to the hearth was 11,765 persons.[13] If we assume that the city was a third less than in the pre-plague period, its pre-plague population would have been about 17,647. With an area of 104 hectares within its walls, the density would have been 170 to the hectare, assuming no suburbs, a rather high density. Lyon was not so large even though it had been a great Roman city with an area of about 163 hectares in the first century AD. It had declined by the fourth century to 113 hectares, which was about its size in the thirteenth century. In 1320 when it became a self-governing commune, some 3,000 persons took the oath. Allowing 3.5 to the oathtaker would give a population of about 10,500. In 1389 the number of *aisées* (householders) was down to 1,470.[14] If we assume five to a householder and a loss of a third from the plagues we reach about 11,000 for Lyon's pre-plague population.

Once past the first two cities the problems of estimating population are serious. In table 9 they are arranged in order of area with the exception of Geneva, where the tax of 1356 seems to give a relatively small figure with respect to the walled area. Geneva, of course, grew very rapidly in the fifteenth century but was quite small in the preceding century. One problem is that local needs should have raised the centres to about 3–4,000 without the help of inter-city activities. In any case the evidence would show that Dijon was head of a very modest region.

In the region of Dijon, as with all others which do not have natural boundaries, the area is ill-defined and very tentative. We assume that it included about twelve French departments: Ain, Allier, Doubs, Haute-Loire, Haute-Savoie, Isère, Jura, Loire, Puy-de-Dôme, Rhône, Saône-et-Loire, and Savoie. In addition it would probably include the four western Swiss provinces: Geneva, Vaud, Valais, and Fribourg. The French area then would have been about 71,848km^2 and the Swiss 13,000 for a total of about 84,848. For the most part it was a high area, quite mountainous. It should have been lightly inhabited since there were no basic resources for maintaining a large population. Two methods for estimating its population exist. One is to assume that its metropolis, Dijon, had about 1.5% of the total. Thus if Dijon had about 17,000 inhabitants, the total of the region should have been about 1,130,000. This was probably a maximum since commerce may have concentrated more people at Dijon than the region itself would have located there. The other method would be to compare for density somewhat similar areas such as Provence. The density of the region would have been about 13 to the km^2, which is about the density for the entire region of Montpellier.

THE REGION OF COLOGNE

The region of Cologne was the heart of Germany, as illustrated by the Rheinische Bund of 1254.[15] Mainz and Worms, with a lesser partner in Oppenheim, formed a *Bundnis* which spread rapidly over most of Germany. The leaders of the league met four times a year at Cologne, Worms, Mainz, and Strasbourg, all Rhine cities, closest to the original trio. The political possibilities of the region were clear. To these cities were joined the three great archbishops of Mainz, Cologne, and Trier, many other bishops and several lay lords. The subsequent break-up over the election of the German king on the death of William of Holland shattered the unity of Germany with its obvious centre in the region of Cologne. Had William lived and made a capital at Mainz or Worms, it is possible that he might have united Germany, assuming that the archbishops had remained as his supporters, that the interests of the cities had persisted, and that a reasonable number of lay lords remained loyal. The promotion of the King of Germany to Roman Emperor made the royal office so attractive that outsiders like Richard of Cornwall, earl and brother of the English king Henry III, and king Alfonso X of Castile, were willing to bid for the place. Perhaps if one of the central Rhine cities (Mainz, Worms, or Frankfurt) had been one of the greater German cities, this could have led toward a strong German union. The region of Cologne was essentially the Rhine Valley, excepting its extreme stretches. Apart from the north-east area about Dortmund and Soest, it was a very fertile, if hilly, area.

In these cities of the region of Cologne, the patriciate which was important was generally open to the wealthy, regardless of their origin.[16] By and large few had been *ministeriales*, but many had been proprietors of lands. In some cities, Basel, Frankfurt, Regensburg, Mainz, and Trier among them, wealthy families had towers in the cities, much as had the great families of some Italian cities. Again the importance of the noble or near noble class as an element in the city patriciate and ruling class in this period is evident.

For a city of its importance, as the largest of west Germany, and possibly of all Germany, Cologne has preserved singularly little demographic information. It was a portal city up the Rhine river, towards the Hanse cities of Westphalia and into the Low Countries. It was the seat of a great archbishop and had a long and important history. It was an early textile manufacturing centre,[17] and was one of the two great European centres of the wine trade. The first German university was there. After the thirteenth century, its parish of St Columban increased from only 887 to 984 houses although the houses were larger. Yet Mols suggests that it had not many more than 15,000 in the thirteenth century although between 30,000 and 40,000 in the sixteenth century.[18] Fortunately, its walled area has been studied carefully; about 100 hectares in the tenth century, 185 by about AD 1106, 320 by AD 1180, and 397 in the fourteenth century. Now it may be true that Cologne was like quite a number of other cities of the fourteenth century in building walls far in excess of those that were necessary.[19] But it is unlikely that Cologne did so earlier, and so the walls of 1180 really should have housed a population of at least 32,000. The later walls would indicate that the population had already outgrown those walls and thus it is likely that Cologne just before the plague had at least 40,000 persons (Table 10). Indeed, it seems unlikely that a place of its great importance could have had fewer than that number.

Strasbourg has preserved a complete census, or rather several censuses for the years 1473–7, showing a population of 20,612 in the first year and a slightly larger number in succeeding years. Since 1473 should have seen a slight rise from the medieval low, its population may have sunk as far as 19,000. This should mean that its pre-plague population was

TABLE 10: REGION OF COLOGNE

Rank, City	Pop Est 1,000s	Hyp Est 1,000s	Area hectares	Base	Deutsche Städtebuch
1 Cologne	40	40	397–401		vol 2, 3, 251
2 Strasbourg	25	23.8	270	1473– 20,612–722 p	
3 Aachen	18	15.6	175		3, 3, 33
4 Worms	16	12	170		4, 3, 451
5 Frankfurt-am-Main	12	9.6	128	1387–2,904 m	4, 1, 123
6 Trier, Trèves	10.5	8.2	133	1363–2,106 t	4, 3, 422
7 Mainz	10	7.1	120	1463–5,750 p	4, 3, 258
8 Soest	8	6.3	101–20		2, 2, 330
9 Dortmund	7	5.7	72		3, 2, 108
10 Speyer	6	5.2	66	1536–7,230 p	4, 3, 384
11 Heilbronn		4.8	28?	1399– 5,501–5,235 p	4, 2, 112

Cologne: East 125; Püschel 209; Weczerka 71. Strasbourg: Püschel 209; Spruner-Menke, *Atlas* by AD 1374 270 hectares; *WEC* EAF. Aachen: *WEC* 371. Worms: Mols 1, 292; 2, 390. Trier: Herzog 146. Soest: Mols 3, 235; Niemeier-Tothert 31; *WEC* 372; Weczerka 71. Dortmund: Mols 3, 235; Püschel 211. Speyer: Herzog 190. Heilbronn: Mistele 55.

at least 25,000. For dates earlier than the first census only the record of wall building gives demographic data. The wall was enlarged quite a number of times from its early Roman form, and by 1374 had included 270 hectares, according to the map in Spruner-Menke. Püschel suggests 193 hectares as the area.[20] Even the smaller area could have held 25,000 without too much difficulty. Strasbourg was, like Cologne, a kind of portal to the traffic of the Rhine and was on the great highway from Paris to Augsburg. Like Cologne also, its position would be one of permanent importance, persisting even after the introduction of modern rail and road systems.

A natural question is whether Strasbourg might not be regarded as a metropolitan centre for a region of its own; the present author at one time held Strasbourg to be probably larger than 25,000,[21] and did not set up the network of subordinate cities which any metropolitan area should have. When this was in fact done it seemed clear that the Rhineland was a natural region and Strasbourg just a portal city of an area in which Cologne was clearly the largest city. In a straight line Cologne and Strasbourg are about as far apart as London and York, while transportation by river was obviously cheaper than by land. For cities of the 25–40,000 class, they were not too far apart to share in commerce.

The next three cities of the region were probably Aachen, Worms, and Frankfurt-am-Main; all three said to have had walls much too extensive for the city,[22] respectively 175, 170, and 128 hectares. Aachen (Aix-la-Chapelle) was one of Charlemagne's capitals, if that august term can be applied to his rather frequent stopping places. Certainly its small size in his time (less than 10,000, probably closer to 5,000) indicates the primitive state of his government, in that it could support no larger city. It developed as an early textile centre.[23] At about 1500 it was said to oscillate around 20,000 [24] and it had probably been about the same just before the plague. It is unlikely that it had much less than one hundred to the hectare. The same can be said for Worms about which even less is known; the evidence that it was strongly rural is greater,[25] yet the fact that its walls were much longer than those of Mainz and Speyer may be significant.

Much more is known about Frankfurt-am-Main. In 1387 it had 2,904 men and boys over the age of eleven.[26] This should have been about a third of the city of about 8,700, and should indicate a city which had at least 12,000 before the plague. Now the totals of new members for the four decades 1311–1350 run for a yearly average in each decade 28.6, 41.4, 84.0, and 105.9. For a city of 12,000 at .007 or .008 a year the new members should have numbered 84 or 96, about the point reached just before the plague. The city was obviously increasing rapidly in the period.[27]

Bücher's famous study, *Die Bevölkerung von Frankfurt-am-Main*, gives some very interesting information about migration into the city in its lists of new citizens of the city of 1387. The largest number came, as expected, from the neighbouring districts on either side of the Main and from nearby areas of the Rhineland. Of the thousand or so whose place of origin seems to be certain, 235 came from Oberhessen, a district which is some distance from the city, back in the hills. Probably most cities had particular rural areas, not necessarily nearest to the cities, from which they drew especially large numbers. These areas would be parts of the region and illustrate the way in which the rural areas were associated with the larger cities. Only a dozen had come apparently from countries outside of Germany, all from Bohemia and Moravia except one from Poland. From the lower Rhineland and Westphalia there were 49, from Bavaria (some parts of which were near Frankfurt) 38, and from the rest of Germany 18. Thus only about 120 came from beyond the immediate areas about the city.

The next three cities in size appear to have been Trier, Mainz, and Soest. The area of Trier was about 133 hectares in the thirteenth century (Püschel gives 120). In 1363 it had 2,106 heads of houses, quite a number of them women, so that the number should probably be multiplied by no more than four to get 8,424 after two attacks of the plague. If we assume a 20% loss from them, Trier's pre-plague population should have been about 10,500. The area of Mainz was about the same (120 hectares) but its area retained certain agricultural features which suggest a relatively low density of population,[28] so 10,000 is suggested for it. It had an important position on the Rhine and, of course, was a great archiepiscopal seat. It had, however, the rising city of Frankfurt 32 kilometres to the east and Worms about 45 kilometres to the south. The third city was Soest in Westphalia, with walls enclosing about 101 hectares, which might suggest a population of about 10,000 also. However, the number of new citizens was only around 29–37 in the decades from 1301 to 1350, which should indicate about 5,000, so low as to raise the possibility that the new citizens did not include sons or other relatives entering into civic rights.[29] Under the circumstances, particularly since it is hard to believe that a city of the importance of Soest should have had so few citizens, 8,000 is suggested as its population; more might be expected.

After these there appear a number of other cities which seem a little smaller: Dortmund, Speyer, and Heilbronn. Dortmund's walls enclosed about 72 hectares while the number of new admissions averaged about 20.[30] Of the new admissions in the fourteenth century, 24% came from the neighbourhood *(landkreis)* and 64% from the rest of Westphalia, with most of the others from the Rhineland. The same problem of the identity of those admitted occurred as in the case of Soest, an average of about twenty a year with little evidence of change over the period 1301–50. Seven thousand is suggested for its population. Even less is known of Speyer, which had about 66 hectares within its walls. Heilbronn was evidently quite a bit smaller within the walls, but in 1399 had apparently about 5,000 persons and may have been larger than the other two before the plague.

The map of the Cologne region shows some cities very close together—cities so large that their interests should seriously conflict with their neighbours' and which in Italy would certainly have led to desperate struggles on the battlefield. By massing some of these together, however, the following reshaping might appear possible.

		Pop est 1000s	Hyp est 1000s
1	Cologne-Aachen	58	60
2	Frankfurt-Mainz-Worms	39	34
3	Strasbourg	25	23
4	Soest-Dortmund	18	18
5	Trier	10	14

The area to be assigned to the region of Cologne is peculiarly difficult to define. Tentatively, it is assumed to have been composed of Baden (15,065km²), Alsace-Lorraine (14,518 km²), Hesse (7,689km²), Palatinate (about 10,000km²) and a strip about 300 kilometres long and 200 wide in the Rhine area, including to the north-east as far as Dortmund and Soest. This would have been an area of about 107,272km², including the thickly settled Rhineland, as well as the hilly land on either side of the river. If the size of the metropolitan city, Cologne, was about 1.5% of the total, the population of the area would have been about 2.7 millions. This is a case where a wide diversity of interpretations might be expected. If, for instance, Cologne-Aachen is interpreted as a combined metropolis with a 58,000 population, the region might be assumed to have had nearly 4 million inhabitants.

The total of the ten largest cities seems to have been about 152,500 persons. If the total population of the area was about 2.7 millions, the urban index would be about 5.6 which is not very far from the normal of about 5%. The density of population would have been about 25.0 persons to the km^2 for the total population and about 23.4 without the ten largest cities. In an area of vineyards, the hilly character of much of the land should not have been too serious a handicap. The average density appears to have been less than that of northern Italy but it was still greater than many other areas.

5

Frontier Regions:
Prague, Magdeburg, and Lübeck

GERMAN AND SLAV met in the frontier area, and eventually the former dominated in the cities while the latter remained strong in the countryside.[1] German agrarian migration moved strongly in the north and in Austria, while the Slavs remained an important factor in Bohemia, Slovakia, and in the Oder Valley. Even in the period 1250–1348 colonisation continued to be important as Germans moved into the eastern cities, while the Czech ruling class was strengthening itself in Prague. The new communities were taking constitutional ideas from older German cities, such as Augsburg and Nürnberg, as part of the *Drang nach Osten* in the marks along the frontier. The regions then were shaping up around the older centres of Prague, Magdeburg, and Lübeck (Fig 4) but in the same period the new centres of Vienna, Leipzig and Hamburg, as well as others, were growing rapidly. Within the regions there were extensive shifts in population which would eventually reshape the order of the larger cities.

Clues to the definition of a region appeared occasionally in the adoption of sets of laws from parent cities, notably in the twelfth and thirteenth centuries. In this the older established area of the Rhineland did not need to share. First, the towns of the northern coastlands, from Holstein to Pomerania, and beyond in the Baltic lands, adopted Lübeck law, a distribution which is to be associated with that of the trade connections of the Hanseatic merchants, many of whom were of

Lübeck origin. The second was the law of Nürnberg which spread in the western part of Bohemia, Moravia, Austria and Bavaria. In the same area the Austrian law of Vienna spread in the south and the law of Iglau (Jahlava) and Brünn (Brno) in the east. Thirdly, Magdeburg law spread east of the Elbe to include north-eastern Bohemia, and the northern lowlands as far as a line from Königsberg to the Carpathians.[2] This, again, is what might be expected since Magdeburg was the great eastern centre in the early period of expansion. But two problems remain. First, it would appear that Nürnberg belonged to the southern region of which Magdeburg was the centre rather than to the central or eastern group; even the road map of the early period suggests no heavy commerce to the east.[3] However, Bohemia was a part of the great ecclesiastical province of Mainz before it was separated in 1344. The second problem is the lack of such a system in the south, but probably there again the area had been settled so early that the constitutions of the cities were established before the era of imitation by new cities of the constitutions of the old cities.

The influence of Nürnberg upon the German cities of Bohemia was by way of mountain passes toward Eger (Cheb) and Prague. Further south the Danube was the great highway of the east-west trade. The backbone of the three regions was the Elbe River; Lübeck was not far from its mouth, Magdeburg was in its middle course, while Prague was on its upper tributary. To the east the Oder Valley was part also of the three regions.

In language the Lübeck area spoke Low German while Upper High German was the dialect of much of the Magdeburg area. Bohemia and Vienna shared in the dialects of south Germany, while various Czech and Slovak dialects of Slavic existed in the region of Prague in the Bohemian and eastern areas.

THE REGION OF PRAGUE

The region of Prague was essentially Bohemia with the adjacent areas to the north in Germany (Silesia) and to the south in Austria. Much of it was in the upper reaches of the Elbe

River and of the tributaries of the Danube from Linz to Bratislava. In the thirteenth century, the Premyslide dynasty of Bohemia united all of the area except the German parts and thus, to an economic and geographical unity, a political unity was added. Had the dynasty lasted beyond 1278 and kept its centre at Prague, the latter might have attained the same greatness of leadership as Cologne and the western capitals. As it was, the Hapsburgs preferred Vienna, which was an outstanding centre in its own right and which gradually increased in respect of Prague. In 1346 and the years following, Charles IV built up Prague as his capital and for a time it again appeared to have a great future as the metropolitan centre of the area. It had a marked advantage over Vienna in that the latter was hemmed in between Hungary and south Germany—regionally between Budapest and Augsburg and Nürnberg. In a sense, then, Prague remained a kind of inchoate metropolitanate for the thirteenth century.

The linguistic situation of the region of Prague was a dual one which remained for centuries, until Hitler settled it in World War II by bringing German-speaking people into the Reich. Much of the countryside in Bohemia and Slovakia spoke Slavic, while in the cities the population was heavily Germanic. Beside the agricultural part of the *Drang nach Osten*, and far exceeding it, was the urban migration of German merchants which settled German colonies to the east, making cities of strategic Slavic villages. So there was one language for the mass of the people and another for the merchant class of the cities. And, as usual, there was Latin, used in the Church and occasionally for records.

Prague was divided into quarters in the Middle Ages with a total area of about 200 hectares, perhaps even 250.[4] Altstadt was one of these quarters, with about 50 hectares. The Premyslide dynasty increased the size of the wall-enclosed area from about 150 hectares to about 430 in the century before the plague. Like the Low Country cities, Prague had walls which were much too extensive for the fourteenth century. In 1429 a census of Altstadt revealed 641 houses and 1,001 *ménages* or households.[5] If the household were rated at 5 and the total number for the city raised to 4,000 on the theory that the density of population was average, a total of 20,000 for 1429 would be reached. Assuming that the population had suffered a decline of 33% from the pre-plague population, that population should have been about 30,000. This must be a maximum since five to the *ménage* is probably high. On the other hand the average *ménage* of Dresden, although 3.6 apiece, occupied only half a house so that the average to the house was nearly seven. If this was applied to the Prague figures the average to the *ménage* would be about 4.5 persons and the population a little less than 30,000.[6] This assumes also that the other sections of Prague were populated as thickly as Altstadt which was probably not the case. Under the circumstances it seems best to use 30,000 as Prague's pre-plague population (Table 11).

TABLE 11: REGION OF PRAGUE

Rank, City	Pop Est 1,000s	Hyp Est 1,000s	Area hectares	Base	Sources
1 Prague	30	30	198–250	1429–Altstadt 1,001 t	Mols II, 138 ; WEC 197
2 Vienna	20	17.1	96–170		Püschel 210 ; WEC 186
3 Breslau	12	11.7	122–43	1403–2,510 t	Püschel 210 ; Mols I, 241
4 Plsen, Pilsen	10	9	90		WEC 386
5 Olomouc, Olmütz	10	7.2	80		
6 Kutna Hora, Kuttenberg	8	6.1	70		Svidkovskij 147, Rausch 141
7 Brno, Brünn	7	5.3	48–50		Svidkovskij 161
8 Linz	6	4.7	50		Egli 147
9 Bratislava, Pressburg	5	4.3	32(90)		Svidkovskij 250
10 Eger, Cheb	4	3.9	30		
11 Litomerice, Leitmeriz	3	3.6	21		Hoenig 68
12 Jihlava, Iglau					

Prague: Svidkovskij 19. Olomouc: *Provodec po Olomouc*. Kutna Hora: Rausch 141, says 46.5 hectares in the thirteenth century.

In the thirteenth century the Viennese walls seem to have enclosed about 170–80 hectares,[7] which Mols believes indicates a population of about 20,000. This is a very rough estimate, but there seems no other evidence. Vienna occupied an unusual position geographically, near a break in the highlands where the Danube flows through to the Hungarian plain. There is, however, easy access to the Bohemian plain and to the highland of Bavaria, which seems part of the region of Augsburg. Thus Vienna, although part of the German march of the area, still seems to have had stronger political and probably economic ties with the Bohemian plain. At least this provides a tentative reconstruction of the conditions in the thirteenth century. At a later date the strength of the Hapsburg position in Hungary and Styria was so strong that Vienna developed a region about it. Already a considerable number of nobles lived in the city and participated in its commerce[8] but its lack of exportable goods kept its population low.

Of the other cities assumed to be in the region, Breslau was probably the largest. It apparently had an area of about 122–43 hectares and about 10,000 persons in 1403; it had the same tax as Bautzen and Görlitz with some 2,510 inscribed in the army. This should have meant about 12,000 before the plague, allowing for the natural growth of Silesian population in the period. It was the chief city of Silesia. The 'capital', if one may call it that, of Moravia was Olomouc (Olmütz) which apparently had an area of about 80 hectares for which we assume 10,000. The chief city of Slovakia was Bratislava (Pressburg) whose area seems somewhere between at least 30 hectares and a possible 90; presumably it grew rapidly at the end of the Middle Ages. Other large cities in the area were Pilsen, which has always been an iron centre, although it later became more famous for beer; it seems to have enclosed about 90 hectares. Kutna Hora (Kuttenberg) developed as a silver-mining centre in the thirteenth century with a mint and a royal residence; its area seems to have been about 70 hectares. Brno (Brünn) was apparently a city of about 48–50 hectares.

Linz in Austria had about 50 hectares and Eger (Cheb) about 30. Litomerice (Leitmeriz) was pre-eminent for navigation on the Elbe River; lacking other basic factors, it was probably too close to Prague (66km) to grow to a great size, and its 21 hectares suggests only a modest population. Tabor also seemed small, but the size of Jihlava (Iglau) is hard to discover; it may have been among the larger cities of the area. More about the geography of these cities will probably result from the fine archaeological work going on in Czechoslovakia, as illustrated by work on the Great Moravian centres.

The extent of the region of Prague as defined above can be estimated in area only in the vaguest way. One may assume that it included the following:

		km^2
	Bohemia	51,967
	Moravia	22,231
Silesia	(Austrian)	5,153
„	(German)	25,000
Austria	(Upper)	11,994
„	(Lower)	19,854
	Styria	22,449
		158,648

In those lands there were obviously great mountain areas which might not be considered part of the region. If we assume that Prague as the centre had about 1.5% of the total, it should have been about two millions. However, since Vienna was above the general average for the second city, this should be regarded as a minimum. The average density of the region would then be about 12.6 which was a low density, appropriate for such a mountainous area. Without the ten largest cities (estimated at 112,000) the density would be about 11.9 with an urban index of 6.6.

THE REGION OF MAGDEBURG

The problem of the region south of the Baltic city territory is that in the late thirteenth century and early fourteenth century it was in a period of transition. Cities like Magdeburg and Brunswick had got off to a good start in the earlier period. At a later time such cities as Berlin and Leipzig were to be the great cities. There were cross-currents in the area: trade with the north, with the frontier territory to the east, with the growing central area. The very settlement of the agricultural lands and great increase in population was shifting the weight of economic factors. Unfortunately the evidence about the larger cities is also vague. There were few parts of central Europe more fragmented politically than this area: south-west Saxony, Brandenburg, and Thuringia were among its larger fragments. While there had been considerable migration into the area, principally from the older parts of Germany, it was probably not very thickly settled yet.

Despite its politically fragmented character, there was a certain unity of language in the area. It falls generally within the West Middle High German group of dialects, more specifically within the Thuringian, Upper Saxon, and Silesian dialects. This region was created as a part of the *Drang nach Osten*, and as the result of a colonisation movement from the west and north-west. People seem to change their language as they move, and this was the case in the region of Magdeburg. Both of the regions of Magdeburg and Lübeck had large numbers of Saxon type houses which Meitzen[9] thought was just a continuation of the old Celtic house. A movement such as the colonisation of the East March also drew upon a variety of German groups, even of the Dutch, in the west. While Magdeburg was the early centre, it was stranded behind the frontier and thus as a later population increase occurred in the south-west, the centre of the population and larger cities developed there.

Magdeburg was obviously the central city, the *Hauptstadt*, of the region,[10] and even though the population of the city was probably not more than 20,000 in the period (Table 12), it had an interesting development. By 1300 the shipping on the Elbe was largely in its control.[11] It enclosed perhaps 172 hectares,[12] yet its growth must have been inhibited to some extent by its neighbours. Halberstadt was only 50 kilometres away to the south-west. Its bishop was lord of a considerable territory and its 6,000 persons rather larger than a city that close to the metropolitan centre should have had then. Furthermore about 33 kilometres to the south-east was Zerbst with a wall enclosing 120 hectares, obviously a very ambitious undertaking but which can hardly indicate a city of less than 9,000. Across the river from Zerbst was Dessau, a small city, Whether one would be justified in assuming that Magdeburg-

TABLE 12:   REGION OF MAGDEBURG

Rank, City		Pop Est 1,000s	Hyp Est 1,000s	Area hectares	Base	Deutsche Städtebuch
1	Magdeburg	20	20	110–172		vol 2, 593
2	Brunswick	12	11.4	115	1403–3,450 s	
3	Erfurt	10	7.8	120		2, 479
4	Zerbst	9	6	120		2, 757
5	Goslar	9	4.8	96		
6	Görlitz	9	4.1	72	1426–1,560 s	1, 753
7	Göttingen	8	3.5		1393–1,361 t	
8	Bautzen	8	3.2	70	1400–1,060 s	2, 22
9	Mühlhausen	7.5	2.9	50	1417–1,831 h	2, 615
10	Paderborn	7	2.6	70		
11	Halberstadt	6		77–100	1531–1,464 h	2, 518
12	Dresden	5		85	1396–3,745 p	
					+ 1,000 p	2, 47
13	Hanover	5		54		
14	Eisleben				1433–4,000 p	2, 473
15	Leipzig			42	1471–6,000 p	2, 121

Magdeburg: Brandt (Lechner) 470 for 172 hectares; Herzog 21. Brunswick: Mols 3, 106; *WEC* 378. Erfurt: Püschel 210. Goslar: Herzog 58. Göttingen: Kronshagen 395. Bautzen: *IXH*. Paderborn: Herzog 109. Halberstadt: Herzog 72; *WEC*. Hanover: *WEC* 378. Leipzig: Püschel 211.

Zerbst-Dessau constituted a kind of metropolitan nucleus of perhaps 30,000, it does seem that Magdeburg was hemmed in to some extent.

Two other cities are alleged to have had about 115–120 hectares as their area of habitation: Brunswick with 115 and Erfurt with 120. Brunswick was an older city, originally of five villages, which became one of the great cities of the Hanseatic League. It lay on the crossroads of the Lübeck-Hamburg-Nürnberg and the Cologne-Magdeburg highways. Yet it was not a bishop's see and was not even on a river. After 1257, the duke lived some distance away at Wolfenbüttel. In 1403 it had 3,450 soldiers, which should have meant a population of at least 12,000 in the pre-plague period. Erfurt, down the highway from Magdeburg south to Nürnberg, was in a somewhat similar situation, although less favourably located. Although on a fief of the Archbishop of Mainz, it became practically a free city in the thirteenth century. At a guess it had a population of about 10,000 then.

Goslar and Mülhausen present problems. Goslar was an important mining centre and a place where a number of imperial diets met. Yet it joined the Hanseatic League only about 1350, which suggests that it was not much of a commercial centre; 9,000 provides a modest estimate for it. Mühlhausen is alleged to have had 1,875 householders in 1419 and 1,455 in 1447, followed by increasing numbers after that year, until by 1505 it had 1,665. Since populations generally tended to be at their lowest about 1440,[13] the 1419 figure ought to have been only a little larger than the 1447 number and one suspects a mistake, especially since the medieval area of Mühlhausen, 50–60 hectares, was so small. Using Roman numerals the 1419 number would have been MDCCCLXXV, or 1,875, which could easily have been a mistake for MCCCCLXXV or 1,475. Her pre-plague population should have been about 7,500.

Bautzen and Görlitz are about 28 kilometres apart in the March of Upper Lusatia near the south-east edge of the region. They might more appropriately be placed in the region of Prague since they are not far from the Elbe on the other side of the mountains. They shared the same tax, a contribution for soldiers (*Geschuss*). Jatzwauk has estimated from some contributors to the tax in 1400 (multiplying the number of contributors by five), that the population of Bautzen was about 5,300. The percentage of women contributors (7–14%), however, suggests that five was a maximum. In any case the chances are that the population of the city was about 8,000 before the plague. The tax in Görlitz in 1426, its earliest, has been estimated to indicate a population of about 7,800, with a pre-plague population of perhaps 9,000.[14]

The area of the Magdeburg region is quite tentative, set at 100,000km². The clue offered by the population of the metropolitan city would suggest that the population of the region should have been about 1,330,000. This would give a density of 13.3 to the whole region. Without the top ten cities, 97,500, the density would be about 12.4 with an urban index of about 7.5.

THE REGION OF LüBECK

Hanseatic trade, de Roover has noted, extended along a single axis with its centre in Lübeck and two arms: one stretching out west towards Bruges and London and the other east to Riga and far-away Novgorod.[15] Seldom has an institution been as single-minded in his aims and activities as the Hanseatic League, which dominated much of the life of the region of Lübeck. Its interest was its economic life. It made full use of the Baltic and North Seas as well as the lower courses of the Rhine, Elbe, and Oder Rivers. Yet the roads of the region were very important; if they were more expensive to use they were safer from storm and ice in winter and more direct. Before the plague of 1348 the cities of the region, despite their fame, were really not very large. It must be remembered that their countryside was often quite bound up with the city and shared much in its activities, demographically as well as economically.

The area might be expected to have had much the same language, since the population had moved east from the same Low German speech areas. For Lübeck, the place of origin of immigrants just before AD 1259 was, proportionately, 31% from Rhine-Westphalia, 29% from Lower Saxony, 22% from Holstein-Lauenburg-Mecklenburg, and 13% from elsewhere.[16] So the language in general was that of Westphalia, Eastphalia and the countryside about Lübeck. It shared the Saxon-type house with the region of Magdeburg.[17] The cities of the area were associated with the countryside to a considerable distance inland. Like other eastward movements in Germany in the *Drang nach Osten,* there was large-scale colonisation, not merely to the cities but to the countryside as well. The March of the Billungs was largely inhabited by this colonisation in the eleventh and twelfth centuries.

This region possessed the usual peculiar problems of a frontier area and the rapid development of commerce and population. Two types of evidence occur which offer a least a comparison among the cities. The first is lists of new citizens of the cities, for which several cities retained rolls. They are listed in the table for the region. At the same time, the probable complication should be borne in mind that the country areas about the cities doubtless furnished a part of the soldiers in the list of 1293, and furthermore, their relations with possible enemies conditioned their quotas. A city with an increasing population would obviously have more new citizens to its total population than one with a stable population. The second type of evidence is the quotas which five cities of the eastern half assigned to themselves in 1293 and 1361; they should be related to population.

The five cities which shared quotas in their armies also had as a common characteristic, a smaller area within city walls than did their western partners. They all seem to have a density of 140 or more, with the exception of Greifswald. The western group may have had densities of about 100–120 a hectare, presumably because they were built on more spacious sites after longer development.

The city of Rostock has, in addition to information about new citizens and quotas, data that show it had 2,160 hearths in 1378. This, at 4 to the hearth, should have been 8,640. Before the plague, it might well have had about 14,000 persons. Lübeck was an older city with heavier responsibilities as one of the great cities of the Hanse; we are assuming then that the other cities took on more military responsibilites, in part, because the others were growing much more rapidly and thus had more younger men and more new citizens.

Lübeck, burned to the ground in 1157, recovered rapidly with the help of Henry the Lion, and made its second great advance with the development of the Hanseatic League in the middle of the thirteenth century.[18] The area within its walls before the plague seem to have reached 200 hectares. The 196 new citizens of 1259, if representing .007 of the population, would suggest a city of 28,000, which Lübeck would seem to have been then. (Table 13). In truth this year may have been exceptional since the city was growing rapidly then and the average for the fourteenth century before the plague (years of apparent population stability) was only 198.[19] In the years 1350–5, Lübeck added 1,599 new citizens. If the city lost a quarter of its population it must have needed about 150 new citizens a year just to hold even (assuming mortality as before the plague). So that the average of 166 new citizens a year made

TABLE 13: REGION OF LÜBECK

Rank, City	Pop Est 1,000s	Hyp Est 1,000s	Area hectares	Army 1293	Quota 1361	New Citizens		DS
1 Lübeck	28	30	200	100	600	198		1, 417
2 Münster	16	17.1	124–56					3, 2, 251
3 Rostock	14	11.7	98	70	400		1378–2,160 h	1, 323
4 Stralsund	12	9	72	50	400	120		1, 244
5 Bremen	12	7.2	64+				1348–6,966 dead?	
6 Hamburg	9	6.1	80–96	106		60		1, 387
7 Osnabrück	9	5.3	98					
8 Greifswald	8	4.7	72	38	200			
9 Wismar	8	4.3	58	38	200	57		1, 344
10 Lüneburg	8	3.9	56					

Lübeck: *WEC* 378. Münster: *WEC* 374 Prinz. Rostock *IXH*; *WEC* 388. Stralsund: *WEC* 388. Bremen: Mols 2, 434; Schwarzwälder 414 (64 hectares, but two sizeable suburbs) Herzog 94. Hamburg: Weczerka 71 *Untersuchungen* 277. Osnabrück: *WEC* 375. Griefswald: *WEC* 388. Lüneburg: Herzog 86; *WEC* 376. Army Quotas: Mols 1, 295. New citizens per year: Mols 3, 235.

for a recovery of 116 extra to make up the deficit. If the losses had been about a thousand (assuming 4,000 citizens in 1346), the city should have made up its loss in less than ten years, but part of this would have been at the expense of the country-side. Lübeck in 1460 had 5,217 hearths and 5,407 in the next year[20] with a population at five to the hearth of more than 26,000. Lübeck's pre-plague population should have been somewhat larger and thus is brought near 30,000. However, assuming a certain rate of general increase in northern Europe from 1346 to 1460, the number selected is 28,000.

The later prominence of Bremen and Hamburg is evident in history; it is surprising to find them so small in this period when they already had some prominence. Indeed, what is usually regarded as good evidence indicates that Bremen had 6,966 deaths from the plague in 1350.[21] A further suggestion that an additional uncounted 7,000 died in the streets is normally rejected. If the loss of 6,966 from a population of 15,000 is accepted, the choice is between two difficult alternatives; that there were 15,000 within Bremen's walls of 64 hectares and two small suburbs making a density of somewhat less than 234, much too high to be believed easily, or that there was a mortality of about 46.3% (without counting the dead in the street). Even the number 6,966 arouses suspicion. The Black Death inflicted definite physical marks, although not necessarily on the forehead: to those familiar with Revelations 13: 16, the Black Death might seem a mark of the beast, and the number of the beast was 666. The 46.3% mortality would be a minimum figure since doubtless there were some not counted. This seems far too high as a percentage of 15,000. The chances are, unfortunately since accurate numbers of plague mortality are so scarce, that 6,966 was not genuine. It is also likely that the population of Bremen was closer to 12,000 than it was to 15,000.

The low estimate for Hamburg is based upon a number of corroborating estimates and facts. Hamburg's new citizens' lists averaged only about 36 to the year in the first three decades of the fourteenth century, jumping to an average of about 60 in the two decades before the plague. One sees then a rapidly growing city for which allowance must be made in estimating total population from the admission lists. On that basis 9,000 would be a fair estimate, well within its 106 hectares. The lists show, moreover, very heavy migration from the neighbouring areas of Hanover to the west and Holstein to the east, again typical of a relatively small city.[22] Both of its eastern neighbours, the very aggressive Lübeck and Lüneburg, close to Hamburg, must have possessed much of the commerce that Hamburg later acquired. The 8,000 assigned to Lüneberg is a compromise between its number of new citizens which suggest as low as 5,000 and its walls enclosing 108 hectares which might suggest as many as 10,000; the estimate is hardly satisfactory. Another reason for Hamburg's small size was her refusal to accept members of noble classes who were forbidden to reside in the city in 1270.[23]

With some hesitation the Hanse cities to the west of Bremen are suggested for the region: Osnabrück and Münster. Both were seats of bishops; the prelate of Münster presiding over an especially large and wealthy diocese. It is difficult to estimate the population of either of these cities. The medieval section of Münster, probably the larger of the two, would seem to have been between 124 and 156 hectares,[24] for which a population of as least 16,000 is assumed in the pre-plague period.

These two cities are near two others which are assigned to the region of Cologne; Soest and Dortmund. A case could be made for Cologne as head of a district only as far up-river as, say Mainz and Frankfurt or even Worms, and then for adding the eastern cities as far as Osnabrück. In any event these Westphalian cities bear the stamp of border cities, rather like Metz, Basel, and others which share in the activities of adjoining groups. If there was continuous trade and commerce among regions, the border cities frequently had very strong connections in both regions.

Of the three eastern cities Stralsund seems much the largest; the problem is how large. Its area (in terms of its army quota and area with respect to Rostock) would suggest about 10–11,690, but the number of new citizens suggests a much higher population, of the order of 17,000. However, it is better just to assume that persons in very large numbers were being admitted to a rapidly growing city and that the population was about 14,000. Wismar's army quota (compared with Rostock) and new citizens (compared with Lübeck) both suggest about

8,000 inhabitants. The area points to a little more, but this seems a less certain indication. Greifswald had the same army quota and almost the same area as Wismar, so 8,000 is also suggested for Greifswald. They seem to have recruited from the younger sons of neighbouring gentry, but the gentry themselves do not seem to have lived in the cities.[25]

The region provides serious complications for estimates of area and population. The Hanseatic League was definitely an organisation within, but almost independent of, the feudal areas about it. However, it is assumed that the land dominated by the cities, at least on an economic basis, was about 500 kilometres long and 150 wide with an area of about 75,000km². Little data can be used to estimate population. The land was flat and only moderately productive; perhaps 20 to the km² would be a tentatively reasonable estimate, bringing its farming population to about 1.5 millions. If it is assumed that the metropolitan city ought to have had 1.5% of the total, the population would have been about 1.9 millions. However, in an area of sizeable commercial cities, the percentage of urban population in the total should have been somewhat, perhaps even much larger than the 1.5%. The north Italian cities showed a much higher percentage of urbanisation, another indication that the commercial position of the Italian cities was very dominant at the time.

Assuming the farming area of the region of Lübeck had a population of about 1.5 millions, the addition of the ten largest would have added about 112,000 persons and other cities and larger market towns would have brought the total to perhaps 1.7 millions. The urban index would then have been about 6.6% and the total density of the area about 22.7 persons to the km². The urban index is rather low for an area in which the Hanseatic League dominated, but it may merely mean that the cities were really not so very large even in terms of the countryside. It is doubtful if the Hanse shared in enough trade, not originated in or brought into the area, to support a larger portion of the population.

6

Northern Sea Regions:
Ghent, London, and Dublin

COMMERCE IN THIS period was primarily a sea trade in the area, although navigation could be very hazardous. The compass was just beginning to be used[1] and the inventions of rudder, deeper keel and better sails were also new. The use of larger vessels was to deprive the shallower harbours of much of their commerce in the century following the outbreak of the plague. It was an era when the larger and deeper ports increased at the expense of the lesser ones; this was to the profit of Bruges, Plymouth, Southampton, and Dublin, to mention a few cases. Before the plague these regions were seldom ravaged by war and were generally prosperous. Two of the regional centres, London and Dublin, were obvious centres and were both earlier and later than the thirteenth century. Ghent was not so obviously a centre although the cluster of cities of which it was a part in Flanders and Brabant had a very central location and these cities were to remain, first in the Belgian area and later in the Dutch, leaders in the economic life of western Europe.

THE REGION OF GHENT

Next to the Italian regions, the Netherlands presented in the Middle Ages the most populous cluster of large cities in western Europe—probably in all Europe (Fig 5).[2] The high population density was caused by the concentration there of the largest textile guilds of the time. Expansion was very rapid in the thirteenth century. This can be seen in two lists illustrating the sizes of the cities in the early part of the thirteenth century and from their greatly increased sizes in the immediate pre-plague period. Many of the textile cities built walls enclosing vast areas just before the plagues, but the space in

Fig 5   The region of Ghent

which was not utilised until well into the eighteenth century and, in some cases, the nineteenth century.

Although the Low Countries has no general study of its population like those devoted to Italy by Beloch, or to France by Lot, or to Germany by Keyser, or England by myself, the lack is largely offset by the special interest which Mols and Van Werveke have had in their native land, and, of course, by the data which remain from that area. For some of the cities had not only hearth taxes but sometimes poll taxes, which included about two-thirds of the people (those over the age of fourteen) and, in a few cases in the fifteenth century, even total population.

H

The Low Countries included Holland as well as Flanders and Brabant, of course. Although Holland was to have a spectacular history at a later date, in this period it seems to have been agricultural with relatively small cities. The presence of Dutch as a language in the area complicated the linguistic situation. Flemish was the main language of the areas of Flanders and Brabant, but much French must have been spoken there. Moreover, French was the language of the ruling class of western Europe then and had a certain attraction as such. Thus the Low Countries had a situation in which at least three languages were spoken among its agricultural inhabitants. Moreover, it had very strong ties in commerce with both the English-speaking islands to the west and to the German-speaking Hanse cities to the east. Unlike most regions, where the linguistic situation was surprisingly simple, that of the region of Ghent was very complicated. In the thirteenth century it must have been a multilingual region, much as Switzerland is.

A combination of circumstances enabled the cities of Flanders and Brabant to attain great strength in the thirteenth century; they had to struggle against the Empire, France, and their own counts. The interest of the Hohenstauffens shifted to Italy at the death of Henry VI and during the minority of Frederick II. France turned its attention to the south, acquiring most of the Angevin fiefs after King John's indiscretion and continuing that interest with the Albigensian Crusade and further interference in the south. Meantime Baldwin IX, count of both Flanders and Hainault, left the west to help found the Latin empire of Constantinople, dying there in 1206. His two daughters ruled the counties up to the year 1280; Johanna to 1244 and Margaret until she was eighty. Both were astute but they were not empire-builders. As a result of these circumstances, which may be regarded largely as acts of chance, the cities were relatively free throughout the thirteenth century. Since distances between cities were often short, nobles moved into the cities, shared in the economic life, and participated in politics.[3] Although pressure from France developed at the end of the century, the practice and tradition of freedom had been so strongly developed that it persisted well into the next two centuries, helped by the internal troubles of France and Germany in the period. Meantime, the dependence of the English king upon the export tax on wool restrained him from cutting down on that English export, as was done in the early modern period. The weakness within Germany also enabled the Hanseatic cities to make full use of the great textile operations of the Low Country cities. In general it can be said that the counts of Flanders, like that of Champagne, understood the value of the cities within their counties.

At the beginning of the thirteenth century many of the Low Country cities had walls which had been built during the previous century, but beyond which they were rapidly spreading. In size they were as follows:

	hectares
Ghent	80
Liège	80
Brussels	79
Bruges	70
Louvain	60
Tournai	50
Haarlem	48
Antwerp	32
Bois-le-Duc (Hertogenbosch)	20

None was outstanding in size; the largest were probably not much beyond a population of 10,000 at the time of the building of the wall and most were in the range of 10–20,000 at the beginning of the thirteenth century. But even at that size they had surpassed the normal size for cities in a purely agricultural area, unsupplemented by manufactures except those required locally. They made good use of the facilities of the near-by Fairs of Champagne. They were, indeed, in much the same condition as that of contemporary Tuscany with several cities of about equal size.

The great problem of estimating the regional population of the cities is that one must employ figures from the number of hearths of the fifteenth century, usually of about 1430 or 1470 and modify them by what is known of the city walls. There are exceptions, of course and fortunately Ghent is one of them. Thirteenth-century walls themselves constitute a problem: they had generally been constructed at the beginning of the century or even in the twelfth century and were thus well outgrown even by the middle of the thirteenth century. Then in the fourteenth century a wave of enthusiasm allied with great wealth enabled several of the cities to enclose very great areas, much too large since the plague soon reduced the population of many of the cities. For some reason a good part of the region escaped damage by the first plague which may have given a false sense of immunity to the other communities.[4] In view of these qualifications, it can be seen that the estimates can only be approximate until much better studies of the historical demography of most of the cities are available.

The population of Ghent is one of the most certain figures of cities obtainable by indirect methods. Professor Van Werveke ascertained that the number of men available for army service was about 12,250 which he multiplied by four to get 49,000 to which he added another 7,000 for the patriciate, the clergy and guildsmen not associated with the guilds.[5] This brought the total to 56,000 (Table 14). Interestingly, if the weavers and other associated guildsmen are assumed to be the basic element to be multiplied by seven, the total (8,800 by 7) would be about the same (61,600). Van Werveke's calculation was based upon figures for the years 1346 and 1357, which seems to disregard the first attack of the Black Death. However, Ghent appears to have escaped that first attack, one of the odd features of the history of the plague.

For Bruges, the second city in size, there is a remarkably reliable figure for a list of potential soldiers in 1340; 6,044 men capable of bearing arms. The author of the study on this document, De Smet, has suggested that another thousand be added for a garrison and strangers and that the total of about 7,000 be multiplied by five to give a population of about 35,000 just before the plague. The walls gave some indication. Before 1127 Bruges had a wall enclosing 90 hectares and was thus a sizeable city even then. This wall was added to after 1293 and probably before 1370, to include (with the old wall), about 200 hectares, when Bruges sharing the common optimism of the Low Countries, built a wall enclosing a total of about 430 hectares, second only to that of Ghent.[6] In the 1420s and

TABLE 14: REGION OF GHENT

Rank,	City	Pop Est 1,000s	Hyp Est 1,000s	Area hectares	Base	Source
1	Ghent	56	56	644	1356–12,250 s	
2	Bruges	30	31.9	430	1340–6,044 s	*IXH*
3	Tournai	20	21.8	175	1365–3,991 h	Mols 2, 6, 521
4	Brussels	18	16.8	360	1374–7,313+ ; 1437–6,376 h	
5	Louvain	18	13.4	410	1374–5,775 1437–3,579 h	
6	Antwerp	17	11.4	352	1437–3,440 h	
7	Namur	14.4	9.8	75	1298–2,876 h	
8	Ypres	14	8.8	112	1412–3,055 h	
9	Bois-le-Duc, Hertogenbosch	13	8.0		1437–2,883 h	
10	Liège	11	7.3	248	1470–2,000 h	
11	Mechlin, Malines	10	6.7	105		Mols 3, 99 ; Egli 105
12	Hague	10	6.2		1470–1,348 h	
13	Mons	10		150	1283–1,440 h	
14	Amsterdam	8		78	1470–1,869 h	

Ghent: Van Werveke, 283–40

1430s Ghent had new citizens at the rate of 229 and 125 respectively.[7] If this represents .008 of the total population, that total should have been about 25,750. The low rate of the 1430s suggest that the population had levelled off then. Bruges' pre-plague population ought naturally to have been somewhat higher than that of Ghent's 1420s and 1430s, perhaps about 30,000, as Bruges was the great port of the region, the end of the journey of the Flanders Galleys and also the seat of regional banking.[8]

In the course of the two centuries, Mols informs us, from 1350 to 1550, first place among the cities of Brabant was occupied successively by Louvains, Brussels and Antwerp—nevertheless their population was modest: 20,000, 40,000, 80,000 at the epoch of their great splendour. In 1374, Mols thinks, Brussels had already outdistanced Louvain with about 25,000 compared with 15–20,000.[9] In that year Brussels had 7,313 persons—including some infants as well as adults—while Louvain had 5,775.[10] If we multiply the number of adult persons by 1.875 to get an estimate of the whole population, it gives 13,712 for Brussels and 10,828 for Louvain, about 24,000 for both. Now these two cities and Malines form an almost equilateral triangle with the sides about twenty kilometres long. In the year 1383 Brussels and Louvain were to pay the same for a general tax while in that century Louvains built a wall enclosing 410 hectares while its nearby rival enclosed only 360 hectares. Louvain was evidently wealthier per capita than Brussels—the product of a long period of greatness. Their earlier walls had apparently enclosed about 75 hectares for Louvain and 56 for Brussels; both walls were badly outmoded by 1340. If we assume that both had a total of about 24,000 persons in 1374 we can assume a loss of a third in the two plagues to give a total of 36,000 before the plague, or about 18,000 apiece. The plague sometimes caused a marked shifting of population from one neighbouring city to another, creating a problem which is well worth studying. But in this case normally the third city should be in this area.

According to Mols, Tournai, the most ancient great centre of the Low Countries, was only surpassed in the fourteenth century by Ghent and Bruges,[11] and this, in so far as it had 3,991 men in 1365, is probably correct. This should mean that before the first two attacks of the plague it had about 5,500 men representing about 20,000, a figure which accords with its walls holding 175 hectares. On the other hand Ypres is suggested as having 20,000 at its height, which must have been just before the plague, and had a wall of only 112 hectares and even in 1412 had only 3,055 hearths.[12] One doubts if it had over 14,000 at its height. Of Ypres and three others Mols indicates that Lille, Arras and Douai may have attained 15,000 also before the plague.[13] Douai had a large wall, like so many other Netherlands cities of the fourteenth century but only an average of 15 new citizens in the period AD 1318–34 which at .007 to the total, would indicate only about five thousands, while according to Mols Lille with another large area still had only 31 new citizens in the period 1415–70 which hardly indicates more than ten thousands.[14] Arras' wall enclosed apparently only 79 hectares. Mols seems to show here the very human frailty, illustrated elsewhere, of over-estimating the size of cities in one's homeland.

It is difficult to choose among the many energetic and efficient small cities which appeared in Flanders, Brabant, and Holland in this period. Antwerp built some of the most extensive walls (352 hectares) in the fourteenth century, but only then did it get its start; it had 3,440 hearths in 1437. Bois-le-Duc had 2,883 hearths in the same year and probably had a population of at least 13,000 before the plague; it apparently had not grown very rapidly in the interval of time. Liège with a wall enclosing 80 hectares increased its area to 248 hectares but had only 2,000 hearths as late as 1470, while Malines with 1,998 taxables in 1380 may have had a 10,000 population before the plague, at the same estimated ratio as Louvain and Tournai. Namur[15] seems to have had 2,876 hearths in 1298 but walls enclosing only 75 hectares.[16] But there were many others which must have had somewhere near 10,000: the Hague, Cambrai, Valenciennes, Mons, and others, particularly Dutch, cities.

Although not one of the larger cities, Douai preserves records that give interesting information about limits of migration.[17] Douai lay at the extreme south-west of Flanders with Artois just across the border, the Cambresis only 30 kilometres to the south and France another 8 kilometres farther to the west. Yet newcomers to Doui came very largely from Flanders and Hainault, a few kilometres to the east, only a small number from Artois and Cambresis and almost none from Picardy in France. As usual (in 1318–34) a large part (34%) came from within 15 kilometres, another 40% came from 15 to 50 kilometres, and only 17 from greater distances. From the longer distances 25% and 50% respectively came from cities. But it illustrates the territorial limits of migration, which by being selective, gave a definite slant to the region. In this case it obviously was a Flemish and non-French slant.

The Low Country cities, particularly those of Flanders and Brabant, apparently had two advantages which produced medieval industrial centres: nearness to a considerable market and a democratic political system. The Netherland cities had as a near market the heavily populated area of northern France, approached in part through the Fairs of Champagne.

They had the English market through London while the Hanse cities traded with the Netherlands. After the heavily settled Po Valley-Tuscan area this was probably the best market, unless a case can be made for Southern French-Northern Iberian area. The region of Paris is estimated at 5.2 millions, the Netherlands themselves at another million[18] while British and German areas would number several million more. A market of at least ten millions may not be an overestimate. The second reason, the democracy of the cities, is important, because the citizens, mostly merchants, industrialists, and workers, would retain more of their own profits and would flourish as entrepreneurs better in a democracy than under a more autocratic system.

There are serious problems about estimating the population of the Low Countries. The only good evidence comes just after the early attacks of the plague and show about 350,000 for Brabant. Assuming that in 1374 loss of a third had already occurred, the population should have been about a half million before the plague.[18] Brabant had about a third of the Low Countries' population at the end of the fifteenth century. If it had the same before the plague, the Low Countries should have had a pre-plague population of about 1.5 millions. This assumes a rather slow recovery by the Low Countries after the attacks of the plague, an assumption which seems probable since even before the plague they were beginning to decline in comparison with the economic development of England, France, and the Italian cities.

The area in the region of Ghent is assumed to include the following territories:

		km^2
	Belgium	29,455
	Holland	32,000
	Luxembourg	2,590
French *départements*:	Nord	5,774
	Pas-de-Calais	6,752
	Total	76,571

If the total population was about 1.5 millions, the average density of population would be about 19.6 to the km^2. Without the top ten cities in population the average density would have been about 17. Some areas of the region are in quite hilly territory and, at the time, parts of Holland also were relatively unsettled, so the fairly modest density is not too surprising. It makes the urban index of 14.1 somewhat less impressive than the indexes of the regions of Venice and Milan which had such large country populations to back them up.

One might tentatively set up a rank-order series for the north-west of Europe, particularly since Paris, London, and Cologne seem to form numbers 2 to 4 in the series. Obviously a group of cities in the Low Countries would then be number one (Ghent, Brussels, Louvain, Antwerp, Liège, Malines) with about 130,000. The order would then be:

	Pop Est in 1,000s	Hyp Est in 1,000s
Textile cities of Flanders	130	140
Paris	90	90
London	60	60
Cologne	40	40
Bruges	30	30

It gives some idea of the relative importance of these cities in comparison with the Po Valley complex discussed earlier. And in the north there is nothing to compare to the region of Florence so large and so near to the Po Valley group.

THE REGION OF LONDON

The region of London was mostly England, although presumably Wales might have been included.[19] Scotland, however, seemed to be a non-region with its division into the Highlands and Lowlands. A more thorough study might possibly produce evidence for a region of Edinburgh.

From Roman days and perhaps earlier times London has been the largest city of the British Isles. It had consolidated its position over the centuries. Its geographical position is that of a great seaport upon which converge the great roads of the island. The evidence upon which a rank-size pattern can be worked out is, for the Middle Ages, very good. Domesday Book contains sufficient data to give a fair impression of the size of the cities in 1086. The poll tax information offers the sizes of the boroughs in 1377, after several attacks of the plague. We may believe that there was a fairly even decline among the cities of England in the first four plagues. There is additional information about population from the period just before the plague. From the two sets of data the changes in pattern among the cities smaller than London in size emerge. England experienced a great increase in population from about 1.1 millions in A.D. 1086 to about 3.7 millions just before the plague.

These are estimates based upon my *British Medieval Population* (1948). Like all medieval estimates, they are subject to criticism on the basis of differing interpretations of the evidence. However, the fundamental estimate of the size of the household of the landholder was based upon evidence from some hundred villages in 1377 where all members of the household over the exact age of fourteen were recorded, mendicants alone being exempted. These showed an average of about 3.5 persons to the household. This was surprising in view of the usual assumption that a household included about five persons. The smaller average is explained by the housing of the elderly and single persons in cottages by themselves.

The evidence for the boroughs (cities) of England in the time of Domesday Book, AD 1086, would show the following: (a) for the boroughs alone and (b) for groups of them:

(a)		(b)		Hyp Est
1 London	17,850	17,850		17,850
2 Winchester	6.	Norwich	4.4	10.1
		Thetford	2.7	
		Dunwich	1.6	
		Colchester	1.4	
			10.1	
3 Norwich	4.4	Winchester	6	6.8
4 York	4.1	Bristol	2.3	5.4
		Gloucester	2.1	
		Shaftesbury	1.1	
			5.5	

(a)		(b)		Hyp Est
5 Lincoln	3.5	York	4.1	4.3
6 Thetford	2.7	Lincoln	3.6	3.6
7 Bristol	2.3	Canterbury	1.6	
		Dover	1.6	
			3.2	
8 Gloucester	2.1	Cambridge	1.9	
		Huntington	1.3	
			3.2	
9 Cambridge	1.9			
10 Chester	1.9			

Earlier it has been mentioned that the 'over-night' cities usually served local agricultural areas and below certain levels the size tended to be determined by the local agricultural population. Of the Domesday cities, for instance, only about eight cities seem to have had a population of more than 2,000, while twenty-two cities, at least, seem to have had populations between 1,000 and 2,000 in size. One suspects that many others would fall in that class if Domesday had preserved information as faithfully about cities as about the villages. The net result of the study of the Domesday cities is to indicate that the commerce and industrial life of England was at a rather low level at the time of the conquest. London had apparently about 1.5% of the population of the island, just about an average for the metropolitan city of a region, but the other cities had far fewer people than normal and, indeed, the first ten in size would seem to have only about 4.4% of the total population of the region, an urban index much below that of the average.

The estimates are derived from Domesday Book by multiplying the number of units assigned to each borough in Domesday by 3.5 since these often include not merely burgesses or burgages but also types of lesser tenements. The great difference in size between London and the others is obvious (Table 15). But this disparity has been typical of English cities up to the present.

The pattern by population of the cities individually has one peculiarity. The second city in size, Winchester, was not in the most populously settled area. In 1086, that area was East Anglia, where one might have anticipated the second city

TABLE 15: REGION OF LONDON

Rank,	City	Pop Est 1,000s	Hyp Est 1,000s	Area hectares		Grouped		1377 poll tax-over age 14
1	London	60	60.0	288	60.0	London	60.0	23,314
2	York	18.1	34.2	94	28.8	York	18.1	7,248
						Hull	4.0	1,557
						Beverley	6.7	2,663
3	Bristol	16.0	23.4	80+	20.1	Bristol	16.0	6,345
						Cardiff	2.5	
						Newport	1.6	
4	Norwich	13.0	18	85	161.	Lincoln	8.9	3,569
						Boston	7.2	2,871
5	Plymouth	12.1	14.4	72?	14.6	Salisbury	8.1	3,226
						Winchester	3.6	1,440
						Southampton	2.9	1,152
6	Coventry	12.0	12.2		13.0	Norwich	13.0	3,952
7	Lincoln	8.9	10.6	67	13.0	Coventry	12.1	4,817
						Warwick	1	
8	Salisbury	8.1	9.5	72	12.1	Plymouth		4,837
9	King's Lynn	7.8	8.6	70	7.8	King's Lynn		3,127
10	Colchester	7.4	7.8	60+	7.4	Colchester		2,955
11	Boston	7.2	7.2					2,871

Sources: unless otherwise specified, the population figures come from Russell, *British Medieval Population*, p 142. For Norwich, p 293, Cardiff and Newport, p 344. Plymouth presumably included Modbury and Newton Ferrers, that is the port of Plymouth. Salisbury: Jowett at end; Lobel 6. King's Lynn: Richards. Colchester: Cutts.

would have been. If we assume there was a civic function in that area, it must have been divided among East Anglia's larger towns: Norwich, Thetford, Dunwich, and Colchester. Indeed, a combination of these cities is about the right total (about 10,000) for the pattern. This would reduce Winchester to third place, which its access to a great harbour and to the rich south shore lands justifies as well as its position as a kind of capital. To the west the combination of Gloucester, Bristol, and Shaftesbury adds up to about the right size for the fourth city, while York and Lincoln were the appropriate sizes and locations for the fifth and sixth places.

Pope Alexander III commented upon London as the royal city, *regia civitas,* where frequent meetings of barons and great men were accustomed to meet[20] and spoke of it as the most noble and famous city of the kingdom. Not only did they meet there, but many of the nobles had homes there along the river, and spent much of the autumn there. For several weeks and sometimes months the society of the capital was a microcosm of the ruling classes of England: the king at Westminster, the Archbishop of Canterbury at Lambeth, the Earls of Hunting-ton at Scotland Yard, the bishop of London near St Paul's and the great national merchants in the walled city. Drawn first by the Exchequer sessions, the Michaelmas term of the courts, and the Great Council meetings, they developed what must have been a social season which drew the leading men of the region into a common society. The Mayor of London was among the twenty-five barons to enforce Magna Carta. The persistence of a parliamentary system in England through the period of absolute monarchy in Europe must have been caused in part by the community of the realm meeting yearly in London.

A brilliant study by Professor Ekwall shows the areas from which the inhabitants of London came (Table 16). It shows the usual effects of distance with a very considerable percentage of migrants coming from within forty kilometres of London itself. More important, since this state of affairs is well known, is his proof of the shift of influence upon London as it grew larger. Here the increasing influence of the East Midlands and

TABLE 16: HOME AREAS OF ALDERMEN AND SHERIFFS OF LONDON

	Before 1307			1307-1365		
	Aldermen	*Sheriffs*	*Both*	*Aldermen*	*Sheriffs*	*Both*
Home Counties	24	12	36	20	5	25
Southwest-West	14	6	20	12	1	13
Total			56			38
East Midlands	10	7	17	33	10	43
West Midlands	3	1	4	2	0	2
Northern	2	1	3	8	2	10
Total			24			55

Source: Eckwall, lxi-ii.

the North of England upon the capital is evident in the larger number of aldermen and sheriffs from those areas. England was becoming more and more an integrated region with influences to even its farther limits in the early fourteenth century: this was evident in its unity in the English Parliament even during this period. One should add to Ekwall's further suggestion, that this influence tended to make the dialect of the Midlands the official English language, helped by the location of universities at Oxford and Cambridge. Such institutions naturally drew more heavily fom their immediate neighbourhoods, and this would bring to the universities a marked influence from the Midlands.

In the pre-plague period London maintained its superiority in numbers over the rest of the cities of the region. In fact, if Winchester really did have 6,000 in 1086, London had increased its superiority over the others. This superiority was greater than that possessed by any other metropolitan city over its region among those considered in this study. For this supremacy, the central position of London was probably responsible; its advantages of a good maritime and road position have been mentioned. The disadvantages of the other English cities stand out. York was obviously located well for a second city, but England was narrower in the north and less fertile. Bristol had a good port, but its commerce must have been much less than that of the Thames Valley, as it faced only Ireland, whose commerce it had to share with Plymouth and northern local ports. A case might be made for considering Bristol-Plymouth as a second metropolitan complex, except that they are too far apart. Norwich's opportunities were limited by the odd shape of East Anglia. In some ways Coventry occupied a site with the best opportunities, except that to the west the land was so sparsely inhabited.

Probably it was the strong central government which was also in part responsible for the concentration at London. Such bureaucracy as there was, centred at London and eventually, as we have noted, a very remarkable social, political, and economic life developed there. Negatively, the central government prevented the cities from conquering each other and forcing a concentration in the larger cities. If York, for instance, had been free, it would have had a chance to conquer

Beverley and Hull, since they were mostly commerical centres, and would have drawn to York many of the governmental functions which were centred at London for northern England. Occasionally, something of the sort did in fact occur. The Archbishop of York was the second prelate in England. Some parliaments met at York; indeed, one actually drew to York representatives from all of the north of England. But even York had competition in the north. The marcher counties of Durham and Lancashire centred some of the royal functions in their county seats and thus prevented a part of governmental concentration at York, and even in Yorkshire, Richmond served as a sort of local centre.

If the strength of the central government and other attractions drew the gentry and nobility of England to London, the weakness of the other cities was increased in part by the failure of these cities to draw from these classes. It would be unlikely that the greater families would have seats in lesser cities if they already were settled in London in addition to their country estates. In England a substitute for influence in the secondary cities was the opportunity to act through the county courts. Indeed, the amount of energy, money and time demanded of city leaders by the royal administration helps account for some of the failure of the cities to develop.[21] While these were usually held in the larger cities, there was no need for the feudal lords actually to live in the cities and normally they could secure in London during the 'season' what they could not have on their estates. Thus from an early date English cities lacked the colour and activity that was characteristic of the Italian cities and to a less extent of other continental cities. Furthermore, city leadership tended to die out (especially in the plague period) while an occasional city family, like the De la Poles, moved up into the higher feudal ranks. In England dignity triumphed over order and the typical virtues (restraint, order, piety) over more flamboyant characteristics.

The failure of the lesser English cities (from number two to number ten) may be estimated by subtracting from the hypothetical population of those cities the estimated population. That would be to substract 103,400 from 135,100, gives 31,700. If we assume that the basic factor should be multiplied by seven to get the total number of dependents within a city, it would be a little less than 4,700. Using the available poll tax returns of 1377, to give villages by size, we can, on this basis, make certain calculations. We can assume that the percentage of villages with population of about 200–400 should have been about 15% from the clustering on the figure. It is actually 16.5%. In the counties of Cornwell, Essex, Kent, Northamptonshire, Nottinghamshire, and the East Riding of Yorkshire there are 153 more villages in the 200–400 class than should have been there on an average basis. Since those counties had about four-elevenths of the villages of England, there were about 421 more villages in England with 200–400 inhabitants than normal in England: they probably included most of the manufacturing villages. Had, on the average, only eleven basic workers from each of those 421 villages been located in the largest nine cities after London, those cities would have had about the proper rank-size population, with their additional 4,700 persons. It can be seen why the modest industrial revolution of thirteenth-century England was sufficient to prevent the cities from having an appropriate population then.[22]

The population of the ten largest cities of England just before the plague was about 163,400. Divided into a pre-plague population of about 3,700,000, the percentage would be about 4.4, which is somewhat below the average of about 5%. This is in spite of the fact that London was about average for a metropolitan city of a region. Even for these top ten cities, the urban index was only slightly above the 4.3 of the Domesday period, not enough for any real significance. Further, the average size of the village seems to have been smaller than in many parts of Europe. Probably this was a result of the better conditions of life and more security in many parts of the island, which made living in smaller communities sufficiently safe to make the advantages of shorter travel to the fields attractive.

The urban index for England was lower than the average or ideal figure and thus indicates that England was primarily an agricultural country in this period. The population has been estimated as about 3.7 millions just before the outbreak of the plague in 1348. This would give England a density of population of about 28.1 for its 131,738km², a relatively large figure for the Middle Ages. If its population about the middle of the thirteenth century was 2.5 millions, its density would have been about 19 to the km². It can be seen that the population density was quite modest by that time and rose quickly in the next century. Now one question that has been raised is whether English population reached its height before 1300 and whether England was already overpopulated then.

The industrial development probably derived from England's long experience with water mills. Already by Domesday, as that document shows England had about five thousand mills. This not only gave the people experience in the use of machinery (which may have been one of the reasons why the later Industrial Revolution began in the English countryside) but also produced a very considerable amount of energy for various industrial processes.

The English region was fortunate also in its food supply. The north and west had extensive pasture land which produced a very large amount of meat. The streams and mill-ponds provided a constant supply of fish, particularly eels, over much of the land. England apparently shipped food to the continent from her surplus. An estimate of land available for tillage suggests that an Englishman's base of subsistence was about four acres,[23] probably three times the area necessary to sustain life. Despite this there has been a suggestion that England in the early fourteenth century was living on the brink of starvation and that it was a society in which every appreciable failure of harvests could result in large increases in deaths in a society balanced on the margin of subsistence. Of course, if England had the seven millions of population that Postan claims it had before the plague, this argument might have some substance.[24]

In this problem of food supply the yield ratio was of obvious importance. Here the work of Slicher van Bath on the subject presents such material as existed. For England and France there was enough information to draw conclusions. The average yield in the half-century before 1250 was about 3.7, that is, for each unit of grain planted, the returns were 3.7. Now this yield was increased notably in the next century to one of 4.7, a 37% increase. Furthermore, it was higher before 1300 than it was later. This is what might be expected since the half-century, 1250–1300, was a period of climatic amelioration

I

—if somewhat windy and wet conditions prevailed. The end of
the century and to about 1316 Europe, as well as Britain,
suffered from both chill and dampness, ending in the famine
and pestilence of 1315–17. The English yield was higher than
the German and Scandinavian until 1700 (theirs was only 4.2
and 4.3) and than that achieved by Eastern Europe before the
nineteenth century. The combination of high yields, relatively
moderate climate and abundant seafood should certainly have
made for a well-fed England in spite of a moderately dense
population.

The region of London in the thirteenth century enjoyed
singular prosperity which was only slightly reduced by the
worsening climate and the relative density of population at the
end of the thirteenth century. The region was fortunate in that
period to have suffered only one civil war of relatively small
impact and, in the last half century, border warfare along the
northern frontier. The region experienced a security far beyond
that of most European countries and thus the monarchy had
little excuse to advance insecurity as an argument for increased
despotism. Indeed, the kings themselves were largely responsible for that 'self-government at the king's command' which
became the base for English common law and the change from
a royally selected advisory Great Council to a Parliament with
something like regular membership, fixed meeting times, definite agenda and legislative action which the king was
accustomed to accept. The combination of prosperity and
security enabled the English to lay solid foundations for a
democratic government if we assume that there, as elsewhere,
the mass of the peasants did not participate much in government.

THE REGION OF DUBLIN

At first a regional approach to thirteenth-century Ireland might
seem unprofitable for such a primitive area.[25] The mass of the
people were Celtic, often assumed so clannish and pastoral
that there was little need for cities. Its early economy was
based upon a pastoral life invigorated by constant cattle-raids,
following a well-organised and customary pattern. The ordinary Irish leader was probably in no real danger of losing his

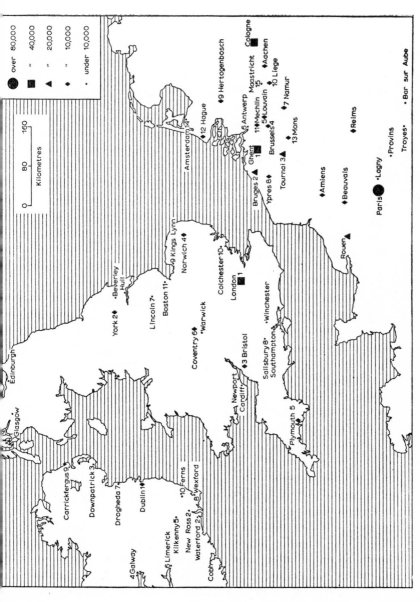

Fig 6 The regions of Dublin, Ghent, and London

land, upon which his flocks grazed, even if he lost many of his animals.The Scandinavian and English invasions ended this security and endangered even his land-holding. What had been a pleasant if sometimes dangerous sport of cattle-collecting now became a grim struggle for existence. By the thirteenth century the Scandinavians seem to have been integrated into the life of the island, bringing some urbanisation and commercial associations with them.

In the thirteenth century the integration of elements in Ireland seemed imminent. King John granted authority to the justiciary of Ireland to hear royal pleas in any but royal courts. Similar measures were taken by his successor, Henry III. Thus Ireland was not to be regarded as a mark or group of counties palatine in the hands of the local Anglo-Irish nobles with the Irish at their mercy. The Irish, about AD 1270–80, sought general inclusion in common law jurisdiction, and many succeeded as individuals in securing the right.

This extension of royal jurisdiction threatened to restrain the Anglo-Irish lords from taking more land from the Irish clans. Common law, of course, did not touch local law, such as rules of hereditary succession, any more than it did the local custom of English or Welsh counties. The movement failed to secure royal approval, probably the result of his distraction from Irish in Ireland as its prince and of his distraction from Irish problems by Scottish developments in the second half of his reign. In any case, the second half of the century saw a more normal Irish-English equilibrium than did any later period.

As was customary in medieval invasions, the conquering group drove out the losing chieftains from all or part of their holdings but did not disturb the actual tillers of the soil to any extent. Following the success of the Anglo-Norman warriors, other groups—merchants, artisans, and even some farmers—migrated to Ireland, especially from Chester, Bristol, Plymouth, London and other English centres. The invasion also brought English clergy, who tended more and more to replace Irish clergy, although the clerical organisation was more widely divorced from the English than the political or economic organisations were. The invasions encouraged urbanisation of the island. The question is whether, by the second half of the

TABLE 17: DISTRIBUTION OF CHURCHES BY
GEOGRAPHICAL AREAS NEAR THE LARGER
CITIES IN THE REGION OF DUBLIN

Area	*Cities*	*Dioceses*	*Taxed Churches*
Eastern	Dublin, Drogheda	Dublin, Kildare, Trim	474
South-eastern	Ferns, New Ross, Waterford, Wexford	Cashel, Ferns, Leighlin, Lismore, Ossory, Waterford	573
Southern	Cobh, Youghal	Cobh, Cloyne, Emly	230
South-western	Bunratty, Limerick	Killiloe, Limerick	214
Western	Galway, Annadown	Annadown, Clonfert, Tuam Kilmacduagh	251
North-eastern	Downpatrick, Carrickfergus	Armagh, Connor, Down, Dromore	250
Northern	Derry	Ardstraw, Derry, Raphoe	90

Source: Russell, *BMP*, pp 323–4 except for the number of Ferns which the *Catholic Encyclopedia* suggests was 150 for the Middle Ages.

thirteenth century, Ireland showed the normal distribution of population for a medieval region.

For the distribution of cities by size the numbers of taxed churches offer rough clues and are given in Table 17. Others might choose to arrange the parishes differently. For instance, the parishes of Cloyne might be regarded as within the sphere of influence of New Ross-Waterford. Many southern churches were possibly too distant from Cobh or Youghal to be in their economic district. Some of Ardfert's 94 churches may have really been in the area dominated by Bunratty-Limerick, while the diocese of Killiloe was relatively near Galway-Annadown. The small number about Derry is largely the result of attributing to the diocese of Ardstraw only one church. Moreover, the list is not all inclusive since it omits churches which were too poor to tax.

Another factor in the determination of the sites of cities would be the transportation system of the region. A study of the medieval roadways, of Ireland shows a concentration within the island, with very few coastal roads. Thus one has to assume that much of the travel went by sea or river. Dublin was obviously the chief centre of the system of roads, with a secondary centre at Derry in the north. The sea trade was largely between the south-western cities of Ireland and the west and south of England, to Bristol and Plymouth, while some trade existed between Dublin and Drogheda and Chester farther north. The coastal trade must have been extensive.

In 1278 a writ was sent to the bailiffs of certain cities in Ireland who were 'appointed to receive throughout Ireland half-a-mark on every sack of wool and half-a-mark on every 300 woolfells, which make one sack, and one mark on every last if hides exported from Ireland'. The order of cities (in the spelling of the writ) was 'Ross, Waterford, Weseford, Dublin, Drogheda, Cnakfergus, del Galuy, Cork, del Yoghel and . . . Limerick'. The arrangement is counter-clockwise around the coast of Ireland, except for the last-named city. The order thus had no significance with respect to the size of the port cities, although the start from New Ross rather than from Dublin or even Waterford might cause some surprise. However, receipts of the great custom for wool were larger at New Ross and at Waterford than at Dublin. The preponderance of southern cities is natural in view of their closeness to England and the Continent and may give an undue impression of the size of such southern cities as Cobh and Youghal. In general the list confirms what other evidence would show.

Into the picture of the distribution of the population of Ireland must be placed the sizes of the larger cities of the island. These estimates will be somewhat tentative because the information upon which they are based is not the most accurate data. Fortunately, the inquest upon holdings so typical of thirteenth-century England was also applied to many landholdings in Ireland. In some cases they included the number of burgages (city lots) in a city; in others the number of burgages can be estimated from the amount of the income from the city. These are the sources of most of the information about the size of the cities, although the areas of the cities and occasionally other items offer evidence of value.

For study of the population of boroughs, maps showing the medieval walls are helpful, largely because the population was often highest in the thirteenth century, when so many of the walls were built. And, in a country where most boroughs were in constant danger of attack, there was little encouragement to waste money by enclosing larger areas than were necessary. In some cases, apparently, the enclosure protected only the burgesses, mostly Anglo-Irish-Norse, and left some of the Irish outside. The small size of some of the boroughs, notably Galway, might be most easily explained in this way. On the average, the medieval boroughs had about 100–120 persons to the hectare. However, in the smaller places, especially those with less than about 3,000, the density tended to be lower than 100 to the hectare. Medieval boroughs were usually built rather solidly, except for a central open area and sometimes a small market. The countryside was so near that the neighbouring land, outside the walls, served the function of recreation ground and public park as well as providing space for the cattle and sheep market and slaughterhouse.

The extents among the inquests as mentioned above often included the number of burgesses or burgages of the city. The usual annual tax for a burgage seems to have been a shilling. The 110 burgesses of Carrick on Slany paid 111s 9d, while the 79 burgesses of Fodereth (Fodered) owed 79s yearly. Nearby, in Carlow, 160 burgesses paid 160s 16½d, a trifle more than a shilling for each. The 134½ burgages at Youghal yielded 134s 5½d, a few pence more than the expected sum. Trillek's 271 burgages paid 271s but there were fewer than 271 burgesses. Thus it would seem that the alleged 226 burgesses on the Clare fief of Bunratty actually should have been 266, since they paid that many shillings. On the basis of this evidence, it is reasonable to estimate burgesses at a shilling apiece, if it is certain that payments contain only the burgages payments.

Some burghal holdings seem to have included adjacent lands outside of the borough walls. One doubts if the shilling per burgess could be applied to the burgesses of Youghal who paid £12 for burgages and for 18 carucates (probably about 2,000 acres) of land, or at nearby Inchocyn, where £11 14s was paid, presumably under the same circumstances. The burgesses of Dungarvon, a relatively small place, paid £13 17s 4d. Although Carrick paid a shilling a burgage, its neighbour, Rosslare, may not have done so; its £9 6s 6d was a high figure for such a small place. Perhaps the sum paid by New Ross included other items than the burgage payment.

The number of burgesses is not that of the entire citizenry.

Fodereth, in addition to its 79 burgesses, had 29 cottagers. Le Ford, near the site of modern Belfast, had about the same proportion—73 burgesses and 29 cottages. One-third of Taghmon in 1358 had about 20 burgesses and four cotters, but this was after the first epidemic of the Black Death. An even smaller proportion of cottagers might be estimated for Dunfort; its 13 cotters were in addition to burgesses who paid £24 9s 4½d, but the payment may have included money for agricultural land as well as for burgages.

The percentage of cottagers thus was somewhat less than 30% of the city population—a smaller percentage than the 40% discovered for the non-burgesses of Domesday boroughs. It seems best then to multiply the number of burgages or burgesses by five for an estimate of the total population of the cities, on the theory that the burgess households would be smaller than in the English cities, with fewer servants and dependent relatives. An exception might be made for Dublin, which had been long established and had a considerable proportion of Scandinavian and English inhabitants; perhaps six to the burgages would be a more accurate estimate.

Even before the Norman conquest, Dublin had been the largest city of Ireland. The old city held perhaps 27 hectares, and Ostmantown across the river another 20; these suggest a population of 4,000–5,000. Dublin's 20 parishes, by Domesday standards, would have been about the same. Under the English it was the capital of the island, whose castle presumably held a garrison, the exchequer and the justiciary's staff. This concentration of administrative officers should have increased the population somewhat. A list of freemen of about AD 1200 shows at least 1,600 names. It assumes a population of at least 6,000–7,000 persons. The general increase in the population of Ireland in the thirteenth century should have caused Dublin's population to increase also.

At the end of the thirteenth century the inhabited area was probably about 112 hectares, which would suggest a population of 11,000–13,000. However, the many churches, the castle area, and the configuration would tend to reduce the size of the inhabited area and the total population to perhaps 11,000. Some documents of the guild merchant remain, but unfortunately the number of new members can be calculated from the membership lists for only three years in the thirteenth century—220 for 1226, 65 for 1256, and 140 for 1257. The average of the last two is about 100 admissions a year; the wide difference in the two years makes this an uncertain average. Theoretically if we could know the average age of the persons on admission and could be certain that they would remain at Dublin the rest of their lives, an estimate of their number could be made. From their names, it would appear that they were a migratory group with a relatively high age entrance. Assuming an expectation of about twenty years, a guild membership of 2,000 and a total population of about 11,000 might be expected (Table 18).

By leaving out mention of the one solid bit of evidence about Dublin's population, the list of 1,600 members of the guild merchant, Hollingsworth[26] avoided one serious problem, its relationship to the three instances of year entries. Suppose we

TABLE 18: REGION OF DUBLIN

Rank,	City	Pop Est 1,000s	Hyp Est 1,000s	Area hectares	Base	Russell, BMP
1	Dublin	11	11	112	1200–1,600 f	
2	Waterford,	2.7–3	6.3	27		
	New Ross	3		30	–506 b	
3	Downpatrick	5	4.3	60		
4	Galway, Annadown	3.8	3.3	10?	1283–717.5 b	355
5	Kilkenny	3	2.6	45	351 b	
6	Bunratty,	3	2.2	21	1288–266 b	352
	Limerick			11–12		
7	Drogheda	3	1.9	31.5		
8	Wexford,	2.4	1.7	18	1307–442 b	356
	Rosslare				186 b	
9	Carrickfergus	2	1.5	23		
10	Ferns,	2	1.4		213 b	353
	Cork,			12		
	Clonmel,			12		
	Carlow,					
	Youghal					

Downpatrick: Government of North Ireland, *An Archaeological Survey of County Down* (Belfast, 1966) 272–4: called to the author's attention by Bruce Proudfoot.

accept his fantastic assertion that guild members might be members for 32 years or perhaps less fantastic, 25 years, Dividing 32 into 1,600 would suggest that the city had about 50 new guild members each year, but the samples are 220, 65, and 140. Suggesting a term of 25 years in the guild reduces the yearly acceptances to 64, near the AD 1256 list. However, assuming that the city had grown somewhat, the average between the 65 of 1256 and 140 of 1257 would appear to be reasonable. The 220 list of 1226 would then appear, as lists of new citizens or guild members often do, as the result of a very exceptional year. If 100 were added a year, the expectation could hardly be for more than 20 years, which may well have been too high, since men could enter or leave at any age, the group was obviously migratory, and the highest possible total expectation at about age 22 could hardly have been more than 25 years. Furthermore, the comparison in size between London and Dublin is misleading, since Dublin's area included the river between parts of it, a large number of monastic and secular religious buildings, and probably housing of a much less dense character. In that period the smaller the city, the fewer persons to the hectare. Finally, it is very unlikely that a city in the very agricultural and not very commercial country of Ireland had 4% or 5% of the total population.

If one could be certain that 'Irishmen were excluded from the guild merchant', room might be made for a large number of them in the city. However, among the guild member names 'Gillefintan' looks very Irish. Many others bore surnames of other Irish cities; it is doubtful if all of them were English emigrants who were moving to the capital. Furthermore, the tendency of parents to give Anglo-Norman names to their children, a change which was typical of twelfth-century England, would, if true also of Ireland, make the separation of Irish from others on the basis of their Christian names alone, difficult. The question needs more research than has been given it.

The next centre, assuming that the largest city had about 11,000 persons, should have had about 6,300 inhabitants. It ought obviously to have been in the south-east of Ireland, probably on Waterford Haven into which flows the rivers

Suir, Nore, and Barrow. Two cities shared the commerce of that estuary and may be considered together as the second city: Waterford and New Ross.

Waterford was a royal borough, had a mint and was apparently a secondary centre of the island's government. The bishop of Waterford was frequently a royal official of importance; his small diocese of only twenty-six taxed churches probably required little supervision. The area within the city was about 27 hectares. The city occupied a favoured position on the estuary and into it should have come most of the commerce of south-east Ireland. Its 27 hectares suggest a population of about 2,700–3,000.

The situation changed drastically when the Marshall family built a bridge about AD 1211 across the Barrow, 25 kilometres above Waterford and 3 kilometres below the confluence of the Nore with the Barrow at the site of New Ross. This presumably forced transhipment at New Ross and thus gave that city an advantage over Waterford, since merchants must move their goods twice to reach there by water from the reaches of the Nore and Barrow but only once at New Ross. Furthermore, merchants could now get 24 more kilometres of water carriage from the sea by going to New Ross. This move by the Marshall family produced a long series of royal acts to protect royal Waterford. These acts seem to have had little effect, since New Ross apparently outstripped Waterford in amount of trade and possibly in size.

By AD 1265 New Ross was a city of some size. In 1279 it paid £2 6s 8d to the Bigod family, who held it then, one of its members having married a Marshall heiress. If this represents burgesses at a shilling apiece, there were about 500 of them. Rosbergen, across the Barrow bridge, paid enough to suggest another 166 burgesses there. However, merely sums are given without any indication whether they include burgage payments. At best then, the sums must be regarded as a possible maximum of the number of burgages. The suggested number would be suitable for an area of about 30 hectares, which seems the size of the city within the walls. Then there is the curious information from the poem, allegedly written by Friar Michael Bernard of Kildare which, subjected to rigorous treatment of the high figures, would suggest at least 375 burgesses and a considerable number of other persons. In all, New Ross probably had a population of about 3,000 persons.

Somewhere among the top cities there should be some north of Dublin. Down (Downpatrick) in the diocese with the most churches in the area, Derry, the focus of the northern complex of roads, and Carrickfergus and Drogheda, the only northern cities in the list of exporting boroughs, seem possible. Recent archaeological research seems to resolve the question of favour of Down, which had an industrial centre of perhaps 60 hectares which, even at a low density, would suggest about 4–5,000 persons. Its walls only included 12 hectares.

Carrickfergus was the site of a great castle, the seat of the powerful Burke (*de Burgo*) family in the north, the Earls of Ulster. At least two churches in the city were in the patronage of that family; there may have been more churches there. One of its merchants carried wine for the king. These are indications that the city was of some size, justified by its position on Belfast Clough and its commerce as well as its Burke connections. Its neighbour, Le Ford, had 75 burgesses and 29 cotters, while its other neighbour, Connor, was the seat of a bishop. Drogheda was about 40 kilometres north of Dublin—so close that one might presume it smaller than the largest city farther north. It drew from the rich valley of the Boyne. Its 31 to 33 hectares were divided by the river, which suggests a relatively thin population within the city.

The choice of Galway as the fourth city in size is based upon the $717\frac{1}{2}$ burgages for which the city paid the Burkes. A major problem is the small size of the city within the walls, perhaps 8–10 hectares. It seems likely then that the average to the burgage would probably have not been more than four to the burgage. However, 13 kilometres away was Annadown, the seat of bishopric which had a cathedral, a monastery and some churches, an arrangement which should assume another thousand inhabitants. The history of the castle perhaps explains why the fortified area was kept small. Built by Richard de Burgh, perhaps in AD 1232, it was demolished the following year, burned in 1247, and rebuilt in 1271. Nevertheless, Galway had no rival in the area and a wealthy hinterland must have supplied it with commerce. This all assumes that between raids there was business as usual.

For fifth place in size, the boroughs of Bunratty and Limerick (together) are suggested; they were only a few kilometres apart. Limerick, seat of a bishop, had an area of at least 12 hectares and perhaps as many as 22. Bunratty, a Clare fort remodelled from an older one about 1275, was about 13 kilometres away and had an area of about 19 hectares with 266 burgages. The two cities dominated the Shannon Valley and south-west Ireland with no rival south of Galway. They should together have had at least 3,000 persons.

For seventh place, Wexford and its near neighbours—Carrick and Rosslare—seem a good possibility. It is the second centre in the heavy concentration of parishes in the south-east. Wexford, like New Ross, was originally a Marshall (Pembroke) holding and at one time had about 440 burgages. However, even before the Black Death, it was so wasted that one suspects original over-colonisation. Its walls enclosed an area of about 18 hectares. Its castle became the seat of the Earldom of Wexford on the division of the Marshall holdings. Rosslare paid a yearly rent of £9 5s 6d, which should represent about 186 burgages, if it paid like its neighbour, Carrick.

Near-by before AD 1200, there were alleged to have been 100 prosperous Ostmen, but by 1283 these had been reduced to 40 men. In any case the combination of Wexford, Rosslare, and Carrick had probably about 2,200 persons even in reduced circumstances.

There are other cities that might well be considered among those in the 1,200–1,600 category. Kilkenny was a bishop's see and had a castle of the Clare family; it seems to have had at least 220 burgesses in the thirteenth century. Yet its fifteenth-century walls, which probably enclosed an area equal to that of its thirteenth-century population, included only 18 hectares for the English population and 6 for the Irish. Somewhat hesitantly it is suggested that it was smaller than Drogheda because of its smaller area. Ferns was a cathedral city which had 213 burgages. Then on the south coast, there were Cobh and Youghal, whose areas were small and the number of burgages uncertain. The cities of this size were primarily local centres, more dependent upon county business opportunities than upon their participation in the regional economy.

The rank-size of the cities of Ireland showed a much nearer approximation to the ideal order than did those of England or France, even when one includes Waterford-New Ross and Bunratty-Limerick as single urban entities. The reason is probably that the Anglo-Irish nobility, like the nobility of Italy, tended to live in the cities rather than in castles or manor houses in the countryside. The hostility of the Irish was probably responsible for this, but it did give the cities a larger size relatively than the English had, at least with respect to total population and the size of the metropolitan city.

By medieval standards, the wealth of Ireland was probably comparable to that of England; it had about as many taxed churches to the population as did its neighbour. It was based upon a pastoral rather than a tillage economy. The size and distribution of boroughs would suggest that the commercial and economic life was normal for the time. Whatever the effects of Celtic culture upon local population, the percentage of the urban, if we may call it that, population indicates no underdevelopment. Evidently the cattle-raids, with the incidental fighting, did not upset or seriously dislocate the general system of economic exchange in the island; it might be regarded as a recreational system rather than as a source of chaos. The raids seldom touched the greater boroughs; they were seldom mentioned in the Latin chronicles. The Irish situation, then, was probably much like that of Germany in the later Middle Ages, when the Hanseatic League kept up commercial lines through a countryside of perpetual warfare. The significance of the Celt-non-Celt alignment was not understood in the Middle Ages by the English and remains difficult to understand today.

There were areas of no integration. One was the separation of bishops' sees from the greater boroughs. Dublin, Down, Kilkenny and Ferns alone were heads of considerable dioceses (with about 180 churches apiece). Waterford's 26 churches constituted a very small diocese. Some of the greater boroughs had cathedrals near them: Annadown near Galway, Limerick near Bunratty, Connor near Carrickfergus. Yet New Ross, Wexford, and Drogheda, not to mention smaller places like Youghal, Kinsale, and Dungarvon, were not bishoprics and this in spite of the relatively large number of dioceses. Ireland had nearly as many as England in spite of her smaller size. Most of the sees were inland: in fact, of the 33 dioceses only Ardfort, Waterford, Dublin, Down, and Derry were on the coast. Even the archbishops of Armagh, Clonmel, and Tuam were inland and in smaller places. The locations of the sees were established before the Norman invasion and represent the dominance of the great religious houses upon the religious organisation of the Irish. The sees had acquired some endowment in the English period, but little had been done to bring the bishops into the greater boroughs; nothing comparable to the shifting of the English sees at the time of William the Conqueror.

The Irish had experienced little of that socio-political integration that was occurring in contemporary London, where the busy autumn Exchequer-Law Term-Parliament season brought most of the important Englishmen to London. Nor had there developed the kind of 'schools' which were already, by 1214, characteristic of Oxford and Cambridge, producing a common intellectual experience for the children of England's leaders. Had the common law been extended to Ireland, schools of law might have arisen at Dublin, like the London Inns of Court, to train lawyers in the combination of law and Irish local custom. In the decade about 1280, there was a chance that, as in the Welsh settlement at the same time, the Irish might be granted equality, leading to integration of the inhabitants of the island. The failure to do so was the choice of the sovereign, Edward I, probably on the advice of his Anglo-Irish vassals. The failure was not as this study would show, because of an inadequate economic development in the island.

The population of Ireland and its condition as a region had importance even for Gaul of Roman days since the Celtic culture was a general one throughout the Celtic areas. Dublin, for instance, had its earlier parallel in Marsala, the Greek colony which became Marseilles. It was a prosperous city despite its refusal to conquer adjacent land and its generally happy relations with the Gallic tribes. And even after the Romans took over the entire country, the new Roman cities or colonies in older Gallic cities must have shared the comparable position of Waterford, New Ross and other Anglo-Irish cities. The Gallic tribes took over the Latin language,

Roman living habits, and Roman culture, except for the Roman type of clothing. The Irish took over the English language and many of the features of English culture even though some Irish retained their independence for a long time. One reason for the acceptance of features of an alien culture was probably the low density of the population. The estimate of 3.4 millions in the parts of Gaul taken over by Julius Caesar would give a density of only 6.3 persons,[27] not far from the density of thirteenth-century Ireland.

The total population of thirteenth-century Ireland must be estimated upon the basis of somewhat unsatisfactory evidence. Unfortunately, that country had neither a Domesday Book nor a poll tax. It was not even as fortunate as Wales, a country for which there is a certain amount of good data. Indeed, the best approach to total population seems to be by comparison with Wales, whose cultural and geographical conditions closely resembled those of her western neighbour. Since Ireland was about four times as large as Wales and had about four times as many clergy and four times the number of political units (cantrefs), it should have had about four times the Welsh population. This would have meant that Ireland had about 400,000 in AD 1100, and twice that many before the Black Death. Assuming a more rapid increase in numbers in the thirteenth century than in either the twelfth or fourteenth centuries, one might suggest a population of about half a million near AD 1200 and three-quarters of a million at the end of the century. However, the political troubles under Edward I probably held back its growth. Perhaps a population estimate of about 675,000 might be hazarded for Ireland around AD 1275–1300.

Another estimate may be made upon the basis of the number of parishes. Ireland in 1320 had about 2,400 parishes—about the same as had existed since the reorganisation of the Irish Church in the twelfth century. The population of the English parishes in Domesday seems to have been about 210–30 to a parish. If one may assume that the English parish had about the same number of people as the Irish, the estimate of Irish population should have been about 500,000–550,000 in the twelfth century. Or approaching the question from a comparison with the number of English churches, Ireland's 2,400 parishes are found to have been about one quarter of the English taxed churches circa 1291. If England had a population of about $2\frac{1}{2}$ million about 1275, the Irish population should have been about one-quarter of that, or 625,000; again not far from the late-thirteenth-century estimate. Another method would be to estimate from the size of the larger cities. Assuming that the cities are distributed as in a normal region, the size of the largest city would be about $1\frac{1}{2}\%$ of the total. Dublin at 11,000 would be head of a region of about 730,000.

If Ireland had a population of 675,000 in the second half of the thirteenth century, the 84,261km² of land would give a density of only 8 persons to the km², a very low density indeed. The urban index (percentage of total population of the ten largest cities) is well above average at approximately 6.1. An economy as primitive as the average density shows in a relatively fertile country, should normally have a much lower urban index. However, a pastoral economy, such as the Celts of Ireland showed even in the thirteenth century, evidently had a higher average prosperity than the usual tillage agriculture of the time. In a sense, it explains why the Irish conducted such a long and successful campaign against the English in the succeeding centuries. The standard of living of the average Irish then was fairly high and remained so until the overpopulation of the late eighteenth and early nineteenth century. It is in accord with the evidence of the export of hides and other goods from Ireland as well as that which indicates an extensive shipping. It is even reflected in the size of Plymouth and Bristol in the time of the poll tax of 1377.

K

7

Western French Regions: Paris and Toulouse

WHILE THERE HAVE been two general histories of French population,[1] much of the best work on medieval population has been by the very great historian, Ferdinand Lot, who, like Beloch, did most of his work on population in his old age. He wrote an exceptional article on the most comprehensive source of French population, the hearth tax list of 1328, and then continued with his comprehensive study of population and areas of French medieval cities, of which he finished a considerable part before his death.[2] Recently, much interest in the subject has appeared with such names as Carpentier, Fourquin, Heers, Renouard, and Wolff, with the best detailed study of a considerable area being the work by Baratier upon the population of Provence.

THE REGION OF PARIS

The most startling political development of the thirteenth century was the rise in extent and power of the Kingdom of France. At the beginning of the reign of Philip Augustus in 1180 more than half of his realm was held of him feudally by one man, Henry II, who was also king of England. John's errors lost the French possessions, except for the duchy held by the aged Eleanor of Aquitaine. Nonetheless, the French royalty experienced a great increase of power, reflected in the increase in the capital city.[3] Under Louis VIII the French

146

king secured a very strong position in the south of France, driving the house of Aragon from its previously strong position in that area. Louis IX (1226–70) followed these moves by a long campaign to strengthen the judicial and personal position of the king there. Philip III and Philip IV (1270–1314) were both strong kings and recovered more of the royal prerogatives which had been lost to local feudatories by the weakness of the later Carolingians and early Capetians.

The increase in the power of the French kings obviously brought on greater prestige, but a case could be made that they merely shared in French prestige before 1200 although contributing to it greatly thereafter. The *langue d'oil* spread over larger areas, becoming popular in Venice, where both Marco Polo and Martin de Canale used it, and in the English law courts as well as by English nobility and gentry. The *chansons de gestes* spread widely over Europe. The intellectual influence of its international university, the new Gothic architecture and perhaps even the styles of clothing and hair did much to promote respect for Paris and help develop it as a great city in the thirteenth century. Of course, Paris was in the centre of a very fertile plain. If its economic life centred in a single city, the city should have grown very large. This is what happened for the city in the thirteenth century.[4] By the beginning of the fourteenth century a lawyer, Pierre de Belleperche, could speak of Paris as the *communior et excellentior* city in the kingdom of France. The identification of Paris with the life of France is clear.[5]

The language of Paris (Ile-de-France) had by 1400 eclipsed the other dialects of the region and had become definitely the regional language as it was later to become the national language. It had been adopted as an official language in the reign of Louix IX (1226–70), but Latin was also used for a long time. Before this, Francien (if this may be used for the language of Paris) was merely one of several dialects, some of which were used even for literary purposes and produced a considerable medieval literature. The Norman was quite important since it was also used in England by its ruling group after the Norman Conquest. To the north of Paris there was the Picard-Walloon, to the east, the Burgundian-Champagne-Lorraine group of dialects, and to the south the Poitevin-Angevin-Saintonge division. For the most part, persons who understood one of these could understand the others without too much difficulty. The advantage Francien had was that it was the dialect of the centre of the area and thus presumably was the dialect most easily mastered by the others.

Even at the beginning of the thirteenth century the city had grown enough to make more inclusive walls advisable, but the city of Louis Philippe included only about 253 hectares. Since the river ran through it and some areas were hardly inhabited, it is unlikely to have had more than 25,000 people. Its growth as capital was remarkable.[6] Perhaps selected, as Fawtier suggests, because of the good hunting about it, the city grew as more and more of the organs of royal government settled there; the Parlement de Paris, the Chambre des Comptes, the treasury at the *Temple* and the archives. Even the Capetian tendancy to decide everything personally instead of deputising effectively brought more and more persons into the city for business. The University would be responsible for several thousands of professors and students (as a basic element) and the non-

TABLE 19: REGION OF PARIS

Rank, City	Pop Est 1,000s	Hyp Est 1,000s	Area hectares	Base	Sources
1 Paris	80	80	237–437	1328–21,089 h	Lot, *L'état* 305
2 Rouen	34	45.6	224		*WEC* 310, 341
3 Tours	26.3	31.2	175		Grenier 424
4 Orléans	22.5	24	150		Ganshof 12, 59
5 Amiens	21	19.2	140		
6 Reims	19	16.3	196	1363–3,779 h	Ganshof 12; *LAMP* 61
7 Bourges	16.3	14.2	115		
8 Beauvais	15.5	12.6	103		Grenier 425
9 Troyes	14.8	11.4	99		Grenier 12, 45, 59
10 Châlons-sur-Marne	10	10.4	100?	1422–1,200 f	Barthelmey 85
11 Chartres	9	9.5	54–60		*WEC* 344
12 Blois	5	8.9	32		*WEC* 40
13 Sens	5		32		Grenier 414, 420
14 Meaux			24		

Troyes: Lavedan *VF* 44.

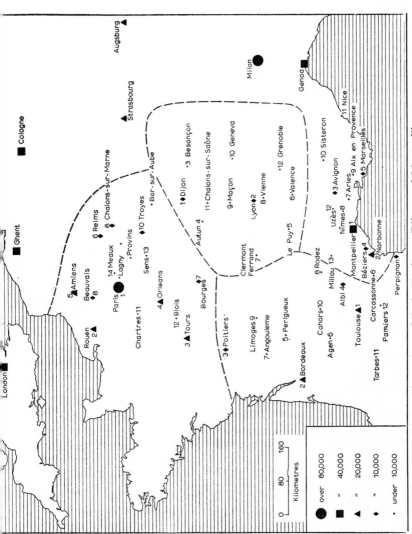

Fig 7   The regions of Paris, Toulouse, Dijon, and Montpellier

basic persons serving them. Presumably there developed there a season when the elite of France found it socially as well as financially and politically advantageous to be at Paris; something worth examining much more carefully. Then, of course, Paris was a convenient trading centre and drew to it an increasingly large mercantile element, to the Fair of the Lendit as well as in other times.

Although Paris was unquestionably the largest city in its region (Table 19 and Fig 7) and in France, its size has been the subject of an odd controversy, The choice is between an estimate of 80,000 as a pre-plague number and about 200,000. The problem is whether to believe that the figure appearing for Paris of some 61,089 hearths in 1328 was correct. One really should not have much difficulty in deciding whether the population of Paris had 80,000 or 200,000; the difference is so great. If 61,089 hearths is correct, then 200,000 is a very low minimum since it assumes 3.27 persons to the hearth. Normally the 'big population' scholars assume at least 5 to the hearth which, in this case, would give 300,000! The wall about Paris built by Charles V enclosed only about 439 hectares which, while it was built after the outbreak of the plague, still must have included the City of pre-plague size. Now 439 hectares is a very small area even for 80,000 in the Middle Ages. The reason for believing that the *livres de taille*,[7] which at their largest seem only to indicate about 19,000 persons, do not contradict the idea of 200–300,000 is the assumption that the taxed are only the commercial people. The evidence is not convincing: in a large city virtually all of the families should fall into the commercial class. Probably 61,089 was a mistake for 21,089; a copyist thought the *xx* had three dots over it.

At 80,000 Paris would have had 182 persons to the hectare, assuming that the walls represented earlier areas of habitation. However, the area may have been larger if the edges of the city had contracted as a result of the plague. One advantage of building walls following an epidemic of the plague was that abandoned houses offered cheap building materials ready at hand. The information about cities other than Paris is mostly about the areas enclosed by walls, as given in Table 19. Rheims also built an early post-plague wall, in 1358, enclosing 196 hectares. Rheims had 2,779 hearths in 1363. At 4 to the hearth, Rheims had then about 11,156. Its population before the plague should have been at least a half higher and thus about 100 to the hectare or about 19,000. The area of Châlons-sur-Marne was so uncertain that it is difficult to estimate its density. Most other French cities had pre-plague walls and probably had a density of about 150 to the hectare.

The second city in the region should certainly have been Rouen. It was the centre of the best organised and most powerful province, that of Normandy. It had a splendid position on the Seine where ocean-going ships of the day could reach. The archbishop of Rouen was an outstanding prelate. Some of the connections with England while her dukes were English kings doubtless helped the city's economy while its position, like that of Paris, as a key frontier city, may have concentrated more military power with its expenses, than would have been normal. At the beginning of the century it may not have been much smaller than Paris itself; there was little more than the general population growth of Europe to bring an increase to it and its subjection to the Capetians, and thus to Paris, may even have hindered its development. Its area of about 224 hectares should have held a population of about 25,000. Actually Rouen does not occupy a position which would be normal for the second city of the size of a region as large as that of the Parisian region; it is about 100 kilometres from Paris with the sea only another 50 kilometres beyond.

At best Rouen seems to have been somewhat smaller than a second city should have been, probably because her history had been more important than her geographical position. The normal second position should have been to the south-south-east in the neighbourhood of Orléans and Tours. During the Roman period this area had actually been the centre of the road system of Gaul, and Orléans had probably been the largest city in northern Gaul away from the eastern frontier. It had the second largest university in the region, the only one with a civil law school. The populations and positions of Amiens and Rheims were about right for the fifth and sixth positions among the cities. The next should probably have been to the east-south-east, but Troyes was apparently too small for that, perhaps because the fairs at the other three Champagne cities attracted a part of the commerce which should have centred on Troyes, especially since Dijon, a city of some size, was beyond.

The schedule of parishes and hearths of 1328 allows a fairly accurate count of the number within the region of Paris. Of that region the area covered by the survey was about 134,000km^2 while another 22,000km^2 was included in the fiefs and apanages not surveyed. If one excludes the areas assigned to the regions of Toulouse, Montpellier, and Dijon, one has about 16,300 parishes and 1,334,227 hearths in the list. Adding about one sixth for areas not included in the schedule would give about 1,520,000 hearths in the region of Paris. Multiplying by the low factor of four would give some 5.2 millions to that region. This still makes that region the most populous of any in Europe in the thirteenth century, as Fourquin has noticed.[8] At 1.5% of the total, its metropolitan city should have had about 78,000. Paris, even at the end of the period in 1328, must have had about 20,000 hearths or perhaps 80,000 persons. She was competing with the great cities of the Low Countries. Paris was only about 270 kilometres from Ghent while she was nearly 600 kilometres from Toulouse. The land which lay between Ghent and Paris was some of the richest in Europe. If Paris attained to anything near the position in France that Venice or Florence had in northern Italy she would be a mighty city indeed.

Let us assume for the moment that the table was approximately that of about 1280 and that in the succeeding years Paris grew rapidly, as she probably did with the increase of the king's power, while the other cities increased quite slowly, adding a few thousands apiece. The result might be something like this:

	Actual	*Hyp*
	1,000s	*1,000s*
Paris	80	80
Tours-Orléans	42	45.6
Rouen	29	31.2
Amiens	18	24
Rheims	16	19
Bourges	13	16
Beauvais	12	14.4

Even here it can be seen that Paris is already outstripping the other cites of northern France as a region, moving toward the time when she would be head of entire France as a kind of super-region.

However, neither Paris nor the other cities seem to have been large in terms of the region's population. The urban index would be then 257,100 as a percentage of the population of 5.2 millions estimated for 1328. However, the figures for the cities were supposed to be for about AD 1280. Presumably the country would have grown somewhat in population, although there are some who feel that 1280–1328 saw a declining population. The urban index calculated on the above basis would have been about 4.9, which is the normal urban index.

Despite the large population and the growth of its capital, the countryside of France and the entire country remained primarily an agricultural area, as it remained for centuries thereafter. Some very fundamental characteristics of France came from a long way back, seeming in part to stem from a very real adjustment to the environment and a strong appreciation of the need to care for the countryside—one of the first nations to appreciate the need for an ecological balance in their country; the wooded hilltops which prevent erosion, the large area still devoted to forest cover, and farming practices to preserve the soil with much use of ponds and water.

By the end of the thirteenth century Paris was definitely larger than its rank-size status in respect of other cities should have been. In part, this is the result of the centralisation of royal activities at Paris, and, in part, the failure of the other cities. Paris was taking over, for instance, the activities which had earlier centred in the Fairs of Champagne. But the Fairs themselves were an indication of the failure of the French cities to develop commercial activities, much as the English had done with respect to industrial possibilities. Futhermore, the French nobility had never taken kindly to the cities who, indeed, tended to dissociate themselves more and more from the cities. As early as AD 1151, St Quentin forbade manor houses within a league of the city.[9] Thus the cities did not get the leadership of the nobility within their walls nor even the growth in population which their presence brought to

Italian and possibly Spanish cities.[10] Gradually then Paris pulled away from the other cities in size, while the cities themselves were more and more subordinate to the French monarchs.

The Fairs of Champagne were more important for the history of trade and commerce than they were for history of population. None of the four cities became large; Troyes succeeding best. The failure of fairs to increase the city populations is not surprising; they were temporary affairs, bringing in money which, for the most part, seems to have been taken away by the visitors. Six weeks or even twelve weeks is only a small fraction of a year; so that one has to divide the number of people who attended by the size of that fraction to get some idea of the permanent effect. Furthermore, the owners of rented property had to keep property in shape all year just for a limited use over a short period. In one way they are of interest to regionalists; visitors seemed to have set up kinds of regional organisations at the fairs.[11] Some of the Italian cities had an organisation. The seventeen cities were from northern France and the Low Countries, while Montpellier seems to have represented the south of France.

The population density of the region of Paris was high, about 33.6 to the km^2, in part the result of relatively high grain yields. Slicher van Bath's collection of information about grain yields shows that several areas (which we hope are representative) had a yield average of about 3.0 before AD 1200, that is, for each unit of seed, 3.0 of grain. The samples after 1300 show that the average had risen to 4.3, an increase of about 65%. This was better than Germany, Scandinavia and eastern Europe were to do before 1500.

THE REGION OF TOULOUSE

The region of Toulouse had the Garonne River and its many tributaries as its central area, with the Charente to the north and lesser streams to the south as peripheral areas, all flowing into the Atlantic. The boundaries, other than the Atlantic. The boundaries, other than the Atlantic Ocean and the Pyrenees, were ill-defined.

Northern France became in the course of the thirteenth

century a fast-growing, well-integrated region and its metropolitan city, Paris, one of the largest European cities. At first sight it might seem that the same would happen in the south and produce a parallel situation at the end of the century or at least before the Black Death of 1348. The Albigensian Crusade and the Battle of Muret in 1213 might seem to have placed south France in the hands of the French kings. Slightly earlier they had taken over Angevin fiefs in the north from King John of England. However, the English still held a centre in Bordeaux and the countryside near it, the inheritance of Eleanor of Aquitaine.

Toulouse remained an important city and was incorporated only gradually into the French kingdom. A series of important cities to the east were lost in the period by Aragon, leaving only Perpignan to the Aragonese king. Meanwhile Burgundy and the east kept their association with the Empire as well as with France. Thus Toulouse and Montpellier remained essentially metropolitan centres of rather modest regions, while Dijon was a quite small centre of an uncertain region in the east. The Albigensian Crusade left bad feelings for France a long time in the south, while differences in language (Languedoc), law (land of the written law), and a general cultural homogeneity held the southern area together, in many ways closer to Aragon than to France.

Nevertheless, the association of Toulouse, Bordeaux, and Poitiers in a single region raises questions. Toulouse had been centre of Languedoc which might seem a region in itself. When France took over the area in the thirteenth century, it broke Toulouse away from the rest of Languedoc and governmentally associated it more with France itself; the more eastern parts became the districts of Carcassone and Nîmes. We are assuming that from this time, despite ancient associations in Languedoc and the English possesson of Gascony, the area did become a region in a real sense. It assumes that the growing commerce, and the textile and wine trades, particularly, tended to knit the south-western part of France into a cultural unit, as well as an economic unit. This, of course, might be questioned and the subject deserves more careful study. It raises questions about the position of Toulouse, especially. Why should it be the largest city when, theoretically, it had broken with the rest of Languedoc? One has to assume that there was still a very heavy commerce from the Mediterranean to Toulouse and on to the north through it. One also had to assume that the Albigensian Crusade, which is thought to have driven textile workers to the region of Barcelona, did not damage Toulouse seriously.

Toulouse has been the subject of careful study by Professor Wolff, who believes that it had a population of about 26,000 in 1385. Given the decline produced by the plague one may assume easily that it had a pre-plague population of 35,000 at least (Table 20). If it had had 1.5% of the hearths of the

TABLE 20: REGION OF TOULOUSE

Rank,	City	Pop Est 1,000s	Hyp Est 1,000s	Area hectares	Base	Sources
1	Toulouse	35	35	289(212)		WEC 110
2	Bordeaux	20	20	120		Lot 2, 551
						Prat
3	Poitiers	15	13.6	200(130?)		Higounet
4	Albi	10.7	10.5	100	1343–2,669 f	Lot 2, 395–6,
5	Perigeux	6	8.4	17.5+	1342–1,500 h	Lot 2, 602
6	Agen	6	7.1	57		Lot 2, 418
7	Angoulême	5	6.2	40		
8	Rodez	5	5.5	21+	1350–996 t	
					1,150 h	
9	Limoges	4	5	32–50		Lot 2, 243,
10	Cahors	4	4.6	25		Mols 1, 255
11	Tarbes	4	4.2	32–48		
12	Pamiers	3.5		33	910 h	Mols 1, 256

Toulouse: Wolff, *Toulouse* 161. Perigeux: Higounet-Nadal. Limoges: *WEC* 120.

region, it would have had about 12,478 hearths or a population of 50,000 if one uses 4 as a multiplier for the hearth. The area of 289 hectares (or is it 212?) also suggests a population somewhere near 40,000. This includes cité, bourg, and suburbs. It had extensive trade connections with northern centres and an early university.

Renouard has suggested that Bordeaux in 1316 had about 20,000.[12] If it had been taxed at the same rate as the country districts in that year, it would have had 40,000 hearths.[13] Even though the city was at the height of its medieval prosperity then, that is a number based on its wine resources rather than its hearths.[14] At about this time in the full flush of its wealth it built a wall enclosing some 120 hectares. Since earlier in the same century it had only added 9–10 hectares to a 32-hectare enclosure, it can hardly have pressed heavily against the new walls; the chances are that it had less than 100 to the hectare and that 20,000 would be a very tentative but reasonable estimate[15] of its population.

Poitiers had been probably the third largest city in Roman Gaul and had enjoyed the largest amphitheatre in the area.[16] This may have given the city, even in the Middle Ages, rather large ideas. The Roman area had been about 42–3 hectares; the city in the time of Henry II (1154–89) built walls to include about 200 hectares. It did, however, occupy a site which should have been that of a sizeable city; the estimate of 15,000 is a pure guess since there seems to have been no other data and the city preserved a rural appearance for centuries. Still, 75 to the hectare is a low density and one can hardly assume a lower estimate for a city built while the countryside was increasing as it was in the thirteenth century.

Much more information is known about Albi since it had 2,669 heads of houses in 1343 and only 952 in 1357.[17] There were 516 female heads of houses in 1343; that is about 19% of the total. Usually if the number of female heads is that high, it means a low density and should be multiplied, as Mlle Prat did, by about 4, giving a total population before the plague of about 10,700. The terrible loss of women heads of households was probably due to their living alone or with one or two others persons; small households suffered severely.

Three other cities seem to have a slightly smaller population: Rodez, Agen, and Cahors. Rodez presents the most serious problems. Its wall is alleged to have held only about 26 hectares, but before the plague its population is said to have been 2,600 hearths. Now a tax of the year 1350 revealed some 966 taxpayers of whom 185 lived outside of the city walls. The number within the city walls would have averaged 186 to the hectare, which was very high and this after the first attack of the plague; at even the same ratio of persons living outside of the city the number to the hectare (18,400 divided by

21) would have been a quite unbelievable figure, about 900 to the hectare. One explanation might be that the 2,300 is a doubled number based upon two payments a year, another that it is just a plain mistake. If we assume that 1,150 hearths before the plague (which would have given a 16% decline for the first plague) at 4 a hearth would have given only 4,600 persons. Agen apparently had an area of about 57 hectares and Cahors about 25 hectares; that is all that is known of them. Agen is set at 6,000 and Cahors at 4,000, on the grounds that two such important cities should have had at least that many. For such a small place Cahors had a tremendous impact upon European trade and finance.[18] Of the three cities which were thought to have had about 10,000,[19] only Albi really seems to have been of that size.

Below those mentioned above, the cities, for the most part, were supported by local sources: Perigeux, Angoulême, Lunel, and Limoges. Perigeux had apparently about 1,500 hearths in 1342, which at 4 to the hearth should have been about 6,000.[20] Angoulême apparently had about 40 hectares within its walls and is assigned 5,000. Lunel had an inquest in 1296 which showed about 1,176 hearths in the city which, multiplying by 4 to a hearth, gives about 4,700 persons at the time.[21] Limoges had about 32 hectares by the thirteenth century and probably had about 4,000 persons.

The region notably lacked cities within the 7,000–10,000 range. The region was in a sort of economic backwater with respect to western Europe. Theoretically the highways from Iberia and the Mediterranean converged at Bordeaux and went north to Paris from there. The Mediterranean lines of commerce seem rather to have gone north through Béziers and Montpellier and the Rhône River, while there probably was not much direct traffic from Iberia due north. Furthermore the strong English connection with Bordeaux and the French pressure on Languedoc must have tended to divide the areas.

Fortunately the schedule of hearths for 1328 includes most of the areas dependent upon Toulouse except the territory held by the English. Renouard has estimated the population of the English holdings in the period at about 625,000 persons or 125,000 hearths from the reports of English officials sent there to solicit money for the war.[22] This seems a reasonable figure.

The other provinces included in the schedule are Saintonge, Rouerge, Poitou, Gascoign, Limousin, Bigorre, Périgord and Cahorsin, and Toulouse, arranged in that order. They include about 7,511 parishes and 780,000 hearths. Adding about 520 parishes for Navarre-Béarne would raise the number to about 8,031 while adding about 53,000 hearths for the additional area would bring a total of 831,914. The area seems to be that of about 21 modern *départements* with limits in the north and east in the following departments: Vendée, Deux-Sèvres, Haute-Vienne, Creuse, Corrèze, Cantal, Lot, Tarn-et-Garonne, Haute-Garonne, and Ariège with a total area of about 135,000km².

The area of the region of Toulouse was about 135,000km² which gave a density of 25.0 persons to the km² including the cities. If the ten largest were omitted, the average density drops to about 24.2 persons. The total for the ten largest cities was about 110,700 which shows an urban index for the region of about 3.3, very low except for a purely agricultural region.

The political situation has been expressed as follows: [23]

The leadership is for a long time held by town nobilities, numerous and turbulent, provided with land revenues. As time goes on, burgher elements, enriched by trade, join this class of leaders, their ideal being to live as nobility. About the middle of the thirteenth century these burghers cease disowning their professional activities, and the nobility having been expelled, they take part in the political organisation of the city, not as landholders or capitalists but as chiefs of corporations.

It will be seen that much of the size and strength of the southern French cities came in part from association with and often joining the ruling feudal class.

8

North-western Mediterranean Regions: Montpellier and Barcelona

THE COUNTRY ON both sides of the eastern Pyrenees has a certain homogeneity in scenery, in history, and in culture. Catalan and Languedoc French are well between Spanish and French and both areas differ in many respects from their national cultures. The documents of the areas have similarities as if the redactors had had an education from the same schools, presumably Bologna, Montpellier and later, other written law centres. For a time it looked as if Aragon might organise an outstanding kingdom in the area and certainly until the end of the pre-plague period she did control much of the coast with her navy or shared it with Genoa. Aragon controlled on land as far north as Millau at times, and with Genoa also managed to keep Marseilles, the natural centre of southern France, as a weak city during the period. Barcelona was definitely the metropolitan centre of one region in the area; at the end of the medieval period Valencia was contesting the leadership. Somewhat surprisingly, the outstanding city of the eastern section was Montpellier, although it arose late as a city and declined precipitously once Marseilles was united with the French Kingdom at the end of the fifteenth century. Much data about the hearth and other similar taxes remain for this region: The Provençal sources have been splendidly edited by Baratier.

THE REGION OF MONTPELLIER

Languedoc and Provence were ancient territorial areas associated primarily with the Mediterranean—a land of many commercial cities. They were good markets themselves and traded with both the Mediterranean and northern cities. The series of large cities along the coast of France from Marseilles to Narbonne and its hinterland obviously suggests the possibility of a region (Fig 7). The maps for the period in Shepherd's *Atlas,* however, suggest as the leading cities in 1190 Marseilles, Arles and Narbonne; in 1328 Marseilles, Nîmes, and Narbonne; and in 1360, Marseilles, Avignon, and Narbonne. Marseilles and Narbonne thus are perennial and there should be another city in the centre. In a sense this is a result of the lack of attention to demography and even to a concept of quantification on the part of medievalists. Historical writing has focused on certain of the cities and missed the others. This was probably the result of concentration upon historical factors, such as archbishops (Narbonne, Arles and Aix, for Marseilles), great ports of the past (Marseilles, Narbonne) and great road centres (Arles, Nîmes, Narbonne). One would hardly guess that Montpellier was by far the largest city in the region; that Béziers was probably larger than Marseilles and Carcassone possibly larger than either Nîmes or Arles. (Table 21).

Montpellier is the great surprise. Its beginning is only in the tenth century. Its port, Lattes, was a rather sad little place a few miles away on an interior water. Its bishop had his title from Maguelonne. It was not even on one of the great medieval highways—for the one important highway then went from the Mediterranean north to Millau and down the Allier or Liger Rivers by Nevers to Orléans and Paris. Its very development was probably the result of a series of accidents. The first was probably the reduction of Marseilles by Genoa, with some help from Aragon, as a great port. That Montpellier took its place is evident from the great jump in size when France took over Marseilles in 1481 and the precipitous decline of Montpellier in the two decades following this event. The counts of Montpellier pursued, for the most part, an opportunist policy and were succeeded by the King of Aragon who

L

TABLE 21: REGION OF MONTPELLIER

Number, City	Pop Est 1,000s	Hyp Est 1,000s	Area hectares	Base	
1 Montpellier	40	40	100	1346–10,100 h	Mols 1, 255
2 Narbonne	25	22.8	70+	1340–6,229 h	Mols 1, 255
3 Avignon	18	15.6	151		Lot 1, 157–9 ; Mols 2, 63
4 Béziers	14.5	12	45(99)	1342–4,336 h	Lot 1, 350–1 ; Mols 1, 255
5 Marseilles	12	9.6	65(84)	–3,000 h	Baratier 66
6 Carcassone	9.5	8.2	68	1304–2,355 h	Lot 1, 405 ; Mols 1, 255
7 Arles	8.4	7.1	36	1319–2,138 h	Baratier 144
8 Nimes	7	6.3	32	1320–2,075 h	Lot 1, 373 ; Mols 1, 255
9 Aix-en-Provence	6	5.7	40	1321–1,500 h	Baratier 65–6
10 Sisterton	5.6	5.2	60	1,400 h	Baratier 65–6 ; Lot 1, 494
11 Nice	5.6	4.8	25	1,400 h	Baratier 65 ; Lot 1, 272
12 Uzès			26		Chauvet

Montpellier: Russell, *L'Evolution* 353–5. Marseilles: Lesage, map on p 33 seems to show 84 hectares: Lot I, 176 gives only 65 hectares for the thirteenth century? Carcassone, see also *LAMP* 56.

possessed the city after 1204. From then on it profited by its membership in the Kingdom of Aragon. Lesser nobles settled in fortified mansions and added strength to the civic leadership.[1] It had also the chief medical school of the south as part of its fine university. It's population has been studied: the city probably was about 40,000 before the Black Death.

Narbonne, the best publicised city in the region, was apparently second in size. In 1340 its hearth tax total was 6,229, which should represent a population of about 25,000 at 4 to the hearth. However, a complication is that the number of hearths may be for the district of Narbonne as well as for the city itself. The 70 hectares, even with some suburbs, is quite small for a city of 24,000 and much too small for one of over 30,000. The same problem arises for its neighbour, Béziers, which is listed at 4,336 hearths and gives about 14,500 at 3.5 a hearth, in 1342. Its walls enclosed only 45 hectares, but there were probably suburbs below the walled hill. The two are only about 30 kilometres apart. However, their economic directions seem different; Narbonne looked toward Carcassone and Toulouse while Béziers seems more toward the north through Lodève. The two cities would then have a combined population of about 39,500. Given the extensive commerce that passed through the area, this does not seem too high.

Avignon gained rapidly after the removal of the Papacy to that city from Rome in 1307. If the Papacy about 1300 had about 450 *curiales*,[2] they should have increased the population by at least 3,000. However, by 1377 the count stood at 2,359 *cortes* and 1,471 *cives* for the city.[3] Among the *cortes* were butchers and other persons obviously not clerical. Presumably these groups were respectively basic and nonbasic; the total is 4,830, which should have given a city at least 3.5 times as large a population, or about 17,000 a number which should not have been too much affected by the plague. The walls of about 1315 took in 40 to 45 hectares, presumably for perhaps 5,000 or 6,000 people. Another set, constructed in the decade following the Black Death of 1348 included 151 hectares. Even with some vacant land, these walls should indicate a density of over 100 to the hectare and should have held the 17,000 postulated above.

Marseilles, known for its great population today as the metropolis of southern France and for its considerable importance in the classical world, can hardly be conceived of as a relatively small city, which is probably why cartographers are so kind to it. The city added to its walls in 1163, 1265 and 1298 and then only had enclosed 65 hectares. However, from the map of the city it would appear that another 20 hectares were inhabited, so 80 hectares is given as its area. Even then, it seems to have declined in the early fourteenth century so that an estimate of 10,000 is generous. But Baratier believes that about 1300 it had 3,000 hearths[4] which was less than its earlier commercial prosperity when, he thinks, Marseilles had 20 to 25,000 persons. In 1359 one part of it had only 807 hearths.[5]

Carcassone enjoyed some of her best days in the pre-plague period. She had 2,355 hearths in 1304 which, at four to the hearth, was about 9,000 persons, very large even for the 18 hectares unwalled together with 12 hectares walled area added to the 38 of the new city across the stream. The 4,325 hearths of 1342[6] seemed to include the population of a considerable district outside of the city. Like Montpellier, its urban areas housed a large warlike nobility[7]; its power and spirit was well typified by its famous walls.

Near the Rhône River were two ancient cities, Arles and Nîmes, which had known better days under the Roman Empire. In 1319 Arles had about 2,138 hearths, which we assume because of its small area of 36 hectares, represent four to the hearth and would have had about 8,400 inhabitants. Arles apparently had been larger in 1271 with 2,270 hearths[8] which, again, would indicate a small number to the hearth. Nîmes also was probably in not too good a condition. It had 2,075 hearths in 1320, but the first attack of the plague reduced the number to 1,526.[9] This was a reduction of about a quarter from the 1320 figure, a little high which probably means that Nîmes had declined some even before the plague.

Three cities in Provence—Aix, Nice, and Sisterton—seem to offer only routine problems. Baratier has made suggestions about all three of them; they were in the neighbourhood of 4,000 to 5,000 in population. The cities of Provence were caught between the greater cities on each side: Montpellier and Genoa. Genoa had a policy of keeping commerce of the area as much in its hands as possible with its great fleet, its control of Corsica and its commerce through the passes to Milan in the north. To offset this a city needed the help of a great land magnate, which the cities of Provence did not have as yet. The hinterland also seemed to be experiencing a depression, especially in the mountains. The deteriorating temperature of the early fourteenth century, as the Little Ice Age came on, must have contributed to the tendency of mountain inhabitants to come out of their villages.

The area of the Montpellier region included the following:

		km^2
	Provence	31,757
Départements	Basses-Alpes	6,988
	Hautes-Alpes	5,643
	Alpes-Maritimes	3,736
	Bouches-du-Rhône	5,248
	Gard	5,881
	Var	6,023
	Vaucluse	3,578
		68,854
West	Aveyron	8,771
	Aude	6,342
	Hérault	6,224
	Lozière	5,180
		95,371

The population of the region may be estimated as follows:

Provence	400,000[10]		
Nîmes	409,072	102,268	hearths[11]
Carcassone	337,084	84,271	hearths
Narbonne	80,000		
Montpellier	70,000		
	1,296,156		

The areas of the vicomte of Narbonne and the county of Montpellier were outside the 1328 count of hearths.

The density of the population of the region of Montpellier would have been about 13.6 persons to the km² for the entire region. Without the ten top cities the density of the rest was about 12.1, since the cities had a combined population of about 146,000. The urban index of the region would have been about 11.3%, a relatively high figure, but then that part of France was a very commercial section of Europe at the time. The density of the countryside was relatively low and suggests that the cities received relatively little support for their population from the country and much from the commerce and perhaps even the industry of the area.

THE REGION OF BARCELONA

For a time in the early thirteenth century the king of Aragon (Peter II) seemed on the verge of constructing an immense empire *occitan* (of Languedoc) comprising Provence, Languedoc, Catalonia, Aragon, Béarn and the smaller part of Gascony, an area where the language, the culture and the customs were so similar that the troubadours lived, sang and were at home in all of them.[12] The Battle of Muret in 1213 ended this possibility; France was to include the south. It illustrates the common character of the three regions of Barcelona, Toulouse, and Montpellier. In spite of the French conquest and French domination, in the thirteenth and early fourteenth centuries, the regions of Montpellier and Toulouse were still very southern rather than French. But Aragon-Catalonia remained a power and expanded south by taking over the Balearics in 1229 and Valencia in 1238. It had a base in the fertile Ebro Valley and the Costa Brava and its heavily populated back country—the one great human concentration in Iberia facing the Mediterranean. Perhaps one could regard both Palma de Mallorca and Valencia in the region of Barcelona even while the Moors possessed them, since in both areas independent emirs were in control. Oddly enough, the incorporation of the places in the kingdom of Aragon was to have a rather deleterious effect on Barcelona, although past the end of the fourteenth century, it remained the metropolitan city of the region.

These conquests shifted the interests of king and especially of the city of Barcelona away from the continent on to the sea, and the city became the naval centre of an increasingly powerful Mediterranean sea-power. So powerful was it that, with its help, Aragon moved into Sicily with little difficulty on the occasion of the widespread insurrection known as the Sicilian Vespers in 1282; the island became an important part of the kingdom of Aragon. Peter III accepted it as the inheritance of his wife, Constance, daughter of King Manfred of Sicily. His powerful navy, with soldiers from Spain, took over Sardinia and even moved into the Morea, setting up the duchies of Athens and Naupatrie. The Spanish profited by these overseas possessions by learning how to govern lands at a great distance from Spain, knowledge which was to come into good stead after Columbus opened the New World to Spanish expansion.

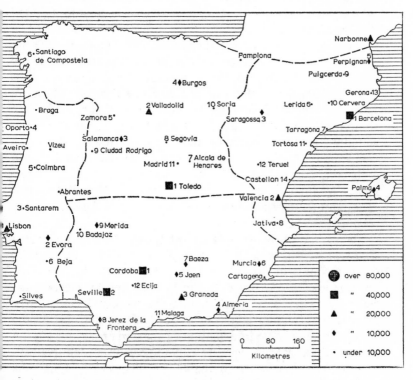

Fig 8 The regions of Cordoba, Toledo, and Barcelona

At first glance the region of Barcelona (Fig 8) including Perpignan in France, the Balearic Islands, Sardinia, Catalonia, Aragon and even the area about Valencia might not be expected to have a very homogenous language. Actually Catalan is the common language, except for the western part of Aragon next to Pamplona, which seems to have been closer to Spanish. Catalan is quite close to Provençal, often considered a branch of it, reminiscent of the chance, even into the thirteenth century, that a great Provençal-Catalan state was possible of the regions of Toulouse, Montpellier and Barcelona.

In 1962 two studies restored order to the tangled state of knowledge of the Catalonian hearth-taxes and revealed much information about the parallel 'monedatge' tax, based on households.[13] D. José Iglesias Fort in his *El Fogaje de 1365–1370* edited a hearth-tax heretofore attributed to 1376 and showed that it actually belonged to the year 1365 (Cortes of Tortosa) and contained some information relating to 1359 (Cortes of Cervera). The prime manuscript is: Archivo de la Corona de Aragon, Real Patrimonio 2590, but some data are at Perpignan in Archives de Pyrénées-Orientales, *B 18*. He also proved that the hearth-tax published by P. de Bofarull as of 1359 from the Archivo de la Corona de Aragon, Varia 28, Petri III, no *1584* actually belongs to the year 1385.[14] He showed also[15] that the hearth-tax ascribed to the year 1378 is actually another version of the 1385 hearth-tax. Thus the Catalonian situation is simplified and the data can be used with confidence. The '1378' manuscripts are both at Barcelona: Archivo de la Corona de Aragon, Real Patrimonio *2,591* and the city archives, series *XIX*, vol *4*. Again, another fragment is at Perpignan.

The second study is my *Medieval Monedatge of Aragon and Valencia* which presented information derived from a series of manuscripts in the Archivo de la Corona de Aragon. This tax was an old one which began in 1205 and by custom was levied every seven years. Although like the Catalonian hearth taxes, the surviving data comes mostly from the post-plague period, there is some information of the earlier period. On the basis of these data it seems possible to set up a tentative estimate of population before the plague (Table 22). It is thus assumed that the cities lost a sixth of their population by 1352 in the initial epidemic, a fifth by 1360 and a third by 1380. It also assumes 5 to the hearth. The experience of Teruel is assumed to be reasonably correct for Spain but not for Portugal. Between 1342 and 1385 it lost about a third of its population. Spain seems to have suffered less from the plague than did most other European countries, probably because of its low humidity and long periods of either high or low temperature on the Meseta.

TABLE 22: REGION OF BARCELONA

Rank,	City	Pop Est 1,000s	Hyp Est 1,000s	Area hectares	Hearths	
1	Barcelona	48	48	260	1359–7,651	Iglesias
2	Valencia	31.1	27.4	142+	1355–5,179	Russell, *MM*, 495
3	Saragossa	19.2	18.7	110	1385–2,560	Russell, *MM*, 497
4	Palma de Mallorca	17.0	14.4	108	1238–3,392	
5	Perpignan	12.3	11.5	52+	1359–1,642	Iglesias 89
6	Lerida	9.6	9.6	50	1385–1,213	Iglesias 65, 86
7	Tarragona	9	8.5	26	1365–1,366	Iglesias 79
8	Jativa	8.5	7.6	30	1361–1,344	Russell, MM 495
9	Puigcerda	7.9	6.9	43	1359–1,232	Iglesias 62
10	Cervera	7.8	6.2	21	1359–1,212	Iglesias 62, 80
11	Tortosa	7.8	5.8	27	1385–1,057	Iglesias 64
12	Teruel	7.6	5.3	28	1342–1,521	Russell, MM 494
13	Gerona	7.5		25	1365–1,590	Iglesias 94
14	Castellon de la Plana	7.0		48	1357–1,110	
15	Huesca	6.5		30	1244–1,347	*CEH* iv 12
16	Morella	5.9			1361– 998	Russell, *MM* 496
17	Catalayud	6.2		31	1346–1,245	Russell, *MM* 498

Reductions: 1/6 to 1351; 1/5 to 1360, 1/3 to 1380–1400.

The problem of the number of hearths in Barcelona is complicated by the situation mentioned above and one additional complication. The data[16] shows the same number, 6,568, for both 1359 and 1365, while the number for 1385 was apparently 7,295. There is another number, 7,651 suggested by Smith[17] for 1378 which is probably the number for 1359 even though it seems a bit too large with respect to the number for 1365. This would give nearly 48,000. However, there would be additional persons, such as the clergy, while the Cortes of Catalonia alternated between Lerida and Barcelona with Barcelona serving in other capacities as a capital.[18] Since 5 to the hearth is probably a bit too high, given the large number of widows in the list, we assume that 48,000 is a reasonable figure for the whole city's population just before the plague.

The *monedatge* records of 1385 preserve the names of the professions and jobs of the hearth holders but unfortunately only for the two quarters (*Mar* and *Pi*) of Barcelona. These included about half of the hearths (3,289 of 7,295) but they may not be entirely good samples of the composition of the entire city: *Mar*, near the sea, had as its most numerous group, sailors and merchants, while *Pi*'s most numerous groups were diggers and farmhands, obviously a working-class quarter. Given this warning let us look at the situation arranged approximately on a basic-nonbasic pattern.[19]

Basic		*Uncertain-both*		*Nonbasic*	
Sailors	227	Merchants	151	Fishermen	94
Seamen	73	Shoemakers	108	Inn-keepers	49
Longshoremen	59	Tailors	96	Carpenters	43
Brokers	45	Wooldressers	70	Bakers	40
Hucksters	36	Weavers	63	Janitors	39
Curriers	29	Tanners	61	Butchers	34
		Scriveners	32	Tavern-keepers	27
		Silversmiths	29	Spicers	26
		Notaries	28	Bargemen	25
	–––		–––		–––
	469		638		377

These are from the largest groups. Altogether there were some 2,000 persons in a total of 100 groups. Generally, the smaller groups indicate specialisation, whose products or services were useful to both Barcelona and the whole region. They also probably should be classed as both basic and nonbasic. The division is between those which bring income from the outside into the city and those which just serve the city itself. The basic also include those for whose services people come into the city. This would give about an even split between the two which is what might be expected; the division (dividing the uncertain evenly between the two) would give 1046 basic (469 + 319 + 258) and 954 nonbasic (377 + 319 + 258), a total of nearly 2,000. Now if the total number of hearths was 3,289 in the two quarters of the city, at 5 to the hearth the number of basic and nonbasic should be about one-seventh or 2,350. The shortage probably was made up of second members of a family who were not listed (wives, sons, etc.). If, however, the large number of women (nearly one-fifth) indicates, as it often does, a smaller number to the hearth, the total actually would be about as expected.

In those quarters of the city, at least, there seem to have been no large concentrations of industrial groups, such as those greater numbers of textile workers at Florence and in the cities of the Low Countries. The chief groups are connected with marine or marketing activities, as one expects of a great commercial city. The city seems to have been highly diversified in its interests, moving goods into its region and probably on beyond into the region of Toledo and perhaps even into the region of Cordoba. It had close connections with the Islamic world and had, for instance, introduced paper into western Europe (through Xativa?). Catalan paper was used in the region of Montpellier[20] and appears in documents of Perpignan. Like most cities, Barcelona was run by a series of great families who were the moving spirits of the commerce and politics of the city and even for the area of Catalonia. Barcelona's government was an early medieval experiment in representation, since some of the city divisions were actually villages many miles from the city. Combine all this with the close co-operation of the King of Aragon and the strength of the region can be appreciated.

The city of Valencia is fortunate in that lists from the tax (monedatge) remain from both 1355 and 1361.[21] The 1355 list gives 4,729 hearths for the parishes within the city and the 1361 list 4,754, thus practically the same. A minor problem is that the numbers vary considerably for parishes, which suggests that the boundaries of the parishes were not as well defined as the limit of collection of the tax-collectors. No *moreria* is listed for the city itself so that presumably Moors and Jews lived outside in the *alqueria,* which had about 450 families. The total then for 1355 was about 5,179 families which should show a city of about 31,000, assuming a sixth loss on account of the plague. Outside of the city was the famed Garden *(orta)* of Valencia which had about 2,000 families. It had (and still has) its own water court which meets at the corner of the cathedral each Thursday noon, reminiscent of the time when it met at the mosque (on that site) just before the Islamic holy day began. Valencia was too large for a second city in the region and was growing rapidly. It remained the seat of the area of the old Moorish emirate of Valencia where the Cortes met.[22] Indeed in the fifteenth century it overtook Barcelona in size.

Saragossa was the great city of the central Ebro Valley. Unfortunately the earliest listing of houses is from 1385; on the basis of that list it is assumed that the pre-plague city had about 19,200. Saragossa had been an outstanding city since Roman days; the outline of the classical city can be seen in the rectangle of city streets in the centre of the modern city. It was also the site of the greatest Moorish emirate of the north. As that area developed in the twelfth and thirteenth century, Saragossa took on an ever greater significance; it had relatively little competition in the area, which probably partially accounts for its considerable size. It was the ecclesiastical capital for Aragon, perhaps more so than its political capital. It was, of course, on the great trade route up the Ebro as well as on another from Barcelona to Toledo. It was perhaps the close connection of the king of Aragon with the sizeable city of Saragossa that caused him to understand and appreciate the city of Barcelona so well since his co-operation with Barcelona, a very independent and energetic city, is one of the fine points in the history of the region.

The data for the cities of Perpignan and Lerida provided some problems. The areas seem to have been about the same about 50 hectares. The data for Perpignan[23] for 1359 show 3,346 hearths, for 1365, 2,678 hearths and for 1385, 1,642 hearths. For Lerida no number is given for 1359 but for 1365, 2,234[24] and for 1385, 1,213. However, Iglesias[25] suggests that the total for 1365 includes part of the villages closely associated with the city and were not properly a part of the city. The same would seem to be true for the 1359 and 1365 figures for

Perpignan, since the physical size of the city suggests that these figures were much too large. Thus the 1385 figures are used as a base for estimating the population of the pre-plague figures. Before 1344 Perpignan was capital of the Kingdom of Mallorca, a sort of sub-kingdom of Aragon, but it was reduced to a subordinate part of the kingdom in 1344 so that one might expect a rather rapid decline in population. But even if it were capital of such a tiny state as Mallorca, its activities were constricted by the nearness of Narbonne and Béziers, which occupied better positions in respect of commerce. Lerida was a sizeable city in northern Catalonia, with a university from which it apparently derived little pleasure, since the city at one time asked to be relieved of it.

Palma de Mallorca was affected adversely by the conquest in 1229; many of its Moorish inhabitants were replaced by Catalonians, whose dialect is still the island dialect. A listing of houses then shows 2,898 occupied and 494 unoccupied, for a total of 3,392. After 1276,[26] Palma de Mallorca had a magnificent age as the centre of international commerce, being part of the important sub-kingdom of Mallorca which included the Balearics, Roussillon and even Montpellier. With Montpellier and Messina, Palma alone is given a position as important for Venetian traffic in the western Mediterranean by the Florentine, Pegolotti, in his *Practica della Marcatura* of circa AD 1330–42. It is assumed that the empty houses were filled during the apogee of the city; by 1559 the houses were reduced in number to 2,155. Nevertheless, Palma was a port visited en route as a convenient stopping-point, but was hardly a portal city for commerce, as were Barcelona, Montpellier and perhaps even Perpignan.

In contrast to the middle Ebro Valley where Saragossa had almost an urban monopoly, the lower valley saw urbanisation distributed among a number of modestly sized cities: Tarragona, Tortosa, Morella, and Castellon de la Plana, perhaps even Lerida. Since the cities are, from their centre at the mouth of the Ebro, about 160–70 kilometres from Barcelona, Valencia and Saragossa, one might have expected in this area a large city, perhaps farther up the list than sixth, probably in the location of Tortosa but it had no good harbour. Tarragona, with its magnificent Cyclopean walls topped by Roman additions, had been capital of a great province during Roman days and still remained the seat of the archbishop. Morella was the centre of the highland back from the sea and Castellon de la Plana had been a part of the economic system of the Moorish state of Valencia before it was captured. Lerida occupied an important position between Barcelona and Saragossa. The wealth of the lower Ebro Valley then supported most of the secondary cities of the region. The region of Barcelona was influenced, as were many parts of Europe, by the textile revolution of the early thirteenth century. One has only to look at the interesting map presented by Gual Camarena[27] to see the heavy concentration of various forms of textile activity in the region. Close to half of the places in Spain lie in the region. Some profited by migration of workers from the north, perhaps stimulated by the Albigensian persecution and some had been in Valencia from Moorish days. The end of the century saw a tremendous variety of types of cloth: wool, cotton, silk, linen, in a wide range of weaves and colours. Society must have presented a contrast in dress from the simpler and more sober appearance of earlier days. Again the region as a whole must have looked different from its neighbours to the west and south, as not only the great cities (Barcelona, Valencia, Saragossa, Perpignan, Mallorca) had their textile industries but nearly sixty smaller places in the region shared in this development. Many of them had famous cloths: Puigcerda, Bañoles, Lerida, Jaca, Huesca. Many, too, were tiny places making use of streams for their power, a little like the situation in England.

Slightly smaller, on the average, were cities outside the Ebro Valley such as Jativa, Gerona, Catalayud, Teruel, Cervera and Puigcerda; all apparently were in the range from 6,000 to 8,000 persons. These cities and the larger cities of the kingdom seem to have been about 83 kilometres apart. Presumably then they were about two days' journey from each other, with a smaller market town between.

A study of population of the region of Barcelona produces an estimate of the size of Aragon and Catalonia after the first attacks of the plague: 213,015 for Aragon and 335,000 for Catalonia. There was some evidence for the area of Valencia but for much of the area evidence was lacking.[28] The density

of population was 4.48 to the km² for Aragon and 10.42 for
Catalonia. A reconstruction of the pre-plague population is
possible by assuming that the loss in the early plague or
plagues was about 40%; it was probably about average for
damper areas but in the interior, as in Teruel, it was definitely
low, with 30% instead of 35–40%. Thus, the average to the
area would have been six to the km² of the interior areas
and thirteen to the coast areas. Another estimate[29] is:

Aragon	47,500km²	×	6	=	285,000	200,000
Catalonia	32,000	×	13	=	416,000	450,000
Balearic	5,000	×	13	=	65,000	50,000
Perpignan	4,100	×	13	=	53,300	18,000
Valencia	26,080	×	13	=	339,040	200,000
Navarre	10,500	×	6	=	63,000	63,000
	125,180				1,221,340	981,000

This gives an average density of about 9.8 to the km², for the
first and 7.8 for the second.

9

Three Iberian Regions:
Cordoba, Toledo, and Lisbon

PORTUGAL AND SPAIN, or Iberia, it is often forgotten, was in the first half of the Middle Ages, the most prosperous and certainly the most progressive area of western Europe. In the sixteenth century under the impact of its very successful colonial policy it was again a most prosperous, and certainly the most powerful, country in Europe. In the first period Cordoba was the capital, the largest city and the head of a very large, well-integrated region. In the sixteenth century for a time, at least, the position of leadership was held by Seville, the great port of the colonial trade. Again Iberia could be considered a region. In between there was naturally a shift from Cordoba to Seville which, since the two are not far apart on the same river (the Guadalquivir), need not have affected the relative position of other cities very much. However, other changes in the period did affect them. Population increased more rapidly to the north and in Portugal than in the south. Aragon and Catalonia, as already seen, were part of the region of Barcelona, which narrowly escaped being a Pyrenees-centred area together with southern France.

The Visigoths, weak as they were about AD 711, still controlled most of the peninsula. They were alien in race, of a different speech and for long were even heretical in religion. Integration was relatively slow since the Visigoths seem to have preserved some areas of fairly dense colonisation and thus avoided the rapid deterioration that occurred to the

Vandals in North Africa at the same period. The Arab forces which so easily conquered in 711 had much the same handicaps, a different race, a very different language, and a religion which some Christian theologians regarded as a Christian heresy (which was even worse in their eyes than an alien religion). They had two advantages, however. They came from lands which had marked geographical resemblances to Spain so that they simply carried over many of their customs as well as their skill in pastoral economics and irrigation practices. Then they were but the first of a long series of invaders from Islam, coming either as sizeable armies or as individuals, bringing all phases of the great Islamic culture to Iberia. In the south at such places as Cordoba, Seville, Malaga, Murcia, and Almeria the Moors built up great industrial and commercial cities, centres of improved agricultural areas,[1] the basis for a great population increase before AD 1000. At that time that culture was certainly superior in most ways to the Visigothic-Romance culture of Iberia. The combination of cultural advance and political-military power placed Iberia at the head of western European progress well into the twelfth century, with its influence extending much beyond that. Probably the mass of documents of AD 1100–1450 in Iberia still constitutes the richest field for historical research in western medieval history today.

The north-east area, including the valley of the Ebro river, was primarily a Mediterranean-oriented country with a distinct climate of its own. The south-east coastline has a distinctly subtropical cast with its date-growing palms; the arab invaders of the eighth century felt very much at home there. They felt at home also on the great central meseta of Iberia which dominates the peninsula. It is both high and dry, while its rivers flow west and thus afford few communications for north-south travel. The west coast areas share in the Atlantic climate with its prevailing west winds and considerable dampness. At first sight it might seem that the peninsula would enjoy isolation from the outside world, particularly since it was at the end of lines of invasion from Eurasia, from Africa and from the Mediterranean itself.

Two conditions have tended to allow it to function as a region despite its poor communications and vastness. First, it

M

was a pastoral area for the most part over which horsemen moved rapidly and in which there had been a fairly fluid society. The second was that the meseta dominated the rest, so that its control by any strong power led to extensive expansion over the fringe areas (Teran y Sabaris). Yet these fringe areas have resisted the controller of the meseta: the Celtiberians against the Romans for long, the Sueves (Suevi) against the Visigoths, the little Christian kingdoms against Cordoba, and Portugal against Spain. When, for some reason, the central power weakened, Iberia easily disintegrated into a series of regions in our sense; perhaps the thirteenth century with a lag in regional conformation saw most division into regions since early Roman days.

The unity of the Moors under the Omayyad dynasty and its political power combined to make Iberia a definite region. Its great cities had a rank-order arrangement somewhat as follows[2]:

	Population *1,000s*	*Area* *hectares*
Cordoba	90	730
Seville	52	286
Toledo	28	106
Jerez de la Frontera	24	96
Badajoz	21	81
Granada	20	75
Murcia	17	65
Saragossa	12	47

The list thus has roughly a medieval rank-size series.[3] The capital, Cordoba, spread out over a great area, much of it, like the suburbs of Bagdad, in gardens with a heavily populated centre. If the Islamic areas had a population of six millions (with another million for the Christian areas in the north) at AD 1000, even the percentage of urbanisation was about the ordinary amount.

For the late thirteenth and early fourteenth century much the best information about Iberian cities comes from the region of Barcelona where a series of taxes on houses and households offers quite good information, even though most of it followed the plague. For some reason the hearth tax was not used in the parts of Iberia dominated by the Castilian dynasties. The next best information then comes from the areas within the city walls. The constant warfare in Iberia tended to discourage the setting up of suburbs outside their protection. The thirteenth century was probably a period of population growth in Iberia as elsewhere in the west and, given the already dense population within the walls of most cities, there must have been some building outside which historical research should eventually be able to define. The areas given in the table on p 178 are those enclosed by the walls.

The volume of Gutkind in the new *International History of City Development* on Spain is a general discussion of the history of the cities, but does usually give areas of cities at particular times and is thus of much help in the study of city population. The cities of the region of Barcelona, as we have seen can be estimated from the number of hearths or householders which appear in tax records. But with the exception of Baeza, Jerez de la Frontera and Soria there seem to be none for the rest of Spain, except Navarre. The latter is not included in any region; possibly it belongs to the region of Barcelona but it was somewhat isolated from it and had stronger connections apparently with the southwest French area. The Navarrese, like the Basques, were a proud, independent group and may not really have shared in any marked regional affiliation.

The distribution of the cities on the map of Iberia sets up, in addition to the region of Barcelona in the northeast of the peninsula, three regions: Portugal, south Spain with Cordoba very definitely as the centre, and a second of the Spanish cities to the north. The two groups of cities are so sharply separated on the map that there seems to be no objection to considering them as two regions. They have different historical backgrounds as well. Toledo was captured as early as 1086 and held not continuously but generally thereafter. Southern Iberia was not securely in the hands of the Castilian kingdom until the battle of Las Navas de la Tolosa in 1212; Cordoba was taken in 1236 and Seville in 1248. Granada, of course, remained in Moorish hands until 1492. The southern part had been well settled under the Romans and had a highly integrated economy as the Caliphate of Cordoba. The northern part was less fertile, a high, dry meseta and had developed only slowly over the centuries. Furthermore, it had developed no real centre or capital in the north. Toledo was an archbishopric and so was Santiago de Compostela; their provinces spread in long strips from the north to the south, along the line of the Reconquista. North and south communications were very poor in the north, and the energies of the people went mostly for resettlement and military activity.

Both sections spoke the Spanish language and the dialects were apparently not so different as in the French north. Perhaps the more mobile character of the pastoral culture of most of Iberia was responsible for this. But there were differences as, for instance, the western coast developed what is known as Portuguese. To the south developed distinct differences in pronunciation, notably the greater prevalence of the 's' sound, which is still noticeable. Moorish occupation seems to have affected other phases of life even more than its language. The peculiar institution of the Mesta, the organisation of sheep growers, who moved their flocks up into the meseta in the spring and back into the valleys in the fall, is primarily a southern region institution, perhaps derived from Moorish experience. Spain was perhaps the first country to adopt the vernacular rather than maintain the Latin language as its official language. It had done this in the reigns of Ferdinand II (1217–52) and of Alfonso X (1252–84). The northern part of the country had had a fairly uniform area since the time of Alfonso VI (1065–1100), while the south came into the control of the Spanish kings only after 1212; Granada, of course, as late as 1492.

The cities of Spain were, in general like most Islamic cities, more densely populated than those north of the Pyrenees, as Torres Balbas has demonstrated.[4] It should be noted that in 1587 Seville with an area of about 385 hectares had 14,381 houses or about 43 houses to the hectare and Madrid with about 185 hectares and 7,016 houses had about 38 houses to the hectare. He believed that the average holding was about 172 square metres which gives 58 to the hectare. However, some allowance must be made for streets and for the patios which are so typical of Islamic apartment house areas. One hundred seventy-two square metres is a space, for instance, of about 17 metres × 10.3 metres, or about 56 × 34 feet, that is, with no space for a patio within the building. Thus probably not over two-thirds of the area would be built over; let us suggest then about 40 holdings to the hectare. Torres Balbas[5] also suggested six to the holding. However, even in the sixteenth century when buildings were even more substantial and solid than in the earlier epoch, only Madrid and Seville of the Spanish samples then, had more than 5 to the house, and Madrid had 6.5. But both were terribly crowded then, Seville with the colonial trade and government and Madrid as the new capital. It seems best, then, to assume about 5 to the house and about 200 to the hectare. Even this seems high with respect to the actual data available.

THE REGION OF CORDOBA

The general plan of Cordoba as a region had been established by the Romans when the province of Baetica was set up as separate from the two other provinces of Tarragonesis and Lusitania about 138 BC. Its heart was the Baetis River (later Guadalquivir Valley with its great cities Cordoba and Ispalis (Sevilla) in the valley and Cadiz near its mouth. The upper course of the Guadiana River was a secondary area in the north. In the east was the almost tropical triangle of Malaga, Almeria, and Granada. Behind the coast and the great valleys were the Sierra Moreno and Sierra Nevada, parts of the Meseta, Thus the region was firmly established for centuries before the Arabs took it over in 711. And, of course, the Arabs found there an area admirably suited to their ways of life: the emirate and later caliphate of Cordoba was one of the gems of Islam, an area profoundly affected by its centuries under Arabic domination. In the thirteenth century, just taken over by Castile, it still was very Islamic in many of its aspects.

At its height Cordoba probably had an area of about 750 hectares and a population of about 90,000; the great extent of the city included some garden areas. With the fall of the Caliphate the city declined as a political factor but remained as a great industrial-commercial centre. The decline in political leadership and population, obvious in the disappearance of some of

TABLE 23: REGION OF CORDOBA

Rank,	City	Pop Est 1,000s	Hyp Est 1,000s	Area hectares	Base	Gutkind, p
1	Cordoba	60	60	385		485
2	Seville	40	27.5	225		498
3	Granada	30	23.4	170		
4	Almeria	18	18	90		447
5	Jaen	16	14.4	84		
6	Murcia	15	12.2	75		
7	Baeza	12.5	10.6	72	1407–1,785 vecinos	
8	Jerez de la Frontera	12	9.5	96	1266–2,058 casas	503
9	Merida	12	8.6	72		
10	Badajoz	9	7.8	50		
11	Malaga	8	7.2	45		
12	Ecija					

Seville: *Al Andalus* 18 (1953) 181. Granada: Torres Balbas, Granada 140. Almeria: Torres Balbas, Almeria 429. Murcia: Teran-Sabaris 380. Baeza: T. Gonzalez 91. Jerez de la Frontera: J. Gonzalez 82. Merida: Murray, 1890 288. Badajoz: Murray, 1890 290.

the suburbs, probably cost it about 15,000 persons which would reduce the population to about 75,000. Its solid area seems to have been about 385 hectares, which would still give it about 200 persons to the hectare, a density which the evidence of population decline would make seem much less. The 1530 census gives it 5,845 *vecinos pecheros,* at five to the *vecino* about 29,000 but that census may be as much as 40% under the actual number (perhaps 48,000). Nevertheless, it was to suffer from the rapid growth of its neighbour, Seville, in the sixteenth century. In the period with which we are dealing (perhaps too optimistically) Cordoba probably still had about 60,000, basing the estimate upon its greatness in commerce and industry. Its Moorish people do not seem to have been as much disturbed as they were in other cities at the conquest.

The second city in size was Seville, which at its height in the tenth century occupied an area of about 286 hectares[6] although its walls included only about 225 hectares.[7] The fighting before its final capture by Castile in 1248 was quite continuous and must have destroyed the extramural areas.

Juan Gil de Zamora[8] a contemporary Franciscan writer, called it a most powerful city, presumably the result of its sturdy resistance in 1248. In that year the Moorish population was driven out and this must have lost to the city a considerable industrial and commercial factor. The replacements came mostly from the central northern areas of Castile[9] and could hardly have been as valuable as industrial and commercial persons as the displaced. There are lists of about 2,500 persons apparently supported by lands outside of Seville given houses in the city.[10] Assuming that these were the new basic factor, the total population indicated by this would be seven times 2,500 or 17,500. However, the 225 hectares should have indicated a much larger population; the estimate is 40,000, largely a guess. In 1530, after the city had commenced a rapid growth as a result of the colonial ventures, it had 6,634 *vecinos pecheros*, 2,229 widows, 64 minors, 74 poor, and 79 exempt. The number of widows is suspect; even 1,229 would be a little large. Furthermore, the census is perhaps 40% under the actual, which would suggest that at this time Seville had about 50,000. It is hard to believe that Seville increased much for a time after her capture; the kings really did not stay there long and it can hardly be called a capital[11] with such a small bureaucracy.

Granada had greatness thrust upon it in this period. As the Moors were driven from one city after another in the thirteenth century, more and more retreated to Granada. The city's walls enclosed about 75 hectares in the eleventh to twelfth centuries but the area of habitation increased to 170 hectares in the thirteenth to fourteenth centuries.[12] It has been suggested by an eminent authority that these areas represent a population of about 26,000 and 50,000 respectively. However, it would take time to build up a city from refugees and, as we shall see, the average number of persons to the hectare was probably not so high in the cases of Baeza and Jerez de la Frontera. On the other hand Granada must have profited by the addition of thousands of highly skilled workers from the captured cities which, in the course of time, should have set up a basic factor there. We have to remember that many of the refugees may have expected to return to such places as Seville and Jerez de la Frontera. They had in folk memory the Almoravid and

Almohad invasions of the twelfth century and might have expected further invasions from Africa in the thirteenth. Probably only well into the fourteenth century were the Moors certain that they must make Granada their permanent home.

Almeria was the favoured port of the Moors and remained as a large emporium in the period, before decline set in after the Black Death. Its area was about 90 hectares which we assume, as a crowded seaport city, would have about 200 to the hectare or about 18,000.[13]

Jaen and Murcia apparently had about 84 and 74 hectares respectively and were well-built cities, strong in the Moorish period. Only about 50 kilometres from Murcia was the seaport of Cartagena, which had been a very important city in the time of the Romans,[14] but under the Moors, as Idrisi noted, it was a small place with ancient ruins and a pretty port.[15]

Fortunately, more information exists about two more which must have been about the next in size. Baeza in 1407 had about 1,785 *vecinos* which should have meant at least 2,500 *vecinos* before the plague and a population of about 12,500. Near Baeza (8 km) was a sizeable city, Ubeda, and to the west at 20 kilometres was Linares, so the urban developments may be considered quite important. The upper Guadalquivir River Valley was the site of extensive mineral and mining activities in the period. The area of Baeza seems to have been about 72 hectares which would give about 174 persons to the hectare. In 1266 Jerez de la Frontera had about 2,000 houses, which should have been a population of 10,000; its 96 hectares would have meant something over 100 to each hectare. The figure for the houses was taken at the time that the city was captured and the Moorish inhabitants driven out. At least the figures for these two cities suggest relatively modest densities even for the Moorish cities in the thirteenth century.

Following these four were a number of other cities, probably between 5,000 and 12,000 in population, which were located, with the exception of Malaga, some distance from the sea. In fact, it is rather curious that an area of such great size as the region of Cordoba should have so few seaports with such a long stretch of sea-coast. Or perhaps that so many seaports should have had such a small population. When one compares the coasts of either the west coast of Italy or the south coast of France, the small number of large seaports in south and east Spain is evident. There is the possibility that Fez in North Africa[16] occupied a spot in the scheme as the third city of the region, taking the place that Cadiz had once held as a major city in the area. Fez was about 240 kilometres from Gibraltar. Even from Roman days the area across from Cadiz had been regarded as almost a part of southern Spain.

The area of the region of Cordoba would appear to have been as follows:

	km²
Albacete	14,863
Almeria	8,778
Badajoz	21,647
Cadiz	7,323
Ciudad Real	19,741
Cordoba	13,727
Granada	12,529
Huelva	10,090
Jaen	13,480
Malaga	7,285
Murcia	11,317
Seville	14,062
	154,842

The census by dioceses of houses in 1597 is the first census which gives a fairly good indication of the population by smaller divisions of government for Spain. For Portugal there is an earlier one of 1527. These are being used on the general assumption that the population of the pre-plague period rose again in the sixteenth century beyond its pre-plague position so that the pre-plague population was about 88% of the 1597 census. In general the plague probably caused less decline in Iberia than in the rest of the continent because of a drier climate in much of the peninsula. Moreover, the Spanish and Portuguese seem to have developed a more permanent culture before much else of Europe and thus its institutions and even settlements, despite the devastations of Reconquista and plague, seem more settled than farther north.

For the region of Cordoba the data, by diocese, from the census of 1597 are:

	hearths
Almeria	3,476
Badajoz	24,014
Cadiz	11,850
Cartagena	20,117
Cordoba	38,463
Guadix	5,747
Granada	20,631
Jaen	34,281
Malaga	19,090
Military Orders	119,761
Seville	37,000
	334,430

The territory of the military order was mostly in the region of Cordoba; the number assigned to Seville is secured by subtracting from its archiepiscopal total (66,929) an appropriate number for its two suffragans of Cadiz and Malaga. The total then at 4.5 for the hearths (*caza*) was 1,505,000. The assumption is that the population of Spain before the plague was about 88% of that at the end of the sixteenth century and thus was about 1,320,000. The density was 8.6 to the km². This gives the city of Cordoba, assuming that it had a population of 60,000, about 4.5% of the regional population. This was a very high percentage, but then it was a famous commercial city. The urban index (224,500 for the largest ten cities) was about 17.0%, also a very high figure, placing that region among the Italian regions in high urban numbers.

THE REGION OF TOLEDO

The region of Toledo was almost unrelieved Meseta, raised even higher in the western Pyrenees. The higher mountains had naturally much more rain and was a natural source for Hispanic migration southward. Communication north and south was difficult since the great mountain ranges ran east and west; the large rivers descended to the Atlantic. Probably the region of Toledo was the most isolated in Europe, at least in the west.

The region of Toledo in the thirteenth century was still in the very transitional period of the Reconquista. The conditions of warfare along the Islamic-Christian frontier and even between those of the Islamic and Christian states themselves were not conducive to building up a large population spontaneously. As a result the states themselves, at least the conquering Christian states, developed interesting policies of re-settlement of the border areas, once they felt secure in their possession of more land. Nobles were given land grants in the newly-acquired, and even older settled, areas. These grants for 'populating' areas defined the limits of the grants, asserted what kinds of workers should be taken to the cities and, in the case of some villages, outlined their form of government. All of this was admirable preparation for the great expansion of the Spanish into the New World when similar problems arose. It explains, in part, the relatively rapid and smooth process by which so many Spanish settled in the New World in the sixteenth century. Of course, the experience which the kings of Aragon gained in the control of their overseas possessions in the late Middle Ages, Sicily, Naples (for a time) and the Balearic Islands, also helped them in the age of colonial expansion.

The region of Toledo was very different from those of Barcelona and Cordoba. No city stood out for its size and the first ten range in area from about 130 hectares within walls to 50 hectares. One reason is that Castile developed no real capital and no extensive bureaucracy. With its power and wealth the establishment of a fixed capital would have surely stimulated the growth of the chosen city. The economic life of the north was always subordinate to the political and military (perhaps even to the religious life) for the period of the Reconquista. The economic life tended to centre in fairs, such as those of Medina del Campo and Medina del Rio Seco, which no more produced large cities than did the Fairs of Champagne. Even the great wagon trains were migratory. The nobles, as more and more territory was opened in the south, tended to live in the country estates rather than in the cities. And, living in the country, they failed to share in city government and participate in business affairs, as did gentry and nobility of Italy or even of the region of Barcelona. The region of Toledo then singularly failed in the development of cities; its regional development was always rudimentary.

The Franciscan writer, Juan Gil de Zamora, wrote, circa 1300, that Toledo was populous beyond other Spanish cities.[17] His ability to judge numbers may be estimated by his further remark that in the city there were 70,000 tribute-paying Jews, a typical medieval exaggeration. The walls of Toledo enclosed 106 hectares and there was a suburb across the river containing perhaps another 25 hectares. We assume that Zamora meant that people were very badly crowded in the city, and suggest 40,000, the city's population in the sixteenth century, as a probable estimate for the pre-plague period. It was an important religious centre since its archbishop was the primate of Spain. It was also a considerable industrial centre and the commercial centre of the Tagus River Valley. However, it had little that resembled a capital for the kings, and the nobles do not seem to have settled there in any numbers. Perhaps it was too crowded and too industrial for them.

The second and third cities in size were probably Salamanca and Valladolid with 119 and 118 hectares respectively within their walls. Nevertheless, there was probably a considerable difference in population before the plague as there is today. Salamanca had a great and respected university but otherwise was in a rather unfavourable economic position in the upper reaches of a tributary of the Duero River, not even on an outstanding trade route. Probably then it had a usual medieval density of 120 to the hectare, or since Islamic influence was still strong there, as much as 150 to the hectare with a total population of perhaps 15,000. Valladolid, however, was in a central position in the Duero Valley. It was a centre for roads: to Soria, farther up the river, to Burgos up one tributary (the Pisuerga, partway), to Avila south on another tributary (the Adaja) down the river itself past Simancas to Zamora. The great fairs of an earlier era were not far away at Medina del Rio Seco to the north-west and Medina del Campo south south-west. The walls were built earlier in the era of fighting in the Duero valley. The chances then are that settlement had

TABLE 24: REGION OF TOLEDO

Rank,	City	Pop Est 1,000s	Hyp Est 1,000s	Area hectares	Base	Source Gutkind
1	Toledo	40	40	130		
2	Valladolid	25	23.8	118		363
3	Salamanca	15	15.6	119		385
4	Burgos	10	12	54		357
5	Zamora	8	9.6	50		380
6	Santiago de Compostela	7	8.2	35		344, *EUI*
7	Alcala de Henares	6	7.1	52		412
8	Segovia	6	6.3	40		268
9	Ciudad Rodrigo	5	5.7	48		
10	Soria	4	5.2	100	1270–777 *vecinos*	317
11	Madrid	3	4.8			

Alcala de Henares: Garcia Fernandez 356 (perhaps 70 hectares?). Soria: Jimeno 207–74. Madrid: Courtenay: *Geography* 24 (1959) 22–34. Medina del Campo had only about 25 hectares.

gone beyond them and that the city itself had at least 25,000 at the time.

Of the other cities none seems very large. Burgos was among the most promising with a fair site in northern Castile which enjoyed a plentiful rainfall, but its 60 hectares probably did not hold ten thousand people. A number of cities with walls enclosing from 40 to 60 hectares probably had about 6,000 to 8,000 inhabitants: Zamora in the Deuro Valley, Segovia and Alcala de Henares on either side of the Sierra de Guaderrama were in this class. Santiago de Compostela, although one of the greatest shrines of the west, second only to Rome, had walls enclosing only 35 hectares and probably a population of 7,000 as a limit. Two cities which in the fourteenth century had larger areas are known to have had quite small populations. Soria within walls about 100 hectares had only 777 *vecinos* (neighbours) in 1270. If *vecino* had the usual connotation of householder, the city cannot have had more than 4,000 people. Similarly the newly-established Madrid with apparently 115 hectares had only 3,000 early in the sixteenth century. The older cities of the north, such as Oviedo, Leon and Lugo, seem to have been even smaller.

For the census of 1597 the following are the number of *cazas* (hearths or houses) for the three archbishoprics of Burgos, Toledo and Santiago de Compostela which were in the region of Toledo:

Burgos		*Santiago de Compostela*	
Burgos	66,732	Astorga	40,622
Calahorra	27,767	Avila	41,977
Palencia	43,316	Ciudad Rodrigo	12,805
		Coria	26,523
	137,815	Lugo	3,872
		Mondoñedo	15,971
Toledo		Orense	28,412
Cuenca	58,190	Plasencia	28,376
Leon	33,544	Salamanca	33,201
Osma	21,518	Santiago de	
Oviedo	80,000	Compostela	33,535
Valladolid	7,691	Tuy	13,834
Segovia	24,598	Zamora	23,284
Siquenza	24,351		
Toledo	20,000		302,412
	269,892		

The totals then are:

Burgos	137,815
Toledo	269,892
Santiago de Compostela	302,432
	710,119

At 4.5 to the *caza* and assuming that the pre-plague population was 88% of the late sixteenth-century population, the pre-plague population would have been about 2,816,000 and the density by km^2 about 15.2, since its area was about 184,000km^2.

The city of Toledo, if it had 40,000, was about 1.43% of the total population of the region, about the average of metropolitan cities then. Similarly the urban index, adding up to

126,000 for the ten largest cities, would have been about 4.5%, again about average. However, both the regions of Cordoba and Barcelona had primate cities larger than the average. It would seem that either sections of the region of Toledo depended upon Barcelona and Cordoba or that the region of Toledo was just not as urbanised as its two neighbours. The taking over of Spain by the people of the region of Toledo thus did not bid fair for the future of that country. Much of its later backwardness may have resulted from the domination by the less urbanised part of the kingdom.

THE REGION OF LISBON

The region of Lisbon was largely the product of its location. It was almost as isolated as Ireland, before the Atlantic became a frequent line of communication. The tendency was to move towards the Mediterranean even though Portugal was a pleasant and fertile land, enjoying the benefit of western winds from the Atlantic and of fishing in that ocean. The rivers opened up valleys but were not navigable (with exceptions) beyond the boundary of the region: the mountains set up a natural eastern limit. In Roman days it had been inhabited largely by one tribe, the Lusitani, and was set up as a province of the Roman Empire, Lusitania, largely but not entirely of the area of Portugal. Although a part of the Visigothic Kingdom and later the emirate and caliphate of Cordoba, it became in the north a separate kingdom from the Castilian kingdom and by 1200 had become a recognized kingdom of its own. Even its language was quite distinct from that of its neighbour by that time. Its population probably grew more rapidly with safer voyages from the Mediterranean to the English Channel after 1280.[18]

The data about the region of Lisbon were relatively good in the form of totals of hearths (*cazas*) for 1417[19] and 1427.[20] For 1417 the density for the km² by the number of hearths is given.

District	Area	Number of cazas 1417	Density in 1417	Number of hearths 1527
Entre Douro e Minho	7,226	22,250	3.1	55,099
Traz os Montes	11,116	21,451	1.9	35,686
Beira	24,000	67,310	2.8	66,804
Estremadura	17,800	50,641	2.8	65,482
Alemtejo	24,390	79,180	3.3	48,304
Algarve	4,850	11,240	2.3	28,410
	89,382	252,072		299,785

It can be seen that, if the figures are accurate, that there was a great change in the population of the several parts of Portugal. The two northern provinces grew rapidly while Alemtejo declined considerably. Estremadura increased modestly while Beira remained much the same. However, the population of the two southern provinces raises a question as to whether the boundaries remained in the same place during the period. The totals of the two are not greatly different if added together for the two periods.

The problem of estimating the number to the *caza* was made easier for the 1527 data because the manuscript gives the number of men stated to be from 18 to 30 as 38,000 in the province of Entre Douro e Minho which has 55,000 cazas. Using the life table for men born of English fief holders, 1426–50 shows the 18–30 age group to have 7,548 of 32,765,[21] which was thus 1/4.34 of the total. This gave an average of three men to the *caza* and since the medieval sex ratio, was apt to be about 120 males to 100 females, a total of 5.5 persons to the house. However, this was in a largely agricultural province where houses were larger than city dwellings, often apartments. Since it was also not certain whether exactly thirty years was meant rather than a rounded thirty and whether the ill were included, five was probably a more accurate number for each *caza*. For 1417, if the situation was like that of Italy at about the same time, four rather than five would seem a fair estimate, given the high mortality of the plague in the period.

The population of Portugal then of about 1527 should have

been about 1.5 millions and about one million in 1417. This conformed to the results for most of the European countries of that day, the recovery from the depths of the depression of the plague. Portugal had been stimulated by the extensive exploration and concomitant commerce since the early part of the fifteenth century and thus probably had grown faster than most countries in the period of recovery. This should have meant that the population of Portugal was somewhat less before the plague than it was in 1527; for the earlier period we assume that Portugal had about 1.25 millions. We might assume also that the damper parts of Portugal, notably the northern parts, had suffered more from the plague since damper areas (humidity 68–80°) usually did suffer more and thus were comparatively larger before 1348 than the more southern areas.

The problem of estimating the area of the larger cities lies in the very limited information about most of them in respect of the area of the walls of the majority and the 1527 population of a few of them. The largest city would seem to have been Lisbon. It had grown rapidly from the time of its capture in 1147 by the Portuguese and the English-German crusading expedition. Its area of about 1373–75 was about 105 hectares which we

TABLE 25: REGION OF LISBON

Rank,	City	Pop Est 1,000s	Hyp Est 1,000s	Area hectares	Base	Source
1	Lisbon	20	20	104		Gutkind 65
2	Evora	12	11.9	104?		Gutkind 32
3	Santarem	7	7.8	75?	1527–1,988 cazas	Da Silva 501
4	Oporto	6	6			
5	Coimbra	6	4.8		1527–1,209 cazas	Da Silva 501
6	Beja		4			
	Abrantes					
	Aveiro	4.5			1527–894 cazas	Da Silva 501
	Braga					
	Guarda					
	Silves					
	Vizieu					

Oporto ; David, *Lisbon* 77.

N

assume to have held about 20,000 persons, since it had been primarily a Moorish city with some suburbs. The figures which the crusaders present about the city are, as usual, fantastic.

Of the other cities of Portugal, Evora seems to have had the largest area, nearly as large as that of Lisbon, but the population was probably less dense than the population of that city. It was centre of the very large and prosperous province of Alemtejo and should have been one of the country's largest cities. Twelve thousand is an estimate based on the size of the city which, after being taken from the Moors, probably was only average in density. The city of Santarem had walls enclosing about 75 hectares. It had a good position in Estremadura but must have suffered from competition from the rapidly growing Lisbon down the river. It probably had 7,000 or 8,000 population before the plague. Coimbra had 1,209 cazas in 1527 and probably had about the same population which should mean about 6,000, before the plague. Its position was not as favourable as those of Evora and Santarem but it had a university much of the time. There were a number of other cities which probably had a few thousands before the plague but more evidence is needed before they can be properly sorted out by size.

Before the Second Crusade of 1147 Oporto had suffered severe devastation, so that the chronicler of the English-low Country Expedition, probably Ranulf de Glanville, wrote in the words of that city's citizen:[22] 'Even this city of ours which you see, once so prosperous, now reduced to the semblance of an insignificant village.' But it revived and had a wall, apparently built about AD 1374 enclosing some 54 hectares. However, Oporto was the chief port of central and northern Portugal although the city was built on forbidding hillsides. As in the case of Siena, much must have been built outside of the walls. It is the one quite favourable place for a sizeable city besides those already discussed, and 6,000 is suggested for the size of the city for its 54 hectares.

Earlier the population of Portugal before the Black Death was estimated at about 1,250,000. Lisbon at 20,000 then should have been about 1.6% of the population of Portugal, a fair figure for as average a country as that state should have been then. The total for the largest ten cities must have been in the neighbourhood of 93,000, assuming that at least ten cities should have had 4,000 persons in that period. This gives an urban index of 7.4, somewhat about the average. The small size of the total population over the area still gives a density of population of 14.0 to the km² of the country.

The state of Iberia in its transition from the Islamic-oriented regional situation was the prelude to its new condition in the sixteenth century when its orientation was essentially trans-atlantic. By then Seville was the centre for shipping and for the governmental agencies which dealt with the new world. The new series of rank-order cities is the following:

	Population 1,000s
Seville	120
Cordoba	71
Lisbon	48
Toledo	41

This was just before Madrid was made capital of Spain by Philip II in 1560; following this its population increased rapidly. By the end of the thirteenth century Iberia was becoming integrated to the point where at least the regions of Toledo and Cordoba were merging. The great wagon companies were creating an all-Iberian communications system. The Meseta was moving sheep from lowland winter quarters to upland summer pastures. Still the Aragon-Catalonian region remained outside for the most part and participated in Mediterranean economy.

The estimate of the population of Iberia based on the regions thus is:

Four regions	Barcelona	1,221,340
	Cordoba	1,320,000
	Toledo	3,540,000
	Lisbon	1,250,000
		6,591,000
Other areas: Alicante, Navarre, Basque provinces, perhaps		400,000
	Total	6,991,000

The total was approximately seven millions just before the plague and probably about the same about AD 1500. This estimate is considerably less than earlier estimates for these two periods[23] of about 9.5 and 8.3 millions. This is in line with the general scaling down of population estimates of the pre-modern world.

The regions of Iberia were already divided by 1348 in their interests and in their historical development. At this stage they seem headed for development of three separate nations which only the accident of the marriage of Ferdinand and Isabella prevented.

10

Two Near-eastern Regions:
Antioch and Cairo

THE REGIONS OF Antioch and Cairo occupy part of one of the oldest settled world areas: the Fertile Crescent. The two are quite different in background. Antioch, lying between the three great centres of population in Mesopotamia, Asia Minor, and the Nile Valley—was the seat of constant warfare and passage between the great centres. Cairo, by contrast, was one of the least invaded and most isolated areas in Eurasia. From the east and north Mesopotamia was easily invaded and so was Syria.

One reached Egypt easily only by the narrow land connection at Suez or by sea. Even over the latter travellers still had the difficult Delta to cross, as St Louis IX discovered after taking Damietta in 1248. From an ethnographic standpoint, Egypt had observed little disturbance over the centuries, while Syria was a melting-pot of racial groups drifting in or driving in from all sides.

From a physical standpoint also, the two were ecologically quite different. The region of Cairo was based almost entirely on the annual flood in the Nile Valley while the region of Antioch was about as varied an area—sea, mountains, plain and desert—as any in Eurasia. One can assume a homogeneity of the Nile Valley just as one can assume that it would suffer relatively few invasions of a serious character but it might be felt that Syria would not have an integrated region as much because of its geographical diversity as because of its position between two areas of potentially heavy population in Egypt and the Mesopotamia.

The period of study of the two regions is not quite the same. For Cairo the two great polyptyques of 1298 and 1315 provide the base for estimating the population for the whole country while the street plans were finished just before the outbreak of the Black Death. The region of Cairo is accordingly examined in the early fourteenth century. The period for the region of Antioch was somewhat earlier. There much of the evidence concerned the Crusades and their fall in the twelfth and early thirteenth century. Saladin had conquered most of even Palestine by 1200 and the general condition of the country did not change much in the course of the period before the Black Death. Probably the population did not change much in the period either.

The region of Antioch was multilingual for most of the thirteenth century. In the east around Damascus there was a relative uniformity of Arabic and its local dialects. However, as long as the Crusaders were in control, its ruling class spoke French and kept records, mostly in Latin. In addition a considerable number of peasant colonists also spoke French dialects. The coastal cities, like the countryside, probably had a majority of Arabic-speaking inhabitants although in the Italian 'quarters' of their cities Italian was much spoken. This area then provides a comparison with the region of Ghent where many languages were also spoken. By the end of the century the Egyptian conquest of the country from the 'Franks' reduced the extent of French-spoken territory. Probably French declined as the Syrian inhabitants absorbed alien elements in the population. By the end of the century Syria began to show the homogeneity so characteristic of most regions.

The region of Cairo had an essential linguistic unity: the mass of the people had in the course of centuries accepted and spoke Arabic. Its great schools were in Cairo. A considerable proportion of the people spoke and wrote Coptic, the ordinary language of the Christians. There were in the commercial cities 'quarters' of Jews, Italians, and occasionally others. The Turkish and Negro garrisons in Cairo were obvious exceptions to the general Arabic outlook. This was a natural result of the century-old isolation of much of Egypt from outside invasion or influence. Louix IX in 1249 captured Damietta but became bogged down in the Delta and lost his army there. It was not much easier to invade from the south. In fact this was a period

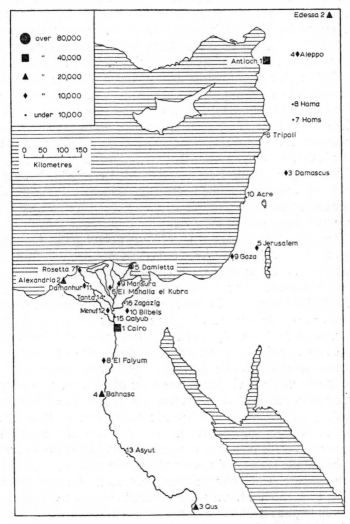

Fig 9 The regions of Cairo and Antioch

of expansion both to the west in the Delta and to the south in the Nile Valley.

THE REGION OF ANTIOCH[1]

Syria was a definite concept for a long time, at least as far back as the Roman Empire under Diocletian when it was the diocese of the East (*Oriens*). It was so described by the great chronicler, William of Tyre. Both included the Cilicias in the north-west and an area in Arabia (Palestine *Salutaria, Arabia*) in the south. Both also included the upper Mesopotamia about Edessa. When the Armenians took over the Cilicias in 1198, they moved it more into the sphere of Asia Minor or at least into a neutral zone, while the southern and south-east areas probably were more closely associated with Arabia than with Syria since they were dominated by the great Islamic highway from Egypt to Bagdad. Under the Crusaders much of Syria was united although they failed to include Damascus and a part of the upper Orontes River Valley, a very important part of the area.

The data about area of cities in Syria is very good. Archaeological research has been very extensive and detailed there, in part because of its Biblical connections as the early site of Christianity and in part because of French interest in it arising out of the Crusades. To convert these data into population estimates of city size, one must assume that population was distributed fairly evenly within the city walls and that there were few suburbs; constant warfare reduced cities to distinctly functional units without suburbs. The characteristic one- or two-storey house made for an evenness of population distribution within the city, while capture and fires reduced even the buildings within the city to rebuildable structures. Few cities had the open spaces which marked Antioch and Baalbeck, the ancient walls of which were built in a more splendid past. Probably the density of medieval cities in general, about 125 to the hectare, would give a reasonable estimate for most Syrian cities, even though Islamic cities tended to have densities running as high as 200 to 300 to the hectare.

In the case of Tyre, a city with a famous past, some idea of density can be obtained from Marsilius Georgius' report upon the Venetian 'third' of that city. It listed edifices (*domus*) containing rooms (*habitationes, camere*) as well as shops (*stationes*)

and stalls (*tabule, banche*). Three storey buildings are mentioned with shops on the ground floor and living quarters
above. The total of 26 *domus*, generally not divided, 33 *camere*
and 27 *habitationes* comes to only 86 and, with 34 *stationes*
added, only to about 120, which can hardly have accommoda-
ted more than 600 persons. Adding a palace and perhaps
other places for which no rent would be paid probably did not
increase the population by more than 300, for a total of 900
for the 'third.' All the city, assuming that Venice had a real
third would have about 2,700. The area of the medieval city
seems about 20 hectares for an average of 135 to the hectare.

TABLE 26: REGION OF ANTIOCH ABOUT AD 1200

Rank,	City	Pop Est 1,000s	Hyp Est 1,000s	Area hectares	Source
1	Antioch	40.6	40	340	Krey 126
2	Edessa	24	22.8	192	Rey 309
3	Damascus	15	15.6	121	mosque 11,000qm Sauveget, *Le Plan* 331–2
4	Aleppo	14	12	102	Sauveget, *Alep* lvi, lviii
5	Jerusalem	10	9.6	82	
6	Tripoli	8	8.2	80	
7	Hims, Homs	7	7.1	56	*Ency. of Islam* 320
8	Hamah	6.75	6.3	54	
9	Gaza	6.1	5.7	48.6	
10	Hebron (or Acre)	5.6	5.8	44	

Edessa: map on p 309, no scale, but chateau said to be 400 by 100m.
Damascus: plan of mosque in G. Le Strange, *Palestine under the
Moslems* (Boston, 1890) 226. Jerusalem: map in W. R. Shepherd,
Historical Atlas (New York, 1923) 63. Tripoli: perhaps same as present
site: Baedeker, *Palestine and Syria* (Leipzig, 1876) 510. Hamah: P. J.
Riis, *Fouilles et recherches*, 1931–38 Copenhagen, 1948), II, 3. Gaza:
D. Mackenzie, 'The Port of Gaza and Excavation in Palestine,' *Pales-
tine Exploration Fund, Quarterly Statement*, 1918, p 72 for plan.
Hebron: L. H. Vincent and E. H. J. Mackey, *Hebron, le Haran, el
Khalil* (Paris. 1923) 132.

In this period Antioch did not enjoy, as it had in Seleucid
and even Roman times, the advantage of being a kind of
capital. The Principate of Antioch could hardly have been

larger in population than either of its neighbours, the counties of Edessa and Tripoli, so that the greater size of the city must have been the result of its commerce. The main trade route was, of course, from the Mediterranean to Mesopotamia; Antioch was a great caravan city. A secondary trade route came in by way of the Cilician Gates and continued up the Orontes Valley to Homs, Hama, and Damascus. Given these trade routes, it is not surprising that it was the metropolitan city of the region. Yet it must have had a considerable manufacturing base as well to overshadow Damascus with its 'damask' and the more northern cities of Aleppo and Edessa. Thus the orientation of the population of the region of Antioch was based primarily upon the trade and industry of the Near Eastern world rather than upon political conditions.

Antioch was recognised by William of Tyre[2] as the greatest city in Syria and one of the largest at the time. Its Byzantine walls enclosed an area of about 600 hectares which included land from the Orontes River well up into the high hills away from the river. The crusaders built a wall at the bottom of the hills. The total area between the new wall and the river was about 325 hectares, the area assumed to have been occupied about 1200. Al-Idrisi, writing about 1154, saw mills, orchards and gardens within the walls, but the mills could have been on the river and the others in the hills. Ibn-Hauqal, writing about 978, reported that there were fields, gardens and mills within the city, which would suggest a smaller city even than in 1154.

Contemporary estimates of the population at the time of its capture in 1268, in typical medieval fashion, ran as high as 100,000. Some 17,000 were alleged to have been killed in action in addition to 100,000 prisoners taken and 8,000 soldiers within the citadel. If we assume a population density of 125 to the hectare for 325 hectares, the total would have been about 40,600 which seems reasonable for the metropolitan centre of Syria. It will be noticed below that, assuming the pattern of Syrian cities conformed to the normal medieval pattern, the population of Antioch should have been about 42,500 as derived from the estimates of sizes of the next two cities, Edessa and Damascus.

Edessa (Urfa) was apparently the second largest city in

Syria and the metropolis of upper Mesopotamia. Its area was about 192 hectares, which, at 125 to the hectare, would give a population of about 24,000. Some 30,000 were alleged to have been killed in two sieges, almost certainly exaggerations. The statement that 12,000 to 16,000 persons, mostly young women and children, were captured, may be more accurate. The children, presumably aged about fourteen and under, should have been about a third of the population. The addition of young women and others might well have added up to more than half of the total, making 24,000 a reasonable estimate for the whole city. Edessa had to pay on one occasion 20,000 pieces of gold to save itself. At two pieces (dinars?) a head, this might represent a male population over sixteen years of age for a city of about 24,000. Two dinars a head was a normal payment a year for Christians and Jews under Islam and thus would be an obvious amount to suggest for a tribute.

A detailed study has been made of the historical geography of Damascus[3] which argues that in the eleventh century, after reconstruction of its walls, it had an area of about 120 hectares, suggesting a population of about 15,000. The great mosque of Damascus had an inside surface of about 11,000m². Such a Friday mosque was expected to accommodate the entire adult Islamic male congregation of the city, perhaps a trifle less than a third of the civic population. Allowing about two m² to each worshipper, since he had to prostrate himself on his knees, there should have been room for about 15,000, thus about the same as the city area suggests. A complication is that Damascus lay in a fertile valley—a typical Islamic 'garden'—in which there was a high density of agricultural population. The question remains as to whether such an area should be classed as a suburb, with men normally worshipping in the Friday mosque.

The fourth city in size was probably Aleppo (Halab) which had an area of about 70 hectares at the end of the eleventh century and increased to about 112 hectares in the middle of the thirteenth century. It was also studied by Sauvaget.[4] Tancred offered 20,000 dinars for it at the time of the first Crusade. Its population was thus probably about 14,000 by 1250.

The most famous city of all, Jerusalem, was smaller than

might be guessed from its historical importance. In 1187 it
had an area of about 82 hectares and almost no suburbs. At
its fall in that year it was alleged that 11,000 to 14,000 persons
were sold into slavery, 2,000 to 3,000 were granted clemency,
and another 7,000 were freed because they were so poor. The
total population, according to the minimum of these figures,
is 20,000. The number is doubtless exaggerated even if the
siege had caught within the city refugees from other places
captured by Saladin as well as neighbouring farmers. Jerusalem
was said to have had 30,000 when it was captured in 1244:
30,000 being a typical medieval symbol for a large number.
Its 80 hectares, however, should have held a population of
about 10,000.

Tripoli became the head of a fair-sized fief in the course
of the twelfth century. A Persian who saw it about 1109 said
that it measured 1,000 cubits square. If the cubit was about
half a metre in length, the area should have been about 25
hectares. However, this was probably old Tripoli (al-Mina or
Tripoli Marine) on the coast. A new city arose near the lord's
castle which reached about 80 hectares. Its density is given
about 100 to the hectare, since the process of moving doubtless thinned the population. The old city may have originally
had a fairly dense population. Nasir-i Khusraw in 1047 said
that Tripoli had a population of 20,000, probably an exaggeration, while the Persians remarked upon hostelries of four
and five storeys. In the thirteenth century it was known for its
schools and was alleged to have had 4,000 employed in its silk
factories which as a basic factor should assume a city of
24–28,000 persons. Despite these statements, the area would
seem to suggest a population of only about 8,000. After these
cities the order by size becomes less clear and, in terms of
estimating total population, of less importance. Homs (Hims,
Emesa) was said by Mukaddasi about 985 to have no superior
in all Syria, probably an over-enthusiastic remark. Homs had
been the capital of one of the Syrian divisions of the government of the Caliphate. In the time of the Crusades, it apparently was about 56 hectares in size, with presumably a
population of about 7,000. It lay in the upper reaches of the
fertile valley of the Orontes River, not far from Hamah, which
had an area of about 54 hectares, assumed to have a popula-

tion of about 6,750. Gaza had an area of about 45 hectares, but the wall may have been an ancient one, protecting a smaller area during the Crusades. Just why there should have been so large a city so near Jerusalem is very uncertain, Acre, even in 12000, was probably among the first ten cities. We have to bear in mind that data from the north-eastern part of Syria is scant and that, for this reason, some of its cities may have been among the list mentioned.

These were apparently the largest cities which maintained their population throughout the period. Another city, Acre (ancient Ptolemais), was among the largest at the end of the period, the result of increasing concentration by crusaders there as they lost the rest of the land. In 1047 Nasri defined it as being 2,000 ells long and 500 wide. If an ell was a metre in length and his measurement was correct, the city enclosed about 100 hectares then. When the Franks captured it in 1191 however, there were said to have been only 3,000 captives. In the thirteenth century, Acre increased until near the end it was about 85 hectares in size. Since it became a kind of capital soon after the crusaders took it in 1191, it probably joined the first ten cities within a few years.

As seen in Table 26, the pattern of Syrian cities conforms with reasonable closeness to the normal pattern of medieval cities. If the numbers of persons to the hectare is considered to be 125, and Antioch had about 2.67 millions, perhaps about 1200. The evidence about Antioch, Damascus and Aleppo would suggest also an increasing population in the period. The ten largest cities thus would seem to have held about 130,000, while an equal number might be expected for another sizeable groups of cities and market towns. Subtracting these from the estimated total population would give about 2.4 millions. The urban index was then about 5.2 and the density of population of Syria's 109,000km² about 24.5.

The estimate assigned to the villages can be tested roughly against information about density of settlement and size of villages in the time of the crusaders. The evidence would show a variation in size of village territory: 100 villages near Caesarea within 1,200 km² with an average of 12.0km², 300 villages near Nieblus within 2,000km² with an average of 6.7km² and 120 villages near Tyre within 450km² with an average of 3.75km². The round numbers give a suspicious quality to the data. All three areas were in relatively settled areas in a country which had much mountainous territory. The inhabited area was probably about 100–110,000km². Dividing the largest estimate (12km²) into the smaller estimate of total area (100,000km²) gives about 8,300 villages, while dividing the middle estimate (7km²) into the larger estimate (110,000 km²) gives about 17,000 villages, certainly a wide variation. Villages near Tyre, for some reason (see Table 27) seem notably smaller than others, so the estimate based on the smaller units near that city seem out of the question.

TABLE 27: ESTIMATE OF SIZE OF SYRIAN VILLAGES

Area Near	Number of Villages	Total units	Average unit	Estimate of average village population
Ascalon	14		46 plows	230
Bira	1	90+50 families	140	700
Nazareth	4	200 plows	40	200
Safad	260	10,000 men	39.2	196
Tyre	11	184 plows	17	85

Sources: Ascalon, Cahen, p 296; Prawer, p 54. Bira, Prawer, p 1087; Eugene de Roziere, *Cartulaire de l'Eglise du Saint Sepulchre de Jerusalem* (Paris, 1899), pp 240–50. Nazareth: Cahen, p 296. Safad, Cahen quoting S. Baluze, *Miscellaneorum Liber Sextus* (1713) VI, 368. The date was 1240. Tyre: Tafel and Thomas, pp 370–83.

The population of the villages, as estimated in Table 27, would be about 200 to 210 to the village. At this size the total village population estimate would vary from a low of 1.67–1.75 millions to a high of 3.4–3.6 millions. Since the villages concerned in the estimate of village size tended to be in the better settled areas, some figure nearer the lesser number of villages seems the better choice. At 200 to the village the suggested village population 2.4 millions would suggest 11,730–12,000 villages, nearer 8,300 than 17,000 villages.

In many respects Syria is a fine example of the importance of the region. As long as the caravan routes from Mesopotamia and Egypt were open, as long as merchants came from Byzantine and the western Mediterranean cities, and as long as Christian, Jewish and even Islamic pilgrims came to the shrines of Jerusalem and the Holy Land, it was the centre of normal activity. The cities maintained a hierarchy of importance as in a well integrated area. To the people, the Crusades were just simply another episode in their subjection to invading foreigners; Saladin and control by Egypt was another. With all of the invaders the local people had certain relations, paid certain taxes, and continued their commerce, their farming, and even their industry as before. The land, the sky, the water were eternal; the rulers were ephemeral.

The thirteenth century was not one of the great ages of the region of Antioch. At about 40,000 the city was perhaps half of the size of Roman Antioch. In contrast to Cairo and Egypt which must by 1300 have been nearly the size of Roman Egypt, it was relatively small. The reasons are not hard to find. The desiccation of great areas next to the desert east and south-east of Antioch reduced the agricultural base for the area. The low state of Mesopotamia in the period reduced the volume of commerce from that very important source, while the reduction in prosperity of Asia Minor helped in the decline in trade from that area. The fall of Constantinople also must have encouraged the decline in the Middle East. It was in the twilight of its greatness. From this time on it suffered from invasions and in the general poor conditions of the Near East.

THE REGION OF CAIRO[5]

The ecological unity of Egypt has been mentioned, a unity so absolutely indivisible that seldom in historical times was the valley below the cataracts divided. Furthermore, its dry climate has preserved treasures of unrivalled quantity and value. The sources for the thirteenth century have not been studied as carefully as earlier data, as is natural, so that much further evidence for the medieval period may be expected.

After conquering Egypt in the seventh century, the Arabs followed their custom of moving capitals inland by setting up Fustat as a capital and then moving it to nearby Cairo about AD 969. Its position at the head of the Delta was as obviously the proper location for a capital in Egypt as such metropolitan centres as Cordoba, London, or Milan were in their regions. Cairo had an area of only about 176 hectares, which, even if it had possessed the usual density of Islamic cities, about 250 to the hectare, would give a population of about 45,000. To this however should probably be added the people of neighbouring settlements on the island, in Gizeh, Babylon and perhaps Old Fustat, bringing a total of perhaps 60,000 which would be about the average 1.5% of the total population estimated for the country.

TABLE 28: REGION OF CAIRO

Rank	Name	Pop Est 1,000s	Hyp Est 1,000s	Area hectares	Document: add to L.C. Doc D, no 88
1	Cairo	60	60	200	
2	Alexandria	30–35	34.2	200	
3	Qus	25?	23.4	54+	
4	Bahnesa		20.0	18	
5	Damietta	18–20	14.4	65–83	685–1898
6	Al-Mahallah al Kubra	18	12.2	63–87	
7	Rosetta		15.0	10.6	60	
8	Medina al-Fayyum	15.0	9.5	54–69	749–50 1933
9	Mansura	13.8	8.6	45–64	720–1935
10	Bilbeis	11.3	7.8	45–64	
11	Damanhur	10.0	7.2	41	679–1932
12	Menuf	10.0	6.7	35–40	851–2–1940
13	Asyut	8.8	6.2	35	685–1914
14	Tanta	7.5	5.8	30	688–1914
15	Qaliub	6.2	5.3	25	
16	Zagazig	5.5			868

Perhaps as large as some of these were Akhmin, Sammanaud, Tinis.

As a new city, Cairo doubtless attracted business ventures only slowly from ancient and well established Egyptian cities. It was very easy to float past the city on the river to the cities and ports of the Nile Delta. Cairo gradually became the political, religious and, finally, intellectual centre before becoming an economic capital. Nevertheless, it profited by favourable water transportation, always cheaper than land travel. Navigation on the Nile was favoured by the current downstream and by a consistent breeze blowing upstream.

The heavily-loaded grain ships could be carried by the current and the returning ships, emptier and standing higher in the water, could take advantage of the winds.

The size of Alexandria is hard to estimate, although it seems to have been larger than Damietta and was probably the second city in size in Egypt. In AD 811 walls enclosing about 300 hectares had been built to hold a city of perhaps 50,000, the capital of Egypt when the country had a population of about 2.5 millions. But since then Cairo had become capital and two other ports, Damietta and Rosetta, more competitive. However, Egypt's population had risen to nearly four million and had become very prosperous. Perhaps 30–35,000 would be a reasonable estimate for Alexandria in the late thirteenth century. Given the great commerce of Egypt in that period, it could hardly have been smaller in size.

Of the other cities, Qus is placed third, even though Abulfeda, contemporary observer, said that after Fustat (Cairo) there was no larger city in Egypt and that it was full of traders from Aden. Maqrizi called it the largest city in the Said (Upper Egypt) and added that during the plague of 1404 it lost 17,000 inhabitants. It was the capital of Upper Egypt and its *wali* (governor) in the thirteenth century was in charge of the Red Sea fleet operating out of Aidab. Qus enjoyed great days, especially when the Crusaders made the Suez area unsafe. Today its site is a small place of about 54 hectares, but its mound has probably been mined for building materials for nearby cities. Qus inherited a key position in that part of Egypt, held earlier by Thebes and Coptas. The estimate is a conjecture based upon the probability that it was not much smaller than Alexandria; at 250 to the hectare its site need only have occupied about 62 hectares.

Below Qus cities are assigned positions largely upon the apparent size of their medieval areas as defined by modern maps. The remarks of medieval travellers, such as Idrisi and Maqrizi, help, but they offer few quantitative estimates. Into the calculations should go the evidence of their administrative positions in Egypt.

Of the cities along the Nile between Cairo and Qus, Bahnesa, the centre of the great province of the same name, was probably the largest. It is difficult to separate its area from that

o

of its Roman predecessor, Heracleopolis Magna, which had covered about 116 hectares. The late medieval city had probably occupied nearly as much ground. In addition to being an administrative centre it was then famous for the manufacture of a fine cloth, whose workers provided a stronger basic element to the economy than Heracleopolis Magna had enjoyed. In Upper Egypt the agricultural wealth of the Fayyum was sufficient to account for the size of its largest city, Medina al-Fayyum, although it was probably smaller than Bahnesa.

The fifth city in size may well have been Damietta, a growing seaport, with a civic area of about 67–90 hectares. Probably the capitals of the four large Delta provinces came next. Al Mahallah al-Kubra, capital of Garbiya, was said to have been for the Delta what Qus was to Upper Egypt, Idrisi mentions the extensive cloth manufacture there and says the same for Damanhur, capital of Baheira. During the thirteenth century Mansura seems to have displaced Aschum al-Rum as the chief city of Dakaliya. Bilbeis is placed lower in the list; it was closer to Cairo. It had been the capital of Sharkiya and an important city even in Roman days. Below these in size apparently was a long list of smaller places, whose trading and manufacturing activities tended to be exaggerated by late medieval chroniclers.[6]

While it can be seen that the top three of the Egyptian cities may have been of about the proper size in relation to Cairo, the remaining cities in the list are much larger than the rank-size formula assumes. The total estimated population of the ten largest cities (about 233,100, using the larger estimates in case of choice) is about 5.7% of the country's total population of four millions. Since the normal is 5.07, the urban index is only about 14% above the average but it does show urbanisation and the industrialisation of the country. It is really surprising, however, since the average density of population is very high: 118.8 to the km^2 for the whole population and even 111.8 without the top ten cities. This region (33,680) was the smallest region, except for the region of Florence (if we assume that it did not include the Roman area) and yet was next in population to the region of Paris. Of course, the region of Cairo could be considered very much larger if adjacent areas of the desert inhabited by nomad groups, which doubtless might be considered a part of the region, are included.

For the fifteen or so larger cities of Egypt the average area of their tributary territory was about 900 square miles with a distance between cities of about thirty miles (48km). This was roughly the distance between secondary cities in England in the later Middle Ages. Here, again, the determining factor seems to have been the length of the one day's journey.

Estimates of Egyptian population of the countryside and villages rest primarily upon some very remarkable polyptyques (land surveys) produced at the end of the thirteenth century and beginning of the fourteenth century and some earlier surveys of taxes. The estimates are based upon the hypothesis that a *feddan* of land (about half an acre) was expected to support a person and that the land tax was close to two dinars a *feddan.* Information about the size of cities is not so good. Excavation by archaeologists has been concentrated heavily upon ancient sites because of the wonderful information which survives from earlier periods. No one would have it otherwise, but it has tended to obscure the interests of the medieval period. Studies like those of Sauvaget on Aleppo and Damascus are needed for medieval Egyptian cities. Not even the size of the Friday mosques are available for most Egyptian cities. Since they were built to hold the total male Islamic population, they often give clues to city population. However, street patterns created in Egypt, as cities grew from the eleventh to the fourteenth centuries, remained much the same until the nineteenth century. During the period after 1348 the declining population merely became less dense within the wider area. Additions of the nineteenth and twentieth centuries have a different street pattern, so that the medieval portions stand out on the maps. Thus in some very careful recent surveys of the cities the size of the fourteenth century inhabited areas can be estimated.

There were some interesting similarities and differences between Egypt and England. The two were about the same in size about AD 1086–90 (1.6 million for Egypt and 1.1 for England) and both rose to 3.7–4.0 millions just before the plague. The size of the capitals was about the same in the fourteenth century and the distance between the day's-journey cities. However, here the differences begin. The 50,000 square miles of England were occupied by perhaps 11,000 villages, an average of about 4.5 square miles to the village. The 2,300 villages of Egypt covered about 13,000 square miles with an average of 6 square miles. However, many of the Egyptian villages were in fact, either a village and its peripheral hamlets or a small group of villages. The radius of a circle enclosing an average village area would be 2.7 miles for Egypt and 2.2 for England; for differently shaped villages the distance would be greater. These distances are about as far as men can walk or ride to their work in the fields; this fact seems to determine the size of the settlements and their fields. In both countries larger-sized villages developed hamlets in the more distant parts of their areas. The average population of the villages differed considerably. Deducting 10% for the cities, the village population of both Egypt and England should have been about 3,330,000. This gives the Egyptian village an average population of about 1,450 and the English about 300 persons. The area of the valley was about 33,700km^2 which gave a density of 121.7 persons to the km^2. It has an urban index of 6.9.

The fundamental difference in the economy of Egypt from that of Europe (or really anywhere else) was in the high fertility of the Egyptian soil. The annual flood of the Nile brought each year (unless there was drought) a fertilising thin layer of soil from the valley above. All Egyptian life adjusted to this flood which started in the spring in the mountains in Abyssinia from the monsoons of the Indian Ocean. Through the summer it passed down the river. At Rueda not far from Qus the Nilometer, a pillar in the bed, registered the progress of the flood and finally indicated just how great it would be. Then messengers hastened down the river, telling the farmers what kind of flood to expect. The height of the flood was reached in the Delta in September and October. This curious phenomenon created a series of unusual conditions for the Nile Valley, the region of Cairo.

In contrast to the region of Antioch, the region of Cairo, the Nile Valley, enjoyed one of its most brilliant epochs at the end of the thirteenth century and the first half of the fourteenth. Under Bibars (1260–77) and Malik al-Nasir (1293–94, 1299–1309, 1310–41) Egypt experienced a kind of golden age under leaders, who, although extravagant at times, still were much interested in the economic life of the country and did their best to encourage commerce and agriculture. The region derived much advantage also from being the centre for a considerable area beyond Egypt itself as a result of political pressure on neighbours and extensive trade to both east and west. This period, however, was much hurt by heavy Nile floods, the plague of 1348–50 and its recurring epidemics, together with a long series of minorities in its ruling family.

11

The Regions of Hiven Tsang's India (AD 629-45)

THE STUDY OF ancient Indian population has a special meaning for demographers as well as for Indian historians. India was alleged to have been overcrowded with a population of 100–140 millions from several centuries before Christ to about AD 1800. That is, for over two milleniums India had no control over the number of its people and was at the mercy of famine, plague, and high birth- and death-rates. Since there is no other well-authenticated case of such a condition, Indian population is of great interest. Generally, societies have taken care of their population in the past and thus the normal inclination is to doubt the construction of overpopulation of India. It is indeed difficult to believe that an overpopulated India could have produced such a remarkable civilisation in the past; perhaps even harder to believe that an India of a 100 millions should have succumbed to foreign armies of modest size over the centuries. As often happens a present condition (great population, military weakness) is easily projected into the past without proper evidence.

TYPES OF EVIDENCE

Some interesting and unused evidence is available in the account of the travels of a famous Chinese Buddhist who spent the years AD 629–45 on a long pilgrimage in India. His primary interest was his religion, so that he gave much

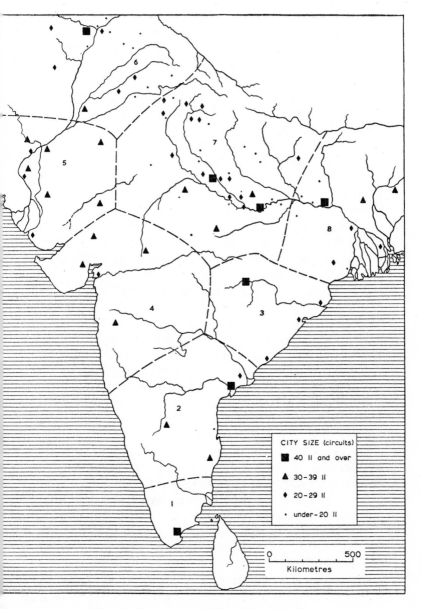

CITY SIZE (circuits)

■ 40 li and over

▲ 30 – 39 li

♦ 20 – 29 li

· under – 20 li

0 ————————— 500
Kilometres

Fig 10   The regions of Hiven Tsang's India

attention to Buddhist shrines and remarked upon the condition of monasteries and other religious groups. However, he also estimated the circuit of many cities, gave the distance between them, and hazarded the area of the country of which the city was a part, often the capital. If the evidence about circuits of cities was accurate and can be used in medieval rank-size patterns of cities within regions, it should give some idea of the size of Indian population in Hiven Tsang's time. This was an interesting period since Harsha, the sovereign of the north at the time, was one of the great rulers of Indian history. We should remember that it was also the period of the plague in the western world (AD 524–700), a plague which is alleged to have come from the east. It was thus a period of low population in the west; the whole European-Mediterranean world is estimated at only about 35 millions then.[1]

The high estimate for Indian population has been presented persuasively as the consensus of several approaches, mostly derived from Buddhist records. All assume a virtually stationary population over two milleniums of history and thus it is assumed that evidence need not really be considered in a chronological setting.[2] They may be summarised:

(1)   India had seven million *gramas* (estates with about 15–20 persons apiece) with a population of 105–140 millions.

(2)   Vaisali, presumably a *janapanda* (one-tenth of a *desa,* a county) had 7,707 *rajans* (estate owners). India had 84 *desas* and 840 *janapandas*. Assuming Vaisali an average *janapanda,* India had 6,473,880 *rajans*, which, at 15–20 persons to the *rajan*, would give a population of 100–130 millions.

(3)   Vaisali, presumably a *janapanda*, is said to have had a population of 168,000. Multiplying by 840 (assuming Vaisali an average *janapanda*) gives 141,120,000.

(4)   One person to the cultivated area (acre) gives 105–140 millions to the seven million *gramas* at 15–20 persons a *grama*.

(5)   Military strength, according to various figures offered suggests about seven million soldiers, one to a *grama,* or 108–144 millions.

Thus almost identical figures are reached, from widely differing bases, yet they must be regarded as approximations arrived at by conjecture.

Hiven Tsang gives an estimate of the army of Harsha—

60,000 elephants and 100,000 cavalry.[3] Now no one could really take the number of 60,000 seriously and it casts doubt upon the 100,000 cavalry as well. Some of the estimates overlap. Numbers (2) and (3) above are based upon the theory that Vaisali was an average *janapanda*, but actually the city, Vaisali, its capital, was one of the largest cities in India. One might estimate its population as perhaps 100,000. Thus to base an estimate for all 840 *janapandas* on this sample is to very seriously overestimate total Indian population. Number (4) is composed of the addition to small rather believable figures for some *janapandas*, several of which seem confirmed by epigraphic evidence, to massive estimates, such as 2.6 millions for Kanyakubja. Similarly, several of the estimates are based on the theory of seven million estates or *rajans* in India. There is no reason to think that the larger figures of these data are any more worthy of belief than the usual run of large guesses coming from the ancient and medieval world. Even the estimates of the Venetian ambassadors, well trained and excellent diplomats, are several times their actual size. In short, the myth of immense overpopulation is raised by using samples which are not average and upon tremendously exaggerated figures.

Now, if one uses the examples of *janapandas* which seem reasonable

One on River Maki	2,200	*gramas*
Konkana	1,414	
Condravati	1,800	
Lata-desa (10 *janapandas*)	21,000	
	26,414	

then he has for thirteen *janapandas* about 26,000 *gramas* or about 2,000 apiece. This would give each *janapanda* about 30–40,000 persons apiece and 840 *janapandas* would bring a total of 25.2–33.6 millions for all of India. Even Hiven Tsang presented one estimate for Harsha's army at 20,000 cavalry, 5,000 elephants and 100,000 infantry which, while awesome for the seventh century, was not quite beyond belief.

HIVEN TSANG'S EVIDENCE

Hiven Tsang's data, covering some eighty places, enable one to set up a pattern of size of cities within several regions of India. Assuming that the Indian pattern was a normal pre-industrial pattern, the cities might be expected to have a typical medieval proportion of total population. The results of such a study will be quite tentative, but should suggest within wide limits what the country should have had, particularly whether the very high estimate of 100–140 millions can be justified.

Before using the data, the question of their meaning and even their validity must be considered. Tsang's statements may be illustrated by one example, as described by Watters:

> The pilgrim relates that from Kosala he travelled south, through a forest, for about 900 *li* to the An-to-lo country. This country was about 3,000 *li* in circuit, and its capital Pingchi (or ki) was about twenty *li* in circuit.

Just how long was the *li*? And, what figure should be accepted for 'about twenty'? Ideally one should check on the length of the *li* by comparing Tsang's statements against actual measurements of the cities. The chief difficulty is shortage of accurate data about large cities of the seventh century. India's early history is so important that its centres, such as Harappa and Mohenjodaro, have attracted the major archae-ological attention, as is both natural and proper. The identifi-cation of many cities is not certain and even if they are identified correctly, their size in the seventh century is uncertain.

An early archaeologist, Alexander Cunningham, did attempt to identify and give estimates of size of many of Hiven Tsang's sites. In his study he seems to have made two miscalculations which partially offset each other. He thought that the *li* was about a sixth of a mile in length (about 280 metres), whereas Fleet has shown that it was probably considerably shorter. We shall consider the *li* to have been about 240 metres in length, although it may have been shorter. Second, the effects of rounding were apparently not considered; that is, 'twenty' or 'above twenty' was, on the average about twenty-four. Thus

TABLE 29: TSANG'S DATA COMPARED WITH CUNNINGHAM'S SITES, LENGTH OF CIRCUITS

Name of site	Page	Tseng's Number of li	Data Metres 100s	Metres 100s	Miles or feet	Cunningham's Sites			Sastri p
						Page	Name	State of site	
Takshasila	I, 240	10(14)	24 – 33.6	32.9	10,800	129	Bir	Mound	681
Sinhapura (cap.)	I, 248	14-15	33.6- 36	32.2	2	145	Ketas	Mound	682
Tsekla	I, 286	20(24)	48 – 57.6	47.5	15,600	221	Azarur	Ruins	687
Pitoshilo	II, 258	20(24)	48 – 57.6	48.3	3	323	———	Hill	692
Stanesar (fort)	I, 316	20(24)	48 – 57.6	43.0	14,000	378	same	Mound	701
Satanissufalo	I, 314	20(24)	48 – 57.6	64.4	4	379	Dara	Mounds	701
Pollyetalo (cap.)	I, 300	14-15	33.6- 36	40.2	2.5	393	Bairat	Mound	702
Srughna	I, 318	20(24)	48 – 57.6	57.9	19,000	395-7	Sugh	Forts	702
Montipulo	I, 322	20(24)	48 – 57.6	56.3	3.5	400	Madawar	Mounds	703
Moyulo	I, 328	20(24)	48 – 57.6	57.9	19,000	404	Mayapura	Old City	704
Kuplsanga	I, 330	14-15	33.6- 36	33.5	11,000	409	Ujain	Ruins	704
Ngohichitalo	I, 331	17-18	40.8- 43	59.1	19,400	414	Ramanagar	Walls	704-5
Piloshanna	I, 332	10, 12	24, 28.8	32.2	2	418-22	Bilsar	Mounds	705
Kapitha	I, 335	20(24)	48 – 57.6	57.6	18,900	425	Sankisa	Earth Rampart	706
Motulo	I, 301	20(24)	48 – 57.6	56.1	18,380	428	Mathura	City Now	706
Kanakubja	I, 341	20×4or5	115 –120	128.7	8	436-7	Kanoj	Monuments	707
Kiaoshangml (cap)	I, 365	30(34)	72 – 81.6	77-80.5	5or23,100	454	Kosambi	Fortress	709
Kashepuio	I, 372	10(14)	24 – 33.6	32.2	2	459	Kusapura	Ruins	710
Shihlofasito	I, 377	20(24)	48 – 57.6	52.7	17,300	470	Sahet-Mahet	Palace/City	711
Vaisall (palace)	II, 65	4-5	9.6- 12	14.0	4,600	507	Betarh	Palace	719
Vipula	II, 154	30(34)	72 – 81	74.7	24,500	532	Old Rampart		—
Kusumapura (ruin)	II, 87	70	168	177.0	11	519		Half of city now	721
Vipula (outer)	II, 148-50	50(54)	120 – 130	125.0	41,000	533		Hills	721
Rajagriha	II, 147	20(24)	48 – 57.6	43.3	14,260	535-6	Rajgir	Fortress/Ruins	725
Capchihchito	II, 251	15	36.0	42.7	14,000	553	Khajuraho	Ruins	725
Wusheyenna	II, 250	30(34)	72 – 81.6	'Little less now'		560	Ujjayini	City now	726
Malwa	II, 242	30(34)	72 – 81.6	56.3	3.5	562	Dhar	Town	728
Chanpo	II, 181	40(44)	96 –105.6		6	596	Chanda	Walls	736

270 metres times 20 (that is 540) is not much different from 240 metres times 24 (or 576) and 240 is probably too long for a metre which would make the estimates even closer. Thus Cunningham's conclusions are quite close to calculations based upon the shorter length of the *li* and the increase for rounding. Some of his identifications have been questioned, but enough were accurate to be a fair test of Hiven Tsang's ability to judge length of city 'circuits'. By and large the archaeological remains corroborate Hiven Tsang's estimates sufficiently for our study.

For two cities Tsang gave length and breadth instead of 'circuits': Benaras and Kanauj. Both were very important; the first as the great Buddhist centre of India and the other as the capital of the great emperor, Harsha. The dimensions of Benaras are given as eighteen and six *li*. At 240 metres to the *li*, that is just about the length of the city today, but its breadth is hardly six *li* in places. Perhaps Benaras had no walls in Tsang's day. Kanauj was also along the Ganges River bank; its dimensions Tsang gave as twenty *li* in length and four or five *li* in width. Even though it had strong walls in Harsha's time, they are now hard to define in the site's deserted state today. From the Benaras data, the accuracy of Tsang's data emerges well. The rest of the data are presented in Table 29; the figures to be compared are on either side of the central line.

There is still the problem of estimating the area within the 'circuits' described by Tsang. In general the cities whose areas were defined were walled cities; he notes occasionally that a city was dilapidated and that only a small population lived within the walls. The shape of the city would determine the area. The largest area produced by a circuit would be a circular wall or something approaching it. But most walls were apt to be square or rectangular; the square would, of course, enclose a greater area than the rectangle. Just to be generous, we assume that the circuit was square and secure the areas by squaring a quarter of the circuit. Perhaps Tsang gave the length and breadth of Benaras and Kanauj because they had such ribbon-like shapes.

The problem of rounding down to the next multiple of ten has been mentioned. The exact lengths would be spread over the range of twenty to twenty-nine, with an average, if spread

TABLE 30: MEASUREMENT AND POPULATION ESTIMATES
OF INDIAN CITIES

Circuit (in li)	Assuming a square, one side in li = 240 m		Area in hectares	Population estimate 60 to hectare	100 to hectare
(44)	11	2640	697	41820	69700
40	10	2400	576	34560	57600
(34)	8.5	2040	416	24960	41600
30	7.5	1800	324	19440	32400
(24)	6	1440	207	12420	20700
20	5	1200	144	8640	14400
17–18	4.5	1080	117	7020	11700
15–16	4	960	92	5520	9200
15	3.75	900	81	4860	8100
13–14	3.5	840	71	4260	7100
11–12	3	720	52	3120	5200
10	2.5	600	36	2160	2900
8–9	2.25	540	29	1740	2900
7–8	2	480	23	1380	2300

evenly, of about 24.4. However, since there are apt to be slightly more cities in the smaller half (20–24) than in the larger (25–9), it seems better to use twenty-four as the average. In Table 30 the calculations are given to secure areas in hectares for the circuits offered by Tsang. These might be modified later if archaeological research should either alter the estimate for the *li* or show that cities were normally another shape, say rectangular with a fairly definite relationship of length and breadth. The present estimates more probably would be revised downward than increased.

To estimate Indian population one must have an estimate for the number of persons to the hectare. As we have seen, in the west, at least in the latter part of the period, the density of cities was about 110–25 to the hectare, but Islamic cities often had a greater density. There the areas within the walls were thickly settled, usually house to house, two or more storeys and with relatively few non-residential buildings. The only open spaces were apt to be central squares. Tsang gives the impression that houses were of wood and wattle and were seldom of more than single storey, so strongly does he emphasise the appearance of multi-storey buildings, such as palaces. Space interjacent between houses was apparently common. Furthermore, many of the establishments can be suspected of housing cowsheds or stables; the cleansing of houses with cattle dung is mentioned; it assumes a relatively large quantity easily available. This type of dwelling, one storey separated from the next, often with corral or stable attached, suggests a low density of population, hardly more than 100 to the hectare and possibly as low as 60. These are the limits suggested in Table 30. Here, again, further archaeological research may provide a more exact estimate of persons to the hectare by determining size of dwellings, their position relative to each other and the number of their storeys.

TOTAL POPULATION ESTIMATE BASED ON RANK-SIZE DISTRIBUTION OF CITIES BY REGIONS

The exact geographical positions of some of the sites are uncertain but are not of real importance since placement within a definite area only is needed. It can be seen from the map and Table 31 that Hiven Tsang reported only unevenly, since he spent much more time in the Ganges Valley than elsewhere, but then that is where the greater part of the population was. Apparently the chief Buddhist shrines were in the larger cities, so that they include most of them and some representation of the others. In areas which he did not examine carefully (as in the south) or seems to have hurried through (West, Indus, East Central, South-east) he reported upon only the largest cities. In three other areas his list is longer and conforms more closely to the expected distribution by rank-size within regions. The very size of the larger Indian cities indicates that the cities ought to have a normal percentage (or even higher than normal) proportion of the total population.

Assuming that Indian cities conformed to the rank-size pattern, the hypothetical distribution is given on the right side of Table 31 for regions with top cities having circuits of 49, 44 and 40 *li* respectively. Since the total population may be

TABLE 31: DISTRIBUTION OF CITIES BY LENGTH OF CIRCUIT AND REGIONS IN HIVEN TSANG'S TRAVELS

Length of Circuit in li	South-Ceylon	South east	West (3 regions)	Indus Valley (3 regions)	North West	Upper Ganges (2 regions)	Lower Ganges	East Central	Total	Hypothetical if largest city is 49 li	44 li	40 li
40+	1	1			1	2	1	1	7	1	1	1
30+		2	5	4	2	2	2		17	2	1	1
20+		2	1	3	6	10	3	2	27	4	3	2
Under 20		1			13	10	5		29			
Total	1	6	6	7	22	24	11	3	80			

estimated from the size of the largest city if the distribution by size seems proper, the problem is to find if they were distributed in an expected pattern. For five of the regions the distribution is reasonable: with one city in top rank (40+) and either no number below (as in the South) or an appropriate small number (South-east, West, North-west, Lower Ganges, and East Central). It is possible that Hiven Tsang entirely missed mentioning some of the larger cities, but he does seem to have made an effort to include them. Of course, cities alone need not determine areas of regions. Geographically, those five regions seem very natural ones, occupying relatively homogeneous areas of the land. All also seem to have been rather sparsely settled.

The Upper Ganges area would appear to be two regions on the basis of the size of the cities, with the two great centres, Benaras and Kanauj mentioned earlier. The Ganges Valley was by far the most thickly settled area in India; it is probable that two regions existed in the Upper Ganges area since the number of larger cities is almost exactly twice the expected number in a regional distribution. Benaras and Kanauj are far enough apart for two regions to be considered for the area.

The most difficult problem is that of the areas, West and Indus Valley, with perhaps what seem to be extra cities in the eastern section of the Northwest region. With nine cities in the 30+ classification the two regions have enough for three regions between the two and so they are considered. The area may have been much like Tuscany in the early part of the thirteenth century when conditions were not well integrated into effective regions. These were the areas which had borne the brunt of the invasions of the Huns in the century before and might have had any regional activity disrupted for a time. It is probably better to consider that there were the equivalent of three regions in the Indus Valley and western India, without attempting to settle with present evidence the configuration of the regions.

If we assume that there were ten regions and that the top cities had about 1.5% of the total population, an estimate of the total Indian population can be made. This assumes that the largest cities had circuits of 44 *li*.

Number to hectare	Total of one city	Total of ten cities	Total for all India
100	67,900	679,000	45,280,000
60	41,820	418,200	27,880,000

In contrast to 100–140 millions the 28 to 45 millions seem small indeed. Even these estimates are probably high since two of the top cities were below the 44 *li* circuits and cities as large as the greater cities normally have a higher percentage of the total population. In any case it is more in line with European-Mediterranean population of the time which, while probably larger than India, had only about 35 millions. If India had an area of about 1.5 million km^2 then its density would be between 18.5 and 30.2 persons to the km^2. However, if the Ganges Valley had four of the ten regions its 120,000km^2 would have had a density between 93 and 37 to the km^2, a density matched in the west only by Egypt.

OTHER EVIDENCE ABOUT SEVENTH-CENTURY INDIAN POPULATION

Some other evidence given by Hiven Tsang and by other sources indicate something about conditions of India in his time. They are worth examining to see if they corroborate or question the low estimate of population based upon the circuits of cities as subjected to rank-size testing. Tsang regularly gave descriptions of the land through which he travelled. In many places he told of going through jungle, heavy forest and other areas of obviously low population density. They show that when the traveller moved out of the Ganges Valley toward the mountains he ran into undeveloped land. Furthermore, the territory to the south seemed largely woodland and jungle; it shows 'that only about half of the total area of India had by that time been surveyed, the remainder probably consisting of hills, forest and jungle, not yet fully explored'.[5] Only the presence of sizeable cities suggests smaller cities to support them. In view of these great areas of low density, the population of India can hardly be regarded as very overcrowded then. And one must admit, that the primitive character of the culture, as also that of the west, makes it difficult to believe in

P

overpopulation. Usually primitive cultures took very good care of their numbers.

A clue to the population of the lower Ganges Valley should be the size of the seaports there if sea commerce was as important as is sometimes stated. Travellers before the time of Tsang wrote of Tanmo-lih-ti (Tomluk near Calcutta) as the chief port, while recently an authority on shipping has written, 'But by far the most impressive emporium of ancient Bengal was Tamralipta, the great Buddhist harbour of the Bengal seaboard.' Tsang wrote of it 'The country formed a bay where land and water communications met; consequently rare valuables were collected in it and so the inhabitants were generally prosperous.' However, Tsang assigned only ten *li* to its circuit which can hardly indicate a city of more than 5,000 to 10,000. To another city in a country near the sea, the capital of Samatata, a twenty *li* circuit is given. Although it was an outstanding Buddhist centre there is no mention of commerce and one cannot even be certain that it was a port. Even taken together the two do not suggest a heavily populated valley. They had together probably only about 20,000 people.

The marriage customs of the time, if actual practice followed the precepts, hardly suggest overpopulation either. Children married at an early age, about the age of ten, but widows did not remarry. It was the latter prohibition that tended to keep down population. Under favourable circumstances the women who lived through the childbearing period (assuming ages 18 to 45 need to have about 5.2 to 6.4 children to keep up the population and actually could have (assuming 30 months to the child) about 5.5 to 7.4, if allowed to remarry. This potentiality was reduced about 6% by deaths of husbands even before the childbearing period (10 to 16); the age of the husband does not make much difference. This brought the average possible down to about 5.2 to 6.6 children. The loss of children as a result of the husbands' death during the childbearing period was another 4% to 7%, so that the potential was lowered to about 4.7 to 5.7 children, just barely enough to maintain the population. However, these estimates are based on male data (usually better than female) for the quite good health conditions of thirteenth-century England. That India could keep up its population under marital conditions like these does not lead one to expect overcrowded conditions. However, it is really too much to believe that, as is sometimes stated, men in general married girls one-third of their age.

The population of the western world was at a low point at precisely this time because the plague, appearing in AD 542 and recurring at regular intervals, had reduced western population to a low of perhaps half of the pre-plague level in the years AD 600–650. The plague seems to have come from the east, and Central Asia has been suspected of being one of the reservoirs of the disease over the centuries. One question deserving study is whether India, like the west, suffered in the same period from epidemics of the plague and whether plague was an endemic disease in the area as it has been in recent times.

At first it seems doubtful if India suffered from plague then. Hiven Tsang did not mention the plague, as one might expect if it had been prevalent in his time. However, he never seemed to write of any disease and apparently just was not interested in conditions of health, except to mention unfavourable weather and climatic conditions. In the west the plague of the fourteenth century produced many cases of dilapidated towns. In that period in the west also the number of monks in the monasteries declined and failed to recover with the population expansion of AD 1470–1550, at least in England. If there was an equivalent loss in India in the century before Hiven Tsang went there, one might expect to find evidence of dilapidated towns and even more of monasteries in India.

References to six cities in ruins may not be to recently destroyed cities. They were capitals of small countries loss of which may have been caused by dynastic shifts or even changes in the location of the capitals themselves. Tsang, primarily interested in visiting Buddhist shrines, naturally went to ancient cities which had connections with Buddha, so that ruined cities had a natural attraction. In one small area, Ganhara, 'The towns and villages were desolate and the inhabitants were few.' The 'Kapilavastu' country contained more than 'ten deserted cities all in utter ruin.' In near-by 'Kusingara' country. 'The city walls were in ruins and the towns and villages deserted.' In the Maghadha area, 'there were few inhabitants in the walled cities, but the other towns were well peopled.' The concentration of ruined towns within fairly narrow limits suggests some local action, military or political, rather than the plague which normally scattered its casualties over a wide area. The towns here and there rather than groups of villages were apt to have been reduced by shifts of population among them. The following account, however, might be a description of plague damage:

> This country, the pilgrim relates, had once been very densely inhabited; a holy rishi possessing supernatural powers had his hermitage in it; he was once offended by a native and cursed the country; as a consequence of this curse the land became, and remained, utterly depopulated. In the lapse of many years since that event it had gradually become inhabited again, but it still had only a scanty population.

This area (Kalinga), according to Tsang, was hot and heavily forested, thus probably damp and ideal for plague mortality.

Certain developments in India look like the rationalisation of declining population, which should depress the position of women; the beginning of child marriage, *sati* system, strong disapproval of remarriage of widows and putting women under the tutelage of men.[6] This was similar to changes in the west, probably in part, the result of declining population: emphasis on monastic and celibate life, reduction of status of women in the Church and discouragement of remarriage. Like the west also, from AD 400 to 800 'it was an age mostly of commentaries and digests and not of original works.' The emphasis seems to have been on the preservation and explanation of the existing fund of knowledge'[7].

As mentioned earlier, Hiven Tsang reported upon the condition of monasteries and 'endeavoured to give a bright picture of Buddhism in India.' 'It appears from his record that the progress of the religion had been arrested, and in many places it had lost its hold upon the people and was, in fact, on the verge of disappearance.' His record specifies some twenty places where dilapidation appeared and these were scattered throughout the north-west, north-east and south. In sixteen of these places, in addition to statements of ruin, the existence of 'few brethren' were noted. Yet the pilgrim noticed a satisfactory condition of monastic life in some 37 areas, many of which were provinces rather than cities. It is somewhat difficult to secure a figure for the total number of monasteries and monks even of the cities which he visited. About 1,530 monasteries are suggested. In addition to three areas which he alleged had 'hundreds': if we allow 200 for each of the three areas, it gives a total of about 2,100 monasteries of Buddhists. The number of monks is roughly 160,000; this gives about 80 monks to the house. The large numbers, as usual raise questions as to the accuracy of the figures. If their numbers were in the same proportion as English clergy of 1377, they would number about 1.5% of the population. The number of Buddhist monks then would suggest a population for India of about 11.3 millions. However, this does not count the residents of Deva-Temples and, of course, places which Tsang did not visit. It all suggests a considerable dilapidation of the preceding time, whether the result of plague or other conditions.

Much more, primarily in archaeology, will have to be done before the history of Indian regions stands out more clearly than these vague outlines. Indian population, apparently much like western population in the seventh century, probably resembled western culture in other centuries. This should mean that population varied considerably over the centuries. Vaisali, for instance, must at one time have been larger than any Indian city of the seventh century, probably as capital of a much larger area and population than Harsha ruled in the seventh century, just as ancient Rome and Alexandria were larger than seventh-century Constantinople and Antioch. The centuries succeeding the seventh probably did not see much change in the population of India which means that India, like the west, saw the rapid expansion of population only in very late medieval or early modern times. For historians this is a relief, for a vastly overpopulated India of a hundred millions was hard to fit into the overall picture of the medieval world.

12

The Significance of Pre-plague Regions

THE STUDY OF individual regions has considered primarily the size of the cities and their relationships within areas. Cities have been given more exact figures for their population than had been attempted previously. In the tables the relationship of actual population sizes to the hypothetical rank-size pattern has been presented: the correlation has generally been quite close. The area represented by the cities often seemed the area of regional significance. In many cases additional similarities appeared which indicated the reality of these regions as areas of sufficiently common characteristics to justify their being classed as regions. With these data it is possible now to consider groups of cities within regions and understand them better, in the period when they had such considerable growth and influence.

Not least cartography in historical atlases should improve as a result of more careful estimates of city size, assuming that one wants to map the larger cities rather than the sites of battles, churches, royal residences, or universities. Existing maps contain many anomalies. If Armagh appeared on an Irish map, its early importance as a Christian centre can be assumed the reason, but if Cobh, its modern importance more than its medieval status. In England Chester has sometimes been emphasised in reference to Coventry, showing an unawareness of rapid population growth in the thirteenth century. Hamburg and Bremen appeared on maps of northern Germany rather

than Lübeck and Münster or Rostock which were probably
larger in the pre-plague period. Marseilles, in eclipse during
the late Middle Ages, still appears on maps rather than Montpellier unless university cities were recorded. In Italy great
cities like Bologna and Siena were eclipsed by Padua and Pisa
on the maps. Even more misleading was the emphasis which
such mistakes made about importance of areas. One might
gather from the concentration of three large-type names—Lyon,
Avignon, and Marseilles—that the Rhône Valley was densely
populated instead of being much less so than the great quadrilateral presented by the regions of Venice, Milan, and Florence.
The relative importance of cities and regions can be made
clearer by a study of indices of their size and density of population together with the urban index of the regions.

THE POSITION OF THE LARGEST CITIES WITHIN REGIONS

The largest cities, as the maps of this study show, often appear
away from the centre of regions. This may seem somewhat surprising since the rank-size pattern is often called the *Central-
Ort* series. As a matter of fact, only three of the metropolitan
cities are clearly central with no claim to being portal cities.
These were Cairo, Cordoba, and Paris, although even here,
all three were on rivers which provided some transportation.
It was quite unlikely however, that ocean-going ships went up
the rivers to these cities: they normally stopped at such trans-
shipment centres as Alexandria, Seville, and Rouen. They were
capitals of heavily-settled, well-integrated areas and important
governments.

Several regional capitals were very obviously portal cities.
In this period Pisa had already lost out to Florence, a more
central although still a portal city with respect to the mountain passes. Venice eventually converted herself from a portal
city to a central city between her maritime possessions and her
new continental holdings, but at this period she still held to her
initial purpose of being only a maritime and therefore a portal
city. Palermo, Dijon, Magdeburg, and Augsburg all were losing
to more centrally located cities (Naples, Lyons, Dresden, and
Nürnberg) although this was not yet clear in the case of Augsburg. In fact, of all the portal cities of this period, only

one, Dublin, was to remain permanently a portal city.

The longest list was of the cities which had claims of being both central and portal cities. This condition was naturally favourable for large growth since the city enjoyed the advantages of both types. The basic factor of the jobs provided by trans-shipment to points within the region often added political administration advantages to central location. Six of these enjoyed direct sea commerce: Barcelona, Ghent, Lisbon, London, Lübeck, and Montpellier, although only Barcelona and Lübeck had ports on the sea itself. Florence and Milan were cities near passes which made them in part portal cities. Perhaps Prague is in this class if the Elbe be regarded as a pass to Bohemia. Toulouse was near the Montpellier and Barcelona districts by overland routes, while Antioch had access both to the sea on the Orontes and to the desert by caravan routes.

A physiographic influence which was often overlooked was that of mountain passes, sometimes in surprising regions. Tuscany, for instance, was dominated largely by passes across the Apennines. Milan probably owed its importance in large part to the fact that roads from several Alpines passes converged on the city. Augsburg in southern Germany lost its position as metropolitan centre when the area developed its resources until they overshadowed the importance of the Alpine passes. Perhaps Barcelona was helped by the block which the Pyrenees set up against direct traffic north from such cities as Saragossa and Pamplona. Perhaps Iberia had so many mountains that its passes were discounted by the value of rivers and the sea: the passes seem to have determined the sites of very few important cities.

The expense of overland travel enhanced the importance of water transportation. The great trade routes were still in the Mediterranean: Venice-Genoa-Montpellier-Barcelona to Palermo-Alexandria and Antioch. The Atlantic and its rivers were second in importance: Garonne, Thames, Loire, Seine, Weser, Elbe, and Oder. Then the inland systems: Rhine, Danube, Rhône and their tributaries. These tended to emphasise river valleys as the cores of regions: Cologne with the Rhine, Toulouse with the Garonne, Dijon with Saône-Rhône upper reaches, Milan with the upper Po, Barcelona with the

Ebro and, most of all, Cairo with the Nile. Far to the east the great regions of India were in the Ganges Valley. Some simply had river valleys as important factors: the Seine for Paris, Guadalquivir for Cordoba, Orontes for Antioch, Rhône for Montpellier and the Elbe for Prague and Magdeburg.

Among man-made developments which affected city locations, Roman roads were among the most important. Their purpose was originally military and administrative, so they were built straight and often in defiance of such obstacles as swamps and hills. While rivers and seas provided cheaper transportation if all else was equal, this was not often the case. The storms of the seas and the ice of the northern winters often kept shipping by water tied up for months during the colder part of the year. Furthermore, the roads were often straighter and shorter than water routes. The Roman roads, then, made for a pattern of land communication that tended to persist. Even when they paralleled rivers they often were the cause of cities being built for preference on that side, as on the Roman side of the Romano-German frontiers of the Rhine and Danube and on the east side of the Rhône from its mouth to Lyons.

The Roman roads often caused cities to remain in a direct line: the most famous case was probably that of the Via Aemilia from Rimini to Piacenza in Italy. A great highway of Iberia: Cadiz, Sevilla, Merida, Salamanca and Lugo to the north-west coast helped fix one important line of commerce and cities. Another led across the peninsula from Tarragona to Lisbon through Saragossa, Toledo, and Merida. The great road centres of Roman Gaul were Lyons and Orléans which were bypassed by the rise of the Fairs of Champagne, Paris and the cities of the Low Countries. The great commercial centres were the most important whatever the type of highway to them.

If the portal city has proved to be of unexpected importance, a second unexpected situation was the grouping of large cities together in certain localities instead of being spread evenly over the area of the region. The density of cities in Flanders and Brabant was probably the outstanding illustration, although the line of cities on the River Arno from Florence to Pisa was impressive. The row of cities between Barletta and

Bari on Trajan's Way was again somewhat unexpected: the collection of cities about Naples had been normal for centuries. In southern France there was the line between Montpellier and Perpignan, mostly along the coast and another rather thickly spread over the countryside from Perpignan to Tortosa in the region of Barcelona. There were many cases where neighbouring cities of considerable size seemed to suggest a divided civic function in the area: the clearest case was that of Venice and Padua. In some cases the concentration seemed not so much a divided function as the attraction of cities with similar interests to each other in much the same way that industries and businesses group in cities. The great textile cities of the Low Countries and the Perpignan-Tortosa complex are probably the best illustrations of this.

In seeking to understand the reasons for the distribution of cities within regions, the factor of chance must be considered, as in all historical possibilities. The loss of the Battle of Muret by King Pedro of Aragon drew southern France more and more into the realm of France, while the sudden death of Frederick II produced a new alignment in Italy. Or there was an unpredictable change in style or interest, often of short duration, such as the intense interest in Carrara marble which tied up so much capital of Renaissance princes[1] or the even greater interest in expensive clothes: wool, linen, silk, which created the great textile industry of the thirteenth century and was one of the chief factors in the rise of the large industrial cities—perhaps the chief cause of great population concentrations of the period. All of these affect regional development but were largely unpredictable before they developed.

The position of the largest cities, the metropolitan centres, tended to emphasise the economic importance of the region and even of medieval society as compared with the political or even the religious aspect. The central cities, such as Paris, Cairo, and Cordoba depended, at least originally, upon their position as political capitals. But other and even larger cities, such as Venice and Florence, were primarily economic and exerted inter-regional influence of vast importance in their great days. Furthermore, it was rather commerce than industry for the greatest cities. The textiles did produce a kind of lesser industrial revolution, but it spread to no other occupation at

TABLE 32: COMPARATIVE DATA ON AREA AND POPULATION OF REGIONS

Rank, Region		Area 1,000 km²	Population 1,000s	Density to km²	Top ten cities 1,000s	Urban index
1	Toledo	184.0	2,800	15.2	128	4.5
2	Prague	158.6	2,000	12.6	112	6.6
3	Paris	156.0	5,226	33.5	257	4.9
4	Cordoba	154.8	1,320	8.6	224.5	17.0
5	Toulouse	135.4	3,372	25.0	111	3.3
6	London	131.8	3,700	28.1	163	4.4
7	Augsburg	130.9	1,667	12.7	117	7.0*
8	Barcelona	125.2	1,221	9.8	170	14.0
9	Antioch	109.0	2,670	24.5	138	5.2
10	Cologne	107.3	2,670	25.0	152	5.6*
11	Palermo	102.2	2,500	24.5	190	7.6
12	Magdeburg	100.0	1,330	13.3	100	7.5*
13	Montpellier	95.4	1,296	13.6	146	11.3
14	Lisbon	89.4	1,252	14.0	93	7.4
15	Dijon	84.8	1,130	13.3	70	6.7*
16	Dublin	84.3	675	8.0	41	6.1
17	Ghent	76.6	1,500	19.6	211	14.1
18	Lubeck	75.0	1,700	22.7	124	6.6*
19	Milan	51.0	1,745	34.5	337	19.1
20	Venice	38.8	1,473	38.0	357	23.4
21	Cairo	33.7	4,100	121.7	233	6.9
22	Florence	28.0	1,140	40.0	296	26.0

* This has little meaning since the total population is based upon the size of the largest city at 1.5 per cent of the total.

the time. Probably the antagonism to the machine was too strong for such to develop.

REGIONAL SIZE: AREA AND POPULATION

Table 32 gives the size and population of regions together with population density and the urban index. The sizes of areas are, of course, very tentative. About all of them, questions could be raised about their extent. Even the most definite, Ireland as the region of Dublin, might be construed as extending across the Irish Sea into Wales. Mountainous areas bordered or were a part of most regions, except for Ghent. The estimates of population are in many cases tentative and will doubtless be improved by further research and perhaps by the recovery of more data. We have to remember that uncertainties are characteristic of medieval data but not limited to them: loud objections are being made to the published results of the 1970 Census in the United States as cities failed to make the hoped-for gains in population. The data are significant even if not as accurate as might be wished.

The total area of the regions seems to have been about 2,252,200km² which for 22 regions obviously gives a little more than 100,000km² (actually 102,400). The median, since there were 22 regions, was about the same (100,000–102,000km²). From 75,000 to 109,000km² in size there were 10 regions, about half. The smallest four were the three northern Italian regions and Cairo, all of very heavy population density. To all of them might be assigned areas in the neighbouring mountains or desert, so that the range in size might be limited somewhat. The largest was Toledo at 184,000km², followed by Prague, Paris and Cordoba, all with about 155,000–159,000km², again the limits of the regions not being certain. The remaining four ranged from 125 to 135,000km². It is obvious that the greater were large enough, if they had a high density of population in addition to size, to dominate in the feudal power struggles. This assumes, of course, that the region's power would be available to one or a very few political groups.

Regional size also indicates that the medieval homogeneous unit was not anywhere equal to the size of modern great nations, such as France, Germany, Italy and Spain. Whatever the historical and 'national' forces there were to unite these areas into workable political entities, the demographic and economic forces of the regions were considerable hurdles, too great for the period AD 1000–1348 to bring about permanently. The Imperial Diet and the French Estates General developed no enduring place and were never workable vehicles of corporate individuality and power before the plague, even though they did express a consciousness of kind in being German and French. Medieval society seemed at ease only in assemblies representing the size of regions or parts of regions.

Estimates of population must be based upon the size of

demographic unit: family, hearth or house. Recently a very high estimate, based upon five as the unit, would indicate over-population of French and possibly other medieval areas[2]. Five is an only one possible assumption: the scanty evidence for pre-plague society suggests four or less. This includes the ex-tensive information from the Polyptyque d'Irminon and some scattered data from England.[3] Even English and Italian evi-dence in the second half of the fourteenth century suggests four rather than five. Since one way of controlling numbers in areas of high population density was to reduce the size of the unit or family, it is unlikely that thirteenth-century France had larger households than the ninth century. Furthermore, Pro-fessor Pounds' estimate of a density of 87.3 persons to the km^2 for an area in the diocese of Rouen in 1328 is so very high (he estimates 40 to the km^2 as a dense population) that a lower number to the family or *parrochianus* than 5 seemed the only reasonable solution, especially since specific indications of results of overpopulation are not evident.

Even with a modest estimate of the size of the family or holding, four regions had a considerable population. The three largest, except for Cairo with its very special position in the Nile Valley, were Paris, London, and Toulouse, all with over three millions. By modern standards these were not large. If one takes just the crop land of these areas, the food based upon them then, yields might not seem to have provided sufficient sustenance. Medieval society was, however, a heavily pastoral culture, producing quantities of milk and cheese as well as grain. In addition there were the gardens, the orchards and woods with fruit and nuts. Fish and eels were abundant in the streams and ponds.[4] Only one severe famine, that of 1315–7, was recorded from which Europe seems to have re-covered in a year or so. One should not take too seriously the habit of medieval chroniclers of exaggerating hunger, of writing that so many died that the living could hardly bury the dead every time there was an epidemic, or of suggesting a famine whenever the price of grain rose.

The weight of numbers of regions tended to explain some factors. The smaller population of India (smaller than usually assumed) explained why outside forces succeeded in conquer-ing India. The rise of Egyptian population from 1096 to 1315

probably doomed the Crusaders in Palestine. The great population of the Italian regions, especially in the cities, underlay their
dominant position in so many ways. The region of Paris was
too much for the other French regions and showed why the
English invasions of the Hundred Years War were among the
most futile policies of history. No existing map in an historical
atlas gives a hint of the relative importance of population
among countries and political units of the Middle Ages.

DENSITY OF POPULATION AND URBAN INDEX

Two indexes were related primarily to wealth. Density of
population was primarily associated with richness in farmland
when so large a part of the people were on the land.[5] The
urban index, the percentage of total population in the ten
largest cities, was essentially an indication of wealth in the
cities. Medieval culture as yet related jobs to marriage too
closely to pile up great masses of poor in the cities, although
Naples was apparently on its way at the end of the period.

The density of Egyptian population, about 121.7 to the km².
in the Valley, was triple that of north Italian regions even with
their great cities. The fertility of the Nile Valley was just too
superior to that of other farm areas. The relatively small size
of Egyptian cities is rather puzzling in view of the dense population of the countryside and since the cities themselves had
some industry. It may be that the Egyptian cities were too
close together to grow larger than they did.

In terms of density outside of the ten largest cities, the region
of Paris was second only to Egypt. Its density was about 31.8
to the km². However, this was not much denser than those of
Florence (30.0), Venice (29.0) and Milan (27.8). Lack of data
makes it difficult to estimate with much accuracy the density
of the German regions, but it was unlikely to have matched the
Italian or even the French of the west. The region of London
also was quite high (26.8). The lowest densities were those
of Ireland (8.0), Cordoba (8.6) and Barcelona (9.8); the slight-
ness of the agricultural population of the last is rather surprising and it raises some question about the accuracy of the
data for that region. On the other hand, the density of the
region of Toledo, (15.2) so much of which was high and rather

arid meseta, was also surprising. One wonders if that area were not already developing those unfortunate demographic habits, losing its grip on its population, which have plagued Spain since that time. If that were true, then the conquest of Iberia by the region of Toledo promised trouble for the future of that peninsula.

The increase in the urban index, that is, of the populations of the ten largest cities in relation to the populations of the countryside and other cities, was one of the outstanding developments of the period, but it seems to have been true mostly of the north Italian regions and the Low Countries. The region of London and probably of Paris saw population increase at about the same pace in city and countryside, as it probably did elsewhere. In Iberia since Moorish times cities had been of considerable size. The urban indexes of the three north Italian regions were: Florence, 26.0; Venice, 23.4 and Milan 17.1. Cordoba was not far behind with 17.0, with Ghent 14.1, Barcelona 14.0 and Montpellier 11.3. There was a considerable gap between these and the rest, but then lack of evidence among the others may account for some low estimates of their urban indexes. The very low indexes for some regions are also revealing. Toulouse with 3.3, London 4.4, Toledo with 4.5 and Paris 4.9. With the exception of the region of Toledo, they were regions of much wealth in land and of large size. The greatness of size was probably one factor in the low urban index. The cities after the first three or four were larger than normal presumably because they were centres of larger agricultural areas, which raised their size beyond their position in the rank-size pattern.

The relation to the rank-size hypothesis was instructive, since there was considerable diversity in it. It is valuable as a standard by which factors affecting cities, populations can be measured. By this standard many metropolitan cities did not have large enough populations. In general this resulted from a lack of sophistication and slow development within the region which had failed to produce the movements of population bringing in the full rank-size series. Paris and London were larger than the standard: both were heads of regions politically unified with a developing bureaucracy located at the capital, while the concentration of basic factors, economic as

well as political, was great there. Florence, Venice and Toulouse were also larger than some lesser cities assumed in the
rank-size series: the first two were great commercial cities, too
great for ten lesser cities in the series, while the cities of the
Toulouse region suffered from competition from near-by cities
outside of the region: Narbonne, Béziers, and Perpignan.

Four regions show a close correlation for most of the largest
ten cities with the hypothetical series: Antioch, Barcelona,
Dublin, and Toledo. They were all cities of commercial importance with, however, no extreme concentration of bureau-
cratic offices in the capital and sharing commercial and
industrial opportunities with the lesser cities. Thus aberrations
from such a normal situation results in deviation from the
hypothetical series.

TABLE 33: SIZE OF CITIES WITH RESPECT TO RANK-SIZE
PLACE IN REGION

| Rank | Number of cities with respect to hypothetical size | | |
	above	the same	below
2	7	8	4
3	11	5	4
4	11	7	3
5	12	6	3
6	10	9	1
7	12	4	2
8	11	6	3
9	12	3	4
10	11	5	3
11	8	2	1
12	8	1	1

The region of Milan not included. As an example, in the region of
Barcelona the population of Valencia was much larger than the second
city should be and thus is included in the first column.

One of the benefits of understanding a rank-size pattern is
that it facilitates estimating the size of cities and even in loca-
ting sites where suitable cities should be.

The indexes of size corroborate the evidence of the location
of the largest cities in emphasising the importance of commerce
as the chief basic factor of the great regions. Nevertheless, the

figures of population showed the possibilities of the largest regions in the field of politics. Given the acquisition of power of the most populous regions, Paris, Cairo, and Toledo, the holders of power were in a position to advance against neighbouring regions, if a kind of regional imperialism should develop.

THE AGE OF REGIONALISM

Regionalism as a base for culture was probably more widespread in the period 1250–1348 than in any earlier or later time. Before then, units based on feudal land holdings, although occasionally as widespread as a region, showed little demographic organisation comparable to the rank-size series so typical of the pre-plague period. Although at a later date nations have come to resemble regions occasionally, they are more complicated and better explained as a series of regions: the Industrial Revolution has produced a different world. The demographic case for the late medieval region, our primary concern, has been explained in the preceding ten chapters. In conclusion some comments are offered on the economic and political relationship. Regionalism was probably more significant economically than politically. On the latter point, we may note that the rise of great feudal houses sometimes coincided with regions, while the economic base for the growth in strength of the great Italian regions and of the Netherlands was very obvious.

The great days of the Italian regions were made possible initially by the activities of the cities themselves before 1200, activities which included extensive commerce throughout the Mediterranean. There was danger that they would be subordinated to the political forces, much as Amalfi, Gaeta and Naples had been by the Norman conquerors of the south. In the struggle against Frederick I the original leaders had been Cremona, Mantua, Bergamo, and Brescia rather than Milan and Venice. This was before the thirteenth-century orientation, but most of the cities were of the later region of Milan and their activity to that extent was evidence of regional interest. The battle of Legnano in 1176 made certain that there would be no reduction of the northern cities to the kind of passive action which marked the German cities under the Hohen-stauffen. While the league was renewed in 1226 against Freder-ick II, who did endeavour over a long period of years to sub-jugate the cities, he failed with most of them. At his death in 1250 the regional organisation of Venice, Milan, and Florence, although threatened occasionally, was essentially independent. Their large population was, in large part, the result of their great commercial and industrial operations, dominating the economic life of Europe and even of the Near East.

Professor Renouard[6] strikingly demonstrated that three great battles determined the course of the European state system within three years: Las Navas de Tolosa in 1212, Muret in 1213, and Bouvines in 1214. The first saw the driving out of the Almohades from Iberia by the Christian leaders of the peninsula, making possible the development of the regions of Barcelona and Lisbon and the expansion of the region of Toledo over Castille. Muret saw the end of the attempt to create a great south French-northern Spanish land power, but regionally substituted Paris for Barcelona as an intruding force in the regions of Montpellier and Toulouse. Bouvines thwarted England's effort to recover much of the regions of Paris and Toulouse which had been lost by King John's mistakes some years earlier, permitting greater unity to the region of Paris if not of Toulouse. It also frustrated the desire of King Otto IV to interfere in the region of Ghent. Thus the three battles, if they did encourage the 'regional imperialism' of Toledo and Paris, did bring more unification to some regions and release from interference to others.

The regions were like later nations in that the process of unification generated an expansive force within them and led them into 'imperialistic' ventures. Even in the fourteenth century the region-nation of England began the Hundred Years War, unluckily against the even more powerful region of Paris. Earlier, Paris under Philip Augustus went on to take parts of the regions of Toulouse and Montpellier as well as of the nearer region of Ghent. Toledo, as mentioned above, had advanced into the region of Cordoba, while Barcelona, restric-ted to a few south French areas, took advantage of the Sicilian Vespers of 1282 to take over Sicily and to continue its eastward expansion in the Mediterranean. In the Near

East, Egypt had a great age, even setting a limit to the Mongolian advance from Central Asia in 1260. The crusades had failed to produce a unity in the region of Antioch and perhaps just succeeded in preventing any unification of that region, a failure that still haunts the world.

The failure of the Empire brought more confusion to its western half than to the eastern. In the west the Dukes of Burgundy did seem about to unify the region of Dijon and threatened to prevent the unification of France well into the fifteenth century. The regions of Cologne and Augsburg were very chaotic, although Bavaria provided some unity to part of the latter region. The Hanseatic League provided a kind of backbone to the region of Lübeck, but the areas outside of the cities and their lands were hopelessly split among small feudal lords. The Wettins built up a considerable political power within the region of Magdeburg. However, shifts in the relative size of cities within these two regions were to make even the demographic base of them uncertain. The Premyslids unified much of the region of Prague, especially when it included the city of Vienna, a unity lost when the Hapsburgs captured that city. Perhaps the unity which these political leaders brought to the region led to later lack of strength of many of the lesser cities, subjected to the constant interference of fairly strong kings.

Maps can show only with difficulty the features peculiar to regions which made them distinctive. Some of these were of the landscape, the greenness of the Irish fields, the pines of Italy, the aridity of the Spanish Meseta and the differences in types of villages and village architecture. Then there were the typical smells coming from food, or animals or just the earth. Types of sounds were also characteristic; of musical instruments, of dances or of just the differences of voices; the sibilants of Spain, the linguals of Italy and the gutturals of northern Europe. In the Middle Ages, even more than today, would have been the difference in clothing, between persons of different regions as well as between rich and poor. All of these regional characteristics stood in the memory of those who had lived or visited them as vivid recollections of regions and their differences.

One factor that could hardly be missed was the creation

of regional types of physique.[7] In general, mass migration occurred or affected only relatively local areas. The tall Italians around Bologna as well as pockets of larger people in Iberia were apparently the result of earlier Celtic migrations. Usually invading groups became ruling classes, scattered over the countryside as knights, landowners and local officials in groups so small that they were soon swallowed up in the general population, particularly if they lost out as the ruling class.

The streams of migration which have been outlined had an interesting effect upon the physical appearance of the region's inhabitants. The cities tended to die out since they did not replace their dead with births. The reason was apparently that there were more women than men in the cities and men were slow to marry, postponing marriage, marrying less and producing fewer children than men in the countryside.[8] Moreover, men probably tended to marry women who were like themselves, either looking alike or sharing common interests. The tendency for those who look alike to marry tended also to force atypical persons, especially women, away from the villages—these were too tall or too different in appearance from the common type. And even in the city they often did not marry and thus the atypical characteristics tended to die out while in the villages the one type, or sometimes two or more types, developed. The peasantry was seldom disturbed, and so the type continued and became more pronounced over the centuries. Since migration was largely within the neighbourhood or at least the region, it saw the development of a regional type.

With so many common features occurring within a region, it naturally had an *esprit de corps*, an enthusiasm for its way of life and a loyalty for it. In England this emerged as something like patriotism.[9] In France, in the region of Paris particularly under the inspiration of Joan of Arc, a somewhat similar spirit appeared in the fifteenth century. The regional spirit had its less attractive side in its dislike for regional nonconformists, aliens in general and Jews and Moors in particular. In the fourteenth century the appearance of a long series of assemblies (*parlements, cortes,* diets, etc.) showed that ever larger groups of people were co-operating politically. It was a typical human phase in the spread of responsibility from the one to the many, from kingship to democracy.

In an age of relative prosperity the cycle moved on: one might even anticipate that, following the example of England, other regional semi-democracies would appear, producing something a little like the ancient series of city state democracies but on a larger and wider scale. With new ideas of personal and group representation available to make such a system work, it had a chance of success.

What made for the success of the more successful regions: the north Italian regions, England and the Low Country cities? In all of these the political base was broader than in the stronger monarchies: in city assemblies and elections and in the Parliament of England and Ireland, even though the poor were excluded from the English and the Celtic from Ireland. In general as the Greeks noted in their study of political cycles, the tendency was from the one to the many, in the use of power. The tendency to spread power was usually accompanied by greater morale and urge to expand. Even within the Church the age of the councils paralleled the secular age of the *parlement* and the diet.

A case can be made that the fourteenth-early fifteenth century was the greatest age of democracy before the nineteenth century. The political theory of even the canonists and Romanists insisted that what affected all must be approved by all and produced an age of proctors and representatives. The position of women rose with love in the romances, the increased veneration or adoration of the Virgin, notably in the thirteenth century, the secularisation of the period and ringside seats at the tournaments. And the remarkable position assigned to Beatrice by Dante, to Laura by Petrarch and Fiametta by Boccaccio replaced the dismal position assigned to women by Jerome and other medieval preachers. Even the poor were getting a break: 'When Adam delved and Eve span, who then was the gentleman?' And this democracy was primarily a city and regional democracy.

THE DECLINE OF REGIONALISM

In 1347 the future of the region as a basis for European life seemed excellent. There were few super-regional powers: the major ones were the Kings of England, France, Castille, and Aragon. In the Hundred Years War, France was threatened with the loss of much of the region of Toulouse and of Dijon as well as of part of the region of Paris. Such a loss might possibly have resulted in the setting up of essentially regional units in the lost areas. The English were losing ground in Ireland. There seems to have been no real centre for the organisation of the region of Cordoba. In Germany the formation of the small confederacy of the Swiss was an illustration of what might have been done elsewhere. There were tremendous obstacles, of course, in the political houses which were strong: the Hapsburgs, the Capetians, Angevins and the Iberian houses. It would have been necessary for a spirit like that of nationalism later to have swept Europe, presaged by that in England.

The continued development of regionalism in the fourteenth century depended in large part upon satisfactory conditions of life as do nearly all expansions of social control. Some have asserted that overpopulation had already created before the Black Death very unfavourable economic conditions which that epidemic only made worse. Still, until more evidence is offered in proof of overpopulation, the allegation may well be doubted. Population had obviously nearly reached a peak in the half-century before the plague, but the controls upon population were rather effective. In the newly settled areas growth was apparently continuous until 1348.

The Black Death, wiping out perhaps a fifth in the first epidemic, 1348–50, and, reducing the population in successive attacks every 3.8 years or its multiples, destroyed half of the people by the early part of the next century. With this went worsening economic conditions and the great depression of the fifteenth century. In these crisis conditions, as usual, individuals, invariably kings or other leaders of the great families, took over. Limitations on the leaders by the masses lessened and finally brought on as its culmination, the Age of Divine Right Monarchy. The chance to create regional democracies was lost. When next restraints upon absolute leadership developed, the Industrial Revolution had made an extensive middle class as well as a working class together with widespread systems of communication and travel. With these it was possible to operate over wide areas: to create nations as easily as it had been to create regions in the Middle Ages.

When one looks at the map of western Europe today, one notices that modern nations resemble either a region or a group of regions more than the political framework of the fourteenth century. France today is closer to the four regions which were French than the kingdom of the Capetians was then. Germany of course, was a chaotic state in that century and even the Empire did not coincide with the regions. Italy, divided among several states in the later Middle Ages, resembled the regions but some were dominated by Aragon or were independent districts. This is not surprising. Nationalism, like regionalism emphasised precisely the same characteristics of common life: it is easy to see the regional limits as later national boundaries. Regionalism thus preceded nationalism in creating widespread loyalties based upon physiographic and demographic conditions.

Thus the Age of Regionalism was strangled by the depression caused by the depopulation of the Black Death. It struggled for a time. The Conciliar Period was one interesting phase, succumbing to papal absolutism. The Estates General of France failed through guilt by association with plague, military defeat, devastation, and civil disturbance. Only in England did the idea of a sharing of royal powers persist, an historical accident, as a royal-parliamentary partnership, an upper-class phenomenon. It persisted also in sub-regions, like Iceland and Switzerland, as an example of what might have been. Royalist and Nationalist points of view have so dominated historical thinking that the possibility of a regionally oriented world in the late Middle Ages has seldom been considered.

Notes and References

Chapter 1   *The Structure of the Medieval Region, pages 15–38*

1   For modern use of basic-nonbasic approach see, for instance, J. W. Webb, 'Basic Concepts in the Analysis of Small Urban Centres in Minnesota', *Annals of the Association of American Geographers,* 49 (1959), 55–72, especially pp 61–63 ; J. W. Alexander, 'The Basic-Nonbasic Concept of Urban Economic Functions', *Economic Geography* 30 (1954) 246–61. For medieval use see my 'A Quantitative Approach to Medieval Population Change', *Journal of Economic History* 24 (1964), 1–21 ; reprinted in *Quantitative History,* ed Don K. Rowney and James Q. Graham (Homewood, Ill, 1969).

2   For an introduction to Urban rank-size relationships there is an extensive bibliography. Perhaps most accessible and convenient is *Readings in Urban Geography,* edited by Harold M. Mayer and Clyde F. Kohn (Chicago, 1959), especially articles by Edward Ullman (pp 202–9), Berry and Garrison (pp 230–9), Charles T. Stewart jr (pp 240–56) and Harris and Ullman (pp 277–86). For an interesting study of reverse rank-size order and a bibliography of other studies see A. R. H. Baker, 'Reversal of the Rank-Size Rule: Some Nineteenth Century Rural Settlements in France', *The Professional Geographer* 21 (1969), 386–92 and note 1.

3   For a long and excellent discussion of migration in the 14th–18th centuries see Mols, R. 'S. J. *Introduction à la Démographie Historique des Villes d'Europe du xive au xviiie siècle,* vol 2 (Louvain 1954), 338–93, especially 374–5 for its theoretical side.

4	Dickinson, R. E. *The Regions of Germany* (New York 1954), 23. For a more recent study of regionalism in modern Europe see R. E. Dickinson, *The City Region in Western Europe* (London, 1967). *The Journal of Regional Science* provides many articles on the subject: a medieval one is my 'Metropolitan City'. The subject now has a vast bibliography, in part because of its interest for regional planners.

5	Smith, C. T. *An Historical Geography of Europe before 1800* (London 1967) pp 303–31 usefully summarises the conditions of cities in the period 1250–1348.

6	Monkhouse, F. J. *A Regional Geography of Western Europe* (New York, third edition 1967), 3–5; Wrigley, E. A. 'The changing philosophy of geography' in Chorley, R. J. and Haggett, P. (eds) *Frontiers in Geographical Teaching* (London, second edition 1970), 7–13.

7	Pounds, N. J. G. and Ball, S. S. 'Core-Areas and the Development of the European States System', *Annals of the Association of American Geographers* 54 (1964), 24–40.

8	Russell, J. C. *British Medieval Population* (Albuquerque 1948), 181.

9	Russell, J. C. 'Late Ancient and Medieval Population', *Transactions of the American Philosophical Society* 43 no 3 (1958), 45–59; Mols, *Démographie Historique des Villes d'Europe* . . . vol 2, 100–163.

10	ibid, 63 n.2, 78.

11	Herlihy, D. *Medieval and Renaissance Pistoia: The Social History of an Italian Town* (New Haven 1967), 1–4.

12	Dickinson, *Regions of Germany*, 27.

13	Mols, vol 2, 510.

14	ibid, 374–5.

15	Russell, *Late Ancient and Medieval Population*, 13–19.

16	Fox, H. S. A. 'Going to Town in Thirteenth-Century England', *The Geographical Magazine* (1970), 658–67.

17	Mols, vol 2, 374–5

18	Meinecke Festgabe, *Das Hauptstadt Problem in der Geschichte* (Tübingen 1952).

19 Marongiu, A. *Il Parlamento in Italia* (Milan 1962), 108–99.

20 Renouard, Y. *Etudes d'Histoire Médiévale* (Paris 1967), 147.

21 Lyon, B. 'Medieval Constitutionalism: a Balance of Power', being pp 161–77 of *Album Helen Maud Cam* (Louvain 1961).

22 Briquet, C. M. *Les Filigranes* . . . (1907).

23 Russell, J. C. 'The Medieval Monedatge of Aragon and Valencia', *Proceedings of the American Philosophical Society* 106 (1962), 483–504.

Chapter 2 Central and Southern Italy: Florence and Palermo, pages 39–61

1 This section is largely republished from the author's 'Thirteenth-Century Tuscany as a Region', TAIUS (Texas A & I University Studies) 1 (1968) 42–52, with some changes. There is a very extensive bibliography of works on late Medieval and Renaissance Italy. On the demographic side, see especially the works of Herlihy, Carpentier, and Fiumi. This is, of course, in addition to Beloch's fundamental *Bevölkerungsgeschichte Italiens*.

2 Herlihy, D. *Pisa in the Early Renaissance: a Study of Urban Growth* (New Haven 1968), 46, 36–7.

3 ibid, *Pisa*, 43.

4 Bowsky, W. M. 'The Impact of the Black Death upon the Sienese Government and Society', *Speculum*, 39 (1964), 11.

5 Herlihy, *Pisa*, 36.

6 ibid, *Pisa*, 1–4.

7 Fiumi, E. *Storia economica e sociale di San Gimignano* (Firenze 1967), 54.

8 Herlihy, *Pisa*, 56.

9 Leroy, 7.

10 Beloch, K. J. *Bevölkerungsgeschichte Italiens*, vol 2, 5.

11 idem.

12 Waley, Daniel *The Papal State in the Thirteenth Century* (1961), 100–9.

13 The fundamental data come, with some modifications, from Beloch, *Bevölkerungsgeschichte Italiens*, vol 1.

14 Beloch, Vol 1, 118–22.

15 Traselli, Carmelo. 'Sulla popolazione di Palermo nei secoli xiii–xiv', Economia e storia, 11 (1964), 328–44.

16 Marongiu, A. *Il Parlamento in Italia* (Milan 1963), 21, 23, 184, 340.

17 Traselli, 338–9.

18 Beloch, vol 1, 122.

19 ibid, vol 1, 136, 159.

20 idem.

21 Marongiu, *Il Parlamento* . . . 182–3, 228, 230–1.

22 Beloch, vol 1, 272.

23 *Cambridge Economic History of Europe*, vol 3, 86.

24 Beloch, vol 1, 200, 272.

25 ibid, vol 1, 93.

26 ibid, vol 1, 199, 203.

27 Marongiu, op cit.

Chapter 3   *Regions of Northern Italy: Venice and Milan, pages 62–76*

1 For both of the regions of Venice and Milan the chief source is still Beloch's *Bevölkerungsgeschichte Italiens*, vols 2 and 3.

2 Russell, J. C. *Late Ancient and Medieval Population* (1948), 128.

3 ibid, 111.

4 Heers, J. 'Les limites des méthodes statistiques pour les recherches de démographie historique', *Annales de démographie historique* (1968), 64–5.

5 Beloch, op cit, vol 3, 288

6 Pistarino, G. 'Genova medievale tra Oriente e Occidente', *Rivista storica italiana* 81 (1969) 44–73.

7 Cipolla, C. 'Profilo di storia demografica della città di Pavia', *Bolletino Storico Pavese* 6 (1943), 9–21.

8 R. de Roover, *Cambridge Economic History of Europe*, vol 3, 43.

Chapter 4   Border   Regions: Augsburg, Dijon,   and   Cologne, pages 77–96

1 The two works of Keyser are paramount in the field, but the historical geography of cities is now much studied in Germany. Much can be drawn from the historical maps in Dickinson's *Regions*. The work of Püschel in verifying the persistence of patterns of streets from the Middle Ages has been valuable in giving confidence in that type of data.

2 Offler, in Hale, J. R., B. Highfield and B. Smalley, *Europe on the Late Middle Ages* (1965), 218.

3 Dickinson, R. E. *The Regions of Germany* (1964), 148–155.

4 ibid, 476.

5 Mols, op cit, vol 2, 294, 510.

6 Schreiber, Adèle, 'Die Entwicklung der Augsburger Bevölkerung von Ende des 14 Jahrhundert'. *Archiv für Hygiene*, 123 (1939) 90–170, 139, 153.

7 Schmiedler, 89

8 Fourquin, G. *Histoire économique de l'Occident médiéval* (Paris 1969), 325.

9 Püschel, A. *Das Anwachsen* . . . (1910), 210 ; Schönberg, G. 'Basels Bevölkerungzahl . . .' (1883).

10 Püschel, 210

11 Renouard, op cit, 701.

12 Laurent, Henri. *Un grand commerce d'exportation au moyen âge* . . . (Paris 1935), 51.

13 Russell, J. C. *Late Ancient and Medieval Population*, 120.

14 Mols, op cit, vol 3, 99.

15 Bielefeldt, E. *Der Rheinische Bund von 1264* (Berlin 1937), 17.

16 Dollinger, in *La Foire* (1953), 383–9.

17 Ammann, H. 'Deutschland und die Tuchindustrie . . .' (1954), 20.

18 Mols, op cit, vol 2, 39, 147, 509.

19 Mols, op cit, vol 2, 63.

20 Püschel, op cit, 209.

21 Russell, J. C. op cit, 112.

22 Mols, op cit, vol 2, 63.

23 Ammann, op cit, 20.

24 Mols, vol 2, 510.

25 Mols, vol 2, 376, 405.

26 Mols, vol 2, 369.

27 Mols, vol 2, 390.

28 Mols, vol 2, 64 note 2.

29 Mols, vol 3, 235.

30 Singer, Elly. 'Untersuchungen über die Bevölkerung Dortmunds . . .' (1936), 125.

Chapter 5   Frontier Regions: Prague, Magdeburg, and Lübeck, pages 97–111

1 For the German areas the works of Keyser are the most important, although much local work is being done. Local history, especially archaeology, is developing well in Czechoslovakia.

2 Dickinson, R. E. *The Regions of Germany* (1945), 168.

3 Dickinson, op cit, 159.

4 Svidkovskij, O. A. *Urbanismus Socialistického* Ceskoslovenska (Praha, 1966), 19.

5 Mols, op cit, vol 2, 138 from Beer, K. 'Zur Bevölkerungsstatistik . . . Prags . . .' (1920), 80–81.

6 Mols, vol 2, 138.

7 Püschel, op cit, 210.

8 *Untersuchungen zur Gesellschaftlichen Struktur der mittelälterlichen Städte . . .* (1963–4), 282–4.

9 Meitzen, A. *Sieldung und Agrarwesen der Westgermanen* . . . (Berlin 1895), vol 3, 292.

10 Meinicke Festgabe (1952) ; Helbig, 34–8.

11 Smith, C. T. *An Historical Geography* . . . (1967), 318–21 ; Gringmuth-Dallmer, H. 'Magdeburg—Haupthandelsplatz der mitteleren Elbe' (1966), 18.

12 Brandt, A. and W. Koppe *Städtewesen und Bürgertum* . . . (1953) 470.

13 Russell, J. C. 'Recent Advances in Medieval Demography' (1965), 100.

14 Mols, op cit, vol 2, 33, 219.

15 de Roover, R. in *Cambridge Economic History of Europe.* vol 3, 106.

16 Brandt, *Untersuchungen* . . . 216

17 Meitzen, vol 3, 296.

18 Reisner, W. *Ein Einwohnerzahl deutscher Städte* . . . (1903), 92–3.

19 Mols, op cit, vol 3, 235.

20 IXe Congrès International des Sciences Historiques (1950), *Rapports*, 78.

21 Mols, op cit, vol 2, 434, from the Bremen Urkundenbuch, vol 3, nl.

22 Mols, op cit, vol 3, 161.

23 Brunner, *Untersuchungen* . . . 281

24 Prinz, *The West European City* (Dickinson), 374.

25 Brandt, *Untersuchungen* . . . 232.

Chapter 6   *North Sea Regions: Ghent, London, and Dublin, pages 112–45*

1 Lane, F. C. 'The Economic Meaning of the Invention of the Compass' (1963), 608–17.

2 The data about many of the cities of the Low Countries are conveniently gathered in *IXH*. Much of the data appear in Mols.

3 van Houtte, *Untersuchungen* . . . 266; Lestocquoy, *Aux Origines* . . . (1952), 187.

4 Van Werveke, Hans, 'De Zwarte Dood . . .' (1950).

5 Van Werveke, Hans, *Miscellanea Medievalia* (1968), 283–90.

6 Dickinson, op cit, 303.

7 Mols, op cit, vol 3, 233.

8 *Cambridge Economic History of Europe*, vol 3, 86, 96.

9 Mols, op cit, vol 2, 520.

10 Cuvelier, cxvi.

11 Mols, op cit, vol 2, 521.

12 Mols, vol 2, 520; *IXH* vol 1, 80.

13 Mols, vol 2, 520.

14 Mols, vol 2, 389.

15 Capelle, J. 'La famille de Gaiffier' (1905), 76.

16 Nicholas, F. 'L'évolution géographique de la ville de Namur' (1925), 184.

17 Mols, vol 2, 383n 5.

18 Russell, J. C. *LAMP*, 122.

19 The data for the British Isles come in part from the author's *British Medieval Population* (Albuquerque, 1948). The English rank-size arrangement appears in his 'Demographic Comparison', which is heavily drawn on.

20 Post, G. *Studies in Medieval Legal Thought* . . . (1964), 389n.

21 Young, Charles R. *The English Borough* . . . (1961), 63–8.

22 Carus-Wilson, E. M. 'An Industrial Revolution of the Thirteenth Century' (1941).

23 Russell, J. C. 'The Pre-Plague Population of England' (1966), 20.

24 ibid 1.

25 This is, with few changes of some importance, the present author's 'Late Thirteenth-Century Ireland', where there are more extensive footnotes about the data used.

26 Hollingsworth, T. H. *Historical Demography* (1969).

27 Russell, J. C. *LAMP*, 7.

Chapter 7 Western French Regions: Paris and Toulouse, pages 146–59

1 Levasseur, E. *La Population francaise* (1889) ; Schöne, L. *Histoire de la population francaise* (1893).

2 For France, the pioneer work of Lot is invaluable. For northern France it is supplemented for the area of cities by the works of Ganshof, Grenier, and Dickinson.

3 Roloff, Meinicke Festgabe. *Das Haupstadt Problem* . . . (1952), 240.

4 Fawtier, Robert. *The Capetian Kings of France* (1964), 216–26.

5 Post, G. op cit, 448, 476.

6 Fawtier, op cit, 186–8.

7 Michäelsson, K. *Le Livre de la Taille* . . . (see Bibliograhy).

8 Fourquin, G. *Histoire économique* . . . (1969), 89.

9 Pernoud, R. *Histoire de la bourgeoisie* . . . (1960), 29.

10 *WEC*, 416.

11 Bautier in *La Foire* . . . (1953), 109–35.

12 Renouard, Y. *Conséquences* . . . (1948), 476.

13 Renouard, Y. *Etudes* . . . (1967), 167.

14 Renouard, Y. *Conséquences* . . . (1948), 473, 475.

15 Lot, Ferdinand. *Recherches* . . . (1945–54), 395–6.

16 idem, vol 2, 580.

17 Prat, Geneviève. 'Albi . . .' (1952).

18 Renouard, Y. *Etudes* . . . (1967), 617–37.

19 Mols, op cit, vol 2, 517.

20 Lot F. op cit, vol 2, 602.

21 Maillard, *Annales du Midi* (1967), 67.

R

22   Renouard, Y. *Etudes* . . . 170.

23   Sautel in *La Foire* . . . 330.

Chapter 8   *North-Western Mediterranean Regions: Montpellier and Barcelona, pages 160–75*

1   *WEC*, 29–30.

2   Renouard, op cit, 147.

3   Denifle, H. 'Liber divisionis . . .' (1885).

4   Baratier, E. *La Démographie provençale* . . . (1961), 66.

5   Lot, op cit, vol 1, 178.

6   Mols, op cit, vol 1, 255.

Lot and Mols contributed much to data about cities in the region of Montpellier.

7   *WEC*, 29–30.

8   Baratier, op cit, 144.

9   Lot, op cit, vol 1, 373.

10   Baratier, op cit, 67.

11   *LAMP*, 106.

12   Renouard, Y. 'Les Principaux aspects . . .' (1962), 238.

13   The estimates of Vives Vicens (*Economic History* 176) should be kept in mind. He was always interested in population. This part draws heavily on my *Medieval Monedatge*'

14   Iglesias Fort, J. 'El Fogaje . . .', 7–21.

15   idem, 21–25.

16   idem, 317.

17   Smith, R. S. 'Fourteenth-Century Population Records . . .' (1944).

18   Marongiu, *Il Parlamento* . . . 112.

19   Smith, op cit, 499.

20   Russell, J. C. MM, 486.

21   idem, 495.

22 Marongiu, op cit, 124–5.

23 Iglesias, op cit, 89.

24 idem, 86.

25 idem, 65.

26 Renouard, op cit, 246–9.

27 Gual Camarena, Miguel. 'Para una mapa . . .' (1967), 128.

28 Russell, MM, 501.

29 Vives Vicens, *Economic History* . . . 176.

Chapter 9   Three Iberian Regions: Cordoba, Toledo, and Lisbon,
pages 176–96

1 Imammuddin, S. M. *Economic History* . . . (1963), 239, 323, 339.

2 Russell, *LAMP*, 92, with modifications.

3 Other estimates of area come from guides and local histories. Estimates of city size appear in Vives Vicens (*Economic History* 176) and Marques de Lozoya, vol 2, 365. 'En la baja Edad Media' (ca 1500?): Seville 70,000, Cordoba 35,000, Jaen 35,000, Baeza 20,000, Ubeda 20,000, Andarjan 15,000, Carmona 15,000; 25–35,000 Valladolid, Medina del Campo, Salamanca, Toledo; more than 10,000: Burgos, Segovia, Cuenca; about 10,000 Madrid, Ocana.

4 Torres Balbas, L. *Studia Islamica*, vol 3, 55–6.

5 idem.

6 Menendez Pidal, R. *Historia* . . . (1966) vol 5, 201.

7 Torres Balbas, *Al-Andalus* 18, 181.

8 Zamora, Fr J. G. de *De Preconiis* . . . (1955), 118.

9 Gonzalez, J. *Repartimiento* . . . (1951), vol 1, 315.

10 idem, vol 2, 36–177.

11 Proctor, E. S. *Alfonso X* . . . (1951), 14.

12 Torres Balbas, Granada, 139–40.

13 Torres Balbas, Almeria, 249.

14   Beltran, A. Cartagena.

15   Bosque Maurel, J. Cartagena, 155.

16   Russell, *LAMP*, 60, 102.

17   Zamora, op cit, 217.

18   Lane, F. C. 'The Economic Meaning . . .' (1963), 617.

19   Da Silva, J.-G. 'Au Portugal . . .' 509.

20   Russell, *LAMP*, 118.

21   Russell, *BMP*, 185.

22   David, C. W. *De Expugnatione* . . . (1936), 77.

23   Russell, *LAMP*, 102, 117.

Chapter 10   Two Near-eastern Regions: Antioch and Cairo, pages 197–213

1   Much of this had been prepared to appear as a chapter in the *History of the Crusades*, edited now by Setton.

2   Krey, A. C. ed *William of Tyre* . . . vol 1, 199.

3   Sauvaget, J. 'Le plan antique de Damas' (1949), *Syria*, 331–2.

4   Sauvaget, *Alep* liv, lviii.

5   Drawn heavily from the author's 'Demographic Comparison' and to a less extent from his 'Population of Egypt'.

6   Lahib, S. Y. *Handelsgeschichte Agyptens* . . . (1965) discusses this.

Chapter 11   The Regions of Hiven Tsang's India (AD 629–45), pages 214–29

1   Russell, *LAMP*, 148.

2   Nath, Pran. *A Study* . . . (1929), 117–23.

3   Watters, T. *On Yuan Chwang's* [Hiven Tsang's] *Travels* . . . (1961), vol 1, 333.

4   idem, vol 2, 209.

5   Ghoshal, 606–7.

6 Sharma, R. S. *Light on Early Indian Society* . . . (1966), 150.

7 Gopal, L. *The Economic Life of Northern India* . . . (1965), 230.

Chapter 12   The Significance of Pre-plague Regions, pages 230–47

1 Klapisch-Zuber, C. *Les maitres du marbre* . . . (1969).

2 Pounds, N. J. G. 'Overpopulation in France . . .' (1970).

3 Russell, *LAMP*, 15, 52–4, 56.

4 Delatouche, R. 'Le boisson d'eau douce . . .' (1966).

5 Pounds, op cit, 232.

6 Renouard, *Etudes*, vol 1, 12.

7 Russell, J. C. 'The Persistance of Physical Type' (1950).

8 idem, 13–22.

9 Keeney, B. C. 'Military Service . . .' (1947), *Speculum*, 548.

Bibliography

Allen, A. M. *A History of Verona* (New York, 1910).

Ammann, H. 'Deutschland und die Tuchindustrie Nordwest-
europas im Mittelalter', *Hanisische Geschichtsblätter* 72
(1954) 1–63.

Baratier, E. *La démographie provençale du xiii⁰ au xvi⁰ siècle*
(Paris, 1961, SEVPEN).

Barthélemy, E. de *Histoire de la ville de Châlons-sur-Marne*
(Châlons, 1854).

Bartlett, J. N. 'The Expansion and Decline of York in the later
Middle Ages', *Economic History Review*, 2nd ser 12 (1959)
17–23.

Bartossi, B. T. 'Crema', *Bollettino della geografia Italiana* ser
8. 6 (1953) 471–510.

Bautier, R.-H. 'Feux, population et structure social au milieu
du xv⁰ siècle; l'exemple de Carpentras', *Annales* 14 (1959)
255–68.

Beer, K. 'Zur Bevölkerungsstatistik (15–16 Jht) Prags und
einiger anderen Städte Böhmens', *Mitteilungen des Vereins
für Geschichte der Deutschen in Böhmen* 58 (1920) 74–87.

Beloch, K. J. *Bevölkerungsgeschichte Italiens* 3 vols (Berlin 1937–39–41).

Beltran, Antonio. 'Topografia de Carthago Nova', *Archivo español de arqueología* 21 (1948) 191–224.
—— 'El plano arqueológico de Cartagena', *ibid*, 25 (1952) 47–82.

Berry, B. J. L. *Geography of Market Centres and Retail Distribution* (1967).

Bertossi, B. T. 'Crema', *Bolletino della Soc. Geog. Ital.* ser 8, 6 (1953) 471–510.

Bielefeldt, E. *Der Rheinische Bund von 1264* (Berlin 1937).

Binz, Louis. 'La population du diocèse de Genéve a la fin du moyen âge', *Mélanges d'histoire économique et social au homage au Professeur Antony Babel* (Geneva 1963) 107.

Biraben, J-N. 'La population de Reims et son arrondissement et la vérification statistique des recensements anciens', *Population* 16 (1961) 722–30.

Bird, R. *The Turbulent London of Richard II* (1949): map by M. B. Honeybourne.

Bosque Maurel, J. 'Cartagena', *Estudios Geográficos* 10 (1949) 579–638.

Bosque Maurel, J. 'Geografía Urbana de Granada', *Estudios Geográficos* 17 (1956) 461–73.

Bowsky, W. M. 'The Impact of the Black Death upon the Sienese Government and Society', *Speculum*, 39 (1964) 1–34.

Brandt, A. and W. Koppe. *Städtewesen und Bürgertum als geschichtliche Kräfte. Gedächtnisschrift für F. Rorig* (Lübeck 1953).

Briquet, C. M. *Les filigranes: dictionnaire historique des marques du papier vers 1282 jusqu'en 1600* (1907).

Bücher, Karl. *Die Bevölkerung von Frankfurt am Main im 14 u 15 Jht* (Tübingen 1886).

Cahen, C. 'Le régime rural syrien au temps de domination franque', *Bulletin de la Faculté des Lettres de Strasbourg* 29 (1950–1) 286–310.

Capelle, J. 'La famille de Gaiffier', *Annales de la societé archéologique de Namur* 26 (1905) 76–82.

Carli, F. 'Il movimento demografico in Italia dal XI al XIII secolo', *Studi in onore di Riccardo dalla Volta* 1 (Florence 1936) 81–109.

Carpentier, Elisabeth. *Une ville devant la peste. Orvieto et la peste noire de 1348* (Paris 1962, SEVPEN).

Carus-Wilson, E. M. 'An Industrial Revolution of the Thirteenth Century', *Economic History Review* 11 (1941) 41–60.

Chauvet, G. *Uzès* (Uzès 1963).

CEHE *Cambridge Economic History of Europe.*

Chorley, R. J. and Peter Haggett, ed, *Frontiers in Geographical Teaching* (2nd ed, 1970).

Cipolla, C. 'Profilo di storia demografica della città di Pavia' *Bolletino Storico Pavese* 6 (1943) 7–69.

Citarella, A. O. 'Patterns in Medieval Economy: the Commerce of Amalfi before the Crusades', *Journal of Economic History* 28 (1968) 531–55.

Courtenay, P. P. 'Madrid: the Circumstances of its Growth', *Geography* 24 (1959) 22–34, map p 31.

Cunningham, A. *Ancient Geography of India*, ed S. H. Sastri (Calcutta 1924).

Cutts, E. L. *Colchester* (1897).

Cuvelier, E. *Les dénombrements des foyers de Brabant (xiv-xvᵉ siècles)* Brussels, 1915.

Dansgaard, W., S. J. Johnsen, J. Moller, C. C. Langway, 'One Thousand Centuries of Climatic Record from Camp Century on the Greenland Ice Sheet', *Science*, 166 (1969) 378.

Da Silva, J-G. 'Au Portugal: structure démographique et développement économique', *Studi in onore di Amintore Fanfani* II, 491–510.

David, C .W. *De Expugnatione Lyxbonensi* (New York 1936). On the authorship of this chronicle see Russell in *Speculum* 45 (1970) 72–4.

Delatouche, R. 'Le boisson d'eau douce dans l'alimentation médiévale', *Compts-rendus de l'Academie d'Agriculture de France* (1966) 793–8.

Denholm-Young, N. *The Country Gentry in the Fourteenth Century* (Oxford 1969).

Denian, J. *La commun de Lyon* (Lyon 1934).

Denifle, H. 'Liber divisionis cortesianorum et civium Romanae Curiae et Civitatis Avinionis', *Archiv für Litteratur—und Kirchengeschichte des Mittelalters* 1 (1885) 627–30.

De Smet, J. 'Les dénombrements des foyers en Flandre en 1469', Bull C. R. H. 99 (1952) 255-333.

Dickinson, R. E. *The City Region in Western Europe* (1967).

Dickinson, R. E. *The Regions of Germany* (New York 1945).

Dickinson, R. E. *Western European City; a Geographical Interpretation* (1951) abbreviated WEC.

Dollinger, Ph. and Ph. Wolff. *Bibliographie d'histoire des villes de France* (Paris 1967).

Dollinger, Ph. 'La chiffre de population de Paris au xive siècle: 210,000 au 80,000', *Revue historique* 216 (1956) 35–44.

Dopp, Wolfram. *Die Altstadt Neapels* (Marburg 1969, Lahn, Marburger geographische Schriften no 37).

DS *Deutsche Städtebuch*, ed E. Keyser *et al.*

Duby, G. *La société aux xie et xiie siècles dans la region mâconnaise* (Paris 1953).

East, W. Gordon. *An Historical Geography of Europe* (3rd ed 1948).

Egli, E. *Geschichte des Städtebaues*, II (Zurich 1959).

Eheberg, K. Th. 'Strassburgs Bevölkerungszahl seit dem Ende des 15. Jahrhunderts bis zur Gegenwart'.

Ekwall, Eilert. *Studies on the Population of Medieval London* (Stockholm: Kungl. Vitterhets Histories och Antikvitets Akademiens Handlingar Filologisk-Filosofiska Serien 2, 1956).

EUI: *Enciclopedia Universala Europeo-Americana* (Bilbao, 1907).

Ewig, E. 'Résidence et capitale pendant le haut Moyen Age', *Révue historique* 230 (1963) 25–72.

Eychart, P. 'Les origines de Clermont-Ferrand', *La Vie Urbiane* 3 (1966) 162–8.

Fahlbusch, O. 'Die Bevölkerungszahl der Stadt Braunschweig im Amfang des 15. Jhdts', *Hansische Geschichtsblätter* (1912) 249–57.

Fanfani, A. 'Aspetti demografici della politica economica nel ducato di Milano (1386–1535)', *Saggi di Storia economica italiana* (1936) p 125.

Fawtier, Robert, *The Capetian Kings of France*, trans. L. Butler and R. J. Adam (1964).

Fiumi, E. 'La demografia fiorentina nelle pagine di Giovanni Villani,' *Archivio storico italiano* 107 (1949) 1–16.

Fiumi, E. 'Fioritura e decadenza dell'economia fiorentina: II Demografia e movimenti urbanisti', *Archivio storico italiano* 116 (1958) 443–510.

Fiumi, Enrico. *Storia economica e sociale di San Gimignano* (Firenze 1961).

La Foire. Recueils de la Société Jean Bodin. 5 (1953), various authors.

Font Rius, J. 'Neuere Arbeitenzur Spanischen Städtegeschichte', *Vierteljahrschrift für Sozial- und Wirtschaftsgeschichte* 42 (1955) 137–51.

Fourquin, G. *Histoire économique de l'Occident médiéval* (Paris 1969).

Fourquin, G. *La population de la région parisienne aux environs de 1328, Le Moyen Age* 62 (1956) 63–91.

Fox, H. S. A. 'Going to Town in 13th-Century England', *The Geographical Magazine* (1970) 658–67.

Ganshof, F. L. *Étude sur le développement des villes entre Loire et Rhin au moyen âge* (Paris 1943).

Garcia Fernandez, J. 'Alcala de Henares', *Estudios Geográficos* 13 (1952) 299–355.

Garnier, J. *La recherche des feux en Bourgogne aux XIVᵉ et XVᵉ siècles* (Dijon 1876).

Ghoshal, V. H. in R. C. Majumbar, *The Classical Age* (Bombay, 1954).

Gil de Zamora, J. See Zamora.

Gill, Crispin. *Plymouth, A New History* (Newton Abbot 1966).

Gonzalez, Julio. *Repartimiento de Sevilla.* (Madrid 1951).

Gonzalez, Tomas. *Censo de Población* (Madrid 1829).

Gopal, Lallanji. *The Economic Life of Northern India c A.D. 700–1000* (Delhi 1965).

Görich, W. 'Gedanken zur Vehrkehrslage und Siedlungenwicklung von Paderborn in frühen und hohen Mittelalter', *Westfälische Forschungen* 10 (1957) 158–67; map on p 164.

Grenier, A. *Manuel d'archéologie Gallo-Romaine* (Paris, 1931, 1934). [Volumes 5 and 6 of J. Dechelette, *Manuel d'archéologique préhistorique et Gallo-Romaine.*]

Grinmuth-Dallmer, H. 'Magdeburg-Haupthandelsplatz der mitteleren Elbe', *Hansische Geschichtsquellen* 84 (1966) 8–19.

Gual Camarena, Miguel. 'Para un mapa de la industria textil hispana en la edad media', *Anuario de Estudios Medievales* 4 (1967), 109–168.

Gutkind, E. A. *International History of City Development*. I Urban Development in Central Europe (Glencoe 1964): II Urban Development in the Alpine and Scandinavian Countries: III Urban Development in Southern Europe (New York, 1967).

Hale, J. R., B. Highfield and B. Smalley, *Europe in the late Middle Ages* (Evanston 1965).

Hamm, Ernst. *Die deutsche Stadt im Mittelalter* (Stuttgart 1935).

Heers, J. *Genes au xvᵉ siècle: activité économique et problèmes sociaux* (Paris 1961, SEVPEN).

Heers, J. 'Les limites des méthodes statistiques pour les recherches de démographie médiévale', *Annales de demographie historique* (1968) 43–72.

Hegel, K. *Chroniken der deutschen Städte, II (Nürnberg)* (Leipzig 1864), 95–120, 317–323, 500–513.

Herlihy, David. *Medieval and Renaissance Pistoia: The Social History of an Italian Town* (New Haven 1967).

Herlihy, David. *Pisa in the Early Renaissance: a Study of Urban Growth* (New Haven 1968).

Herzog, E. *Die ottonischen Stadt* (Berlin 1964).

Higounet, C. 'Cologne et Bordeaux, marchés de vin au moyen âge', *Revue historique de Bordeaux* 17 (1968) 65–80.

Higounet-Nadal, A. *Les comptes de la taille et les sources de l'histoire démographique du xiv siècle* (Paris 1965).

Hoenig, A. *Deutscher Städtebau in Böhmen* (Berlin 1921).

Hollingsworth, T. H. *Historical Demography* (1969).

Homberg, A. K. 'Zur Erforschung des westfälischer Städtewesens in Hochmittelalter', *Westfälische Forschungen* 14 (1961) 8–41.

Iglesias Fort, J. 'El Fogaje de 1365–1370', *Memorias de la Real Academia de Ciencias y Artes* 34 (1962) 247–356.

Imammuddin, S. M. *The Economic History of Spain under the Umayyads, 711–1031* (Dacca 1963).

IXH: IXe Congrès International des Sciences Historiques (Paris 1950), *Rapports*, pp 76–80.

Jastrow, J. *Die Volkszahl deutscher Städte zu Ende des Mittelalter und zu Beginn der Neuzeit* (Berlin 1886).

Jatzwauk, J. *Die Bevölkerungs- und Vermögens-verhältnisse der Stadt Bautzen zu Anfang des 15 Jhdt* (Bautzen, 1912).

Jecht, R. 'Wie lassen sich die Görlitzer Geschussbücher fur die einheimische Geschichtsschreibung nutzbar machen?' *Neues Lausitzisches Magazin* 72 (1896) 284–92.

Jimeno, E. 'La población de Soria y su termino in 1270', *Bull. Real Academia de Historia*, 142 (1958) 207–74.

Jowett, R. L. P. *Salisbury* (Salisbury 1951).

Keeney, B. C. 'Military Service and the Development of Nationalism in England, 1272–1327', *Speculum* 22 (1947) 534–49.

Keyser, E. *Die Bevölkerung Danzigs und ihre Herkunft im 13 u 14 Jhdt*. 2nd ed (Danzig 1928).

Keyser, E. *Bevölkerungsgeschichte Deutschlands* 2nd ed (Leipzig 1941).

Klapische-Zuber, C. *Les maitres du marbre: Carrare 1300–1600* (Paris 1969, SEVPEN).

Koppmann, K. 'Uber die Pest des Jahres 1565 und die Bevölkerungstatistik Rostocks im 14, 15, und 16 Jahrhundert', *Hansische Geschichtsblätter*, 10 (1901) 45-67.

Kowalewsky, M. *Die ökonomische Entwicklung Europas bis zum Beginn der Kapitalistischen Wirtschaftsform* 7 vols (Berlin 1901–14).

Krey, A. C. *The First Crusade, the Accounts of Eye-Witnesses and Participants* (Princetown 1921).

Kronschage, W. *Die Bevölkerung Göttingen: ein demographischer Beitrag zur Sozial- und Wirtschaftsgeschichte von 14 bis 17 Jahrhundert* (Göttingen 1960).

Lacarra, J. M. 'El desarrollo urbano de Navarra y Aragon en la Edad Media', *Pirineos* 6 (1950) Lacarro, J. M. 'Orientation des études d'histoire urbaine en Espagne entre 1940 et 1957,' *Le Moyen Age* 13 (1958) 317-39.

Lahib, S. Y. *Handelsgeschichte Agyptens in Spätmittelalter (1171–1517) (Wiesbaden 1965).*

Lamb, H. H. 'Britain's Changing Climate', in C. G. Johnson and L. P. Smith, *The Biological Significance of Climatic Changes in England* (London, New York, 1965, Institute of Biology).

Lane, F. C. 'At the Roots of Republicanism', *American Historical Review* 71 (1966) 403–20.

Lane, Frederick C. 'The Economic Meaning of the Invention of the Compass', *American Historical Review* 68 (1963) 608–17.

La Plante, Ed. de. *Histoire de Sisteron* (Paris 1844).

Laurent, Henri. *Un grand commerce d'exportation au moyen âge. La draperie des Pays-Bas en France et dans les pays Méditerranéens (xii–xv siècles)* (Paris 1935).

Laurent, J. C. M. 'Uber das älteste und über das Zweitälteste Hamburger Bürgerbuch', *Zeitschrift des Vereins für Hamburgische Geschichte* 1 (1841).

Lavedan, P. *Histoire de l'urbanisme* I, Antiquité, Moyen Age (Paris 1926).

Lavedan, P. *Les villes Françaises* (Paris 19—).

Lechuer, K. *Das Grosse Sterbem in Deutschland in dem Jahren 1348-51 und die folgenden Pest epidemien bis zum schluss des 14 Jahrhunderts* (Innsbruck 1884).

Le Goff, J. *La civilisation de l'occident médiéval* (Paris 1967).

Lesage, George. *Marseille Angevin* (Paris 1950).

Lestacquoy, J. *Aux origines de la bourgeoisie: les villes de Flandre et Italie* (Paris 1952).

Lestocquoy, J. 'Les villes et la population urbaine (l'exemple d'Arras)', *Cahiers de civilisation médiéval* I (1958).

Levasseur, E. *La population Française* I (Paris 1889).

Lewis, A. R. 'Seigneurial Administration in Twelfth Century Montpellier', *Speculum* 22 (1947) 562–77.

Lobel, M. D. *Historic Towns* (London 1969).

Lot, Ferdinand. 'L'état des paroisses et des feux de 1328', *Bibliothèque de l'École des Chartes*, 90 (1929) 51–107, 256–315.

Lot, Ferdinand. *Recherches sur la population et le superficie des cités remontant à la période gallo-romaine*, (3 v Paris 1945–54).

Lozaya, Marques de. *Historia de España* (Barcelona 1970).

Lütge, F. 'Das 14.15. Jahrhundert in der Sozial- und Wirtschaftsgeschichte', *Jahrbücher fur Nationalökonomie und Statistik* 162 (1950) 161–213.

Lyon, B. 'Medieval Constitutionalism: a Balance of Power', *Album Helen Maud Cam* (Louvain, 1961, International Commission for the History of Representation and Parliamentary Institutions).

Maillard. *Annales du Midi* 73 (1961) 65-81.

Mantels, W. 'Uber die beiden ältesten Lübeckischen Bürgermatrikeln', in K. Koppmann, *Beiträge zur Lübisch-Hansischen Geschichte* (Jena 1881) 55–100.

Marongiu, A. *Il parlamento in Italia* (Milan 1962).

Meinecke Festgabe. *Das Haupstadt Problem in der Geschichte* (Tübingen 1952).

Meitzen, A. *Siedlung und Agrarwesen der Westgermanen und Ostgermanen* (Berlin 1895).

Mendl, B. 'Breslau zu Beginn des 15 Jhdt. Eine Statistische Studie nach dem Steuerbuch von 1403'. *Z. des Vereins für Geschichte Schlesiens,* 63 (1929) 154–85.

Menendez Pidal, R. *Historia de España.* Vol. XIV L. Suarez y Juan Reglà Campistol, (Madrid 1966).

Michäelsson, K. *Le livre de la taille de Paris de l'an 1296* (Göteberg, 1958 Romanica Gothoburgensia, 7).

Michäelsson, K. *Le livre de la taille de Paris de l'an 1297* (Göteberg 1962, Romanica Gothoburgensia, 9).

Michäelsson, K. *Le Livre de la Taille de Taille de Paris, l'an de Grace 1313* (Göteberg 1951, Acta Universitatis Gotoburgensis).

Mistele, K-H. *Die Bevölkerung der Reichstadt Heilbronn im späten Mittelalter* (Heilbronn, 1962).

Molinier, A. 'La sénéchaussée de Rouergue en 1341', *Bibliothèque de l'Ecole des Chartes* 44 (1883) 452–88.

Mols, Roger, S. J. *Introduction à la démographie historique des villes d'Europe du xive au xviiie siècle* 3 vols (Louvain 1954, 5, 6).

Nath, Pran. *A Study in the Economic Conditions of Ancient India* (1929).

Neubauer, Th. 'Wirtschaftsleben im mittelalterlichen Erfurt', *Vierteljahrschrift für Sozial-und Wirtschaftesgeschichte* 12 (1914) 521-28; 13 (1961) 132–32.

Nicholas, F. 'L'évolution géographique de la ville de Namur', *Bulletin de la Société Belge de Géographie* 4 (1925), 169–201, map on p. 184.

Niemeier, G. and H. Rothert, 'Der Stadtplan von Soest', *Westfälische Zeitschrift* 163/4 (1954) 30–92.

Ott, K. *Bevölkerungsstatistik in der Stadt und Landschaft Nürnberg in de ersten Hälfte des 15, Jhdts.* Thesis (Berlin 1907).

Otte, J. 'Untersuchung über die Bevölkerung Dortsmund im 13 u. 14 Jahrhundert', *Beiträge zur Geschichte Dortmunds und der Graftschaft Mark*, 33 (1926) 5–53.

Ottolenghi, D. 'Studi demografici sulla popolazione di Siena dal secolo XIV al XIX', *Bollettino Senese di storia patria* 10 (1903) 297–358.

Paasche, H. 'Die städtische Bevölkerung früherer Jahrhunderte . . . Rostock', *Jahrbücher für Nationalökonomie und Statistik* 39 (1882) 303–80.

Pardi, G. 'Il catasto d'Orvieto dell'anno 1292', *Bolletino della Societa Umbra di storia patria* 2 (1896) 225–320.

Pernoud, R. *Histoire de la bourgeoisie en France* (Paris 1960).

Perrin, E. 'Le droit de bourgeoisie et l'immigration rurale à Metz XIVᵉ siècle', *Vierteljahrschrift für Sozial- und Wirtschaftslogie de la Lorraine* 30 (1921) 513–639.

Perroy, E. *Le Moyen Age* (Paris 1967).

Pirenne, H. 'Les dénombrements de la population à Ypres au XIVᵉ siècle', *Vierteljahrschrift für Sozial- und Wirtschaftsgeschichte* 1 (1903) 1-32.

Pistarino, G. 'Genova medievale tra Oriente e Occidente', *Rivista storica italiana* 81 (1969) 44–73.

Post, G. *Studies in Medieval Legal Thought: Public Law and the State* (Princeton 1964).

Postan, M. 'Credit in medieval trade', *Economic History* 1 1928); reprinted in E. M. Carus-Wilson, *Essays in Economic History* (1966) 61-87.

Pounds, N. J. G. 'Overpopulation in France and the Low Countries in the later Middle Ages' *Journal of Social History* 3 (1970) 225–47.

S

Pounds, N. J. G. and Sue S. Ball. 'Core-Areas and the Development of the European States System', *Annals of the Association of American Geographers* 54 (1964) 24–40.

Prat, Geneviève. 'Albi et la peste noire', *Annales du Midi* 64 (1952) 15–25.

Prawer, J. 'Colonisation activities in the Latin Kingdom of Jerusalem', *Revue Belge de Philologie et d'Histoire* 29 1951) 1063–1118.

Proctor, Evelyn S. *Alfonso X of Castile. Patron of Literature and Learning* (Oxford 1951).

Püschel, A. *Das Anwachsen der deutschen Städte in der Zeit der mittelalterlichen Kolonialbewegung* (Berlin 1910). Abhandlungen zür Verkehrs und Seegeschichte, 4.

Rausch, Wilhelm. *Die Städte Mitteleuropas im 12 und 13 Jahrhundert* (Linz 1963).

Reincke, H. 'Bevölkerungsverluste der Hansestädte durch den Schwarzen Tod, 1349–1350'. Hansische Geschichtsblätter. 72 (1954) 88–90.

Reisner, W. *Ein Einwohnerzahl deutscher Städte in früheren Jahrhunderten, mit besonderer Berücksichtigung Lübecks* (Jena 1903, Sammlung national-ökonomischer und statistischer Abhandlungen des Staatswissenschaftlichen Seminars zu Halle, 36).

Renouard, Y. 'Apropos d'ouvrages récents: destin d'une grande métropole médiévale: Pise' *Annales* 17 (1962) 137–45.

Renouard, Y. 'Conséquences et intérêt démographiques de la peste noire de 1348', *Population* 3 (1948) 459–466.

Renouard, Y. *Etudes d'histoire médiévale* (Paris 1967, SEVPEN).

Renouard, Yves, 'Les principaux aspects économiques et sociaux de l'histoire des pays de la couronne d'Aragon aux xiieme, xiiieme et xiveme siècles', Ponencias (VIII Congreso de la Corona de Aragon, 1962).

Rey, E. G. *Les colonies franques de Syrie aux XIIme et XIIIme siècles* (Paris 1883).

Richards, William. *The History of Lynn* (Lynn 1812).

Richter, O. 'Zur Bevölkerungs- und Vermögensstatistik Dresden im 15 Jahrhundert', *Neues Archiv fur Sächisische Geschichte und Altertumskunde* 2 (1881) 279–89.

Roca Traver, A. 'Cuestiones de demografía medieval' *Hispania* 13 (1953) 1–36.

Romani, M. *Pellegrini e viaggiatori nel l'economia di Roma, dal XIV al XVIII secolo'*, (Milan, 1948, Pubblicazioni dell' l'Università cattolica del Sacro Cuore, XXV).

Rossi, A. 'Lo svilluppo demografico di Pisa dal XIIe al XVe secolo', *Bollettino storico pisano* N.Ser. 14 (1945–7) 5–61.

Roulet, A. *Statistique de la ville et banlieue de de Neuchatel en 1353* (Neuchatel 1963).

Ruiz Almansa, J. 'La poblacion de España en el siglo xvi', *Revista internacional de sociologia* 3 (1943) 115–36.

Ruocco, Domenico. 'Profilo geografico de Catania e provincia', *Annali del mezzogiorno* 8 (1968) 297–326.

Russell, J. C. *British Medieval Population* (Albuquerque 1948).

Russell, J. C. 'Demographic Comparison of Egyptian and English Cities in the Later Middle Ages', TAIUS (Texas A & I University Studies) 2 (1969) 64–72.

Russell, J. C. 'L'Evolution démographique de Montpellier au Moyen Age', *Annales du Midi* 74 (1962) 245–60.

Russell, J. C. *Late Ancient and Medieval Population* (Philadelphia, 1958, *Transactions of the American Philosophical Society* 43, no 3).

Russell, J. C. 'Late-Thirteenth-Century Ireland as a Region', *Demography,* 3 (1970) 500–12.

Russell, J. C. 'London and Thirteenth-Century Anti-Royal Methods', *The Southwestern Social Science Quarterly* 12 (1931) 156–68.

Russell, J. C. 'Medieval Midland and Northern Migration to London, 1100–1365', *Speculum* 34 (1959) 641–5.

Russell, J. C. 'The Medieval Monedatge of Aragon and Valencia', *Proceedings of the American Philosophical Society*, 106 (1962) 483–504.

Russell, J. C. 'The Metropolitan City Region in the Middle Ages', *Journal of Regional Science* 2 (1960) 55–70.

Russell, J. C. 'The Persistence of Physical Type', *Social Studies* 41 (1950) 210–13.

Russell, J. C. 'Population in Europe 500–1500', *The Fontana Economic History of Europe*, I, ch 1.

Russell, J. C. 'The Preplague Population of England', *The Journal of British Studies* 5 (1966) 1–21.

Russell, J. C. 'Recent Advances in Medieval Demography', *Speculum* 40 (1965) 84–101.

Russell, J. C. 'Thirteenth Century Tuscany as a Region', TAIUS (Texas A & I University Studies) 1 (1968), 42–52.

Russell, J. C. 'The Triumph of Dignity over Order in England', *Historian* 9 (1947) 137–50.

Santoli, Q. *Liber focorum districtus Pistorii* (A.1226); *Liber finium districtus Pistorii* (A.1255) (Rome 1956, Fonti per la storia d'Italia).

Sauvaget, J. *Alep* (Paris 1941).

Sauvaget, J. 'Le plan antique de Damas', *Syria* 26 (1949) 331–2.

Schaefer, F. *Wirtschafts- und Finanzgeschichte der Reichsstadt Überlingen* (Fribourg i.B. 1893, Gierker Untersuchungen, 44).

Schalk, K. 'Die Wiener Handwerker um die Zeit des Aufstandes von 1462 und die Bevölkerung von Wien', *Jahrbuch für Landeskunde von Niederösterreich*, N.S. 13–14 (1914–1915) 300–46.

Schimmelpfennig, B. *Bamberg im Mittelalter*. (Lübeck 1964). in 15 Jahrhundert', *Zeitschrift für Schweizer Statistik* 36 (1900) 173–89.

Schindler, K. 'Finanzwesen und Bevölkerung der Stadt Bern'.

Schmidt, R. W. *Deutsche Reichsstädte* (Munich 1959).

Schnyder, W. 'Die Bevölkerung der Stadt und Landschaft Zürich vom 14 bis 17 Jahrhundert', *Schweizer Studien zur Geschichtswissenschaft* 14 (1926).

Schönberg, G. 'Basels Bevölkerungszahl im 15 Jahrhundert', *Jahrbücher für Nationalökonimie und Statistik* 40 (1883) 344–80.

Schöne, L. *Histoire de la population française* (Paris 1893).

Schreiber, Adèle. 'Die Entwicklung der Augsburger Bevölkerung von Ende des 14 Jahrhundert', *Archiv für Hygiene*, 123 (1939) 90–170.

Schwarzwalder, H. 'Bremen im Mittelalter', *Studium Generale* 16 (1963) 391–421.

Sharma, R. S. *Light on Early Indian Society and Economy* (Bombay 1966).

Singer, Elly. 'Untersuchungen über die Bevölkerung Dortmunds im 15, Jahrhundert (1401–1510)', *Beiträge zur Geschichte Dortmunds und der Grafschaft Mark*, 42 (1936), 1926.

Slicher van Bath, B. H. 'Yield Ratios, 810–1820', *A.A.G Bijdragen* 10 (1963).

Smith, C. T. *An Historical Geography of Europe before 1800* (New York 1967).

Smith, R. S. 'Barcelona Bills of Mortality and Population, 1457–1590', *Journal of Political Economy* 44 (1936) 84–93.

Smith, R. S. 'Fourteenth-Century Population Records of Catalonia'. *Speculum* 19 (1944) 494–501.

Spont, A. 'Une recherche générale des feux à la fin du XVe siècle', *Annuaire bulletin de la Société d'Histoire de France* 29 (1892) 222–36.

Spruner-Menke, *Atlas*.

Stephenson, Carl. *Borough and Town* (Cambridge, Mass 1933).

Steyert, A. *Nouvelle histoire de Lyon* (Lyon 1897).

Suyvelgheest, C. *Bevolking van Antwerpen in de XIVe an XVe eeuw* (Anvers 1861).

Svidkovskij, O. A. *Urbanismus Socialistického Ceskoslovenska* (Praha 1966).

Tafel and Thomas. *Urkunden zur älteren Handels und Staatgeschichte der Republik Venedig*, ed G. L. F. Tafel and G. M. Thomas Vienna (1856).

Techen, F. 'Die Bevölkerung Wismars in Mittelalter und die Wachtpflicht der Burger', *Hansische Geschichtsquellen* 7 (1890–1891), 65–94.

Teran, M. de y L. Sole Sabaris. *Geografía Regional de España* (Barcelona 1968).

Thomas, L. 'La population du Bas-Languedoc à la fin du XIIIe siècle et au commencement du XIVe siècle', *Bulletin historique et philosophique* 25 (1907) 157.

Torres Balbas, L. 'Almeria', *Al-Andalus* 22 (1957) 429.

Torres Balbas, L. 'Esquema demografica de la ciudad de Granada', *Al-Andalus* 21 (1956) 131–50.

Torres Balbas, L. *Studia Islamica* 3 (1955) 55-6.

Traselli, Carmelo. 'Sulla popolazione di Palermo nei secoli xiii–xiv', *Economia e storia,* 11 (1964), 328–44.

Ullman, E. On rank-size relationships in *Readings in Urban Geography* ed. Harold M. Mayer and Clyde F. Kohn (Chicago 1959), pp 202–9 and 277–86 (with C. D. Harris). *Untersuchungen zur Gesellschaftlichen Struktur der mittelälterlichen Städte in Europa. Reichenau Vorträge, 1963–4,* vol XI.

Vannerus, J. 'Les anciens dénombrements de Luxembourg', Bull. C.R.H. 5th ser 11 (1901) 421–76.

Van Werveke, Hans. 'De Zwarte Dood in de Zuidelike Neder-
landen (1349–1351)'. Brussels, 1950, *Mededelingen van de
Koninklijke Vlaamse Acad voor Wetenschappen, Kl,
Letteren,* XIII, 3.

Van Werveke, Hans. *Miscellanea Mediaevalia.* Ghent, 1968.

Verbeemen, J. 'De demografische evolutie van Mechelen
(1370–1800)', Handelingen v.d. Kon. Kring. v. Oudheidkunde
v. Mechelen 57 (1953) 63–99.

Vives Vivens, Jaime. *An Economic History of Spain* tr by
F. M. Lopez-Morillas (Princeton 1969).

Vrancken-Pirsun, I. 'Demographie liégeoise du XVe siècle',
Bulletin Statistique 37 (1951) 599–600.

Waley, Daniel. *The Papal State in the Thirteenth Century*
(1961).

Watters, Thomas, *On Yuan Chwang's Travels in India*
(AD 629–45), ed T. W. Rhys Davids and S. S. Bushell
(Delhi 1961).

WEC: R. E. Dickenson. *The West European City.*

Weczerka, Hugo. 'Bevölkerungszahlen der Hansestädte (ins-
besondere Danzigs) nach H. Samsonowicz', *Hansische Geschichtsquellen* 18 (1964) 69–80.

Willems, J. F. 'De la population de quelques villes belges au
moyen âge', *Bulletin Academie Royale de Belgien* 6 (1839)
162–9.

Wittmer, C. *Le livre de bourgeoisie de la ville de Strasbourg*
(Strasbourg 1961).

Wolff, Philippe. *Les 'Estimes' Toulousaines des xive et xv^e
siècles* (Toulouse 1956).

Wolff, Philippe and F. Mauro. *L'âge de l'artisanat. Histoire
Général du Travail* (Paris 19—).

Wrigley, E. A. 'Regional Geography', in R. J. Chorley and
P. Haggett, *Frontiers in Geographical Teaching* (1970).

Young, Charles R. *The English Borough and Royal Administration, 1130–1307* (Durham N.C. 1961).

Zamora, Fr Juan Gil de *De Preconiis Hispaniae,* ed M. de Castro y Castro (Madrid 1955).

Zipf, G. K. *Human Behaviour and the Principle of Least Effort* (Cambridge, Mass 1949).

Index